FOR
PROFIT

FOR PROFIT

A History of Corporations

William Magnuson

BASIC BOOKS

NEW YORK

Basic Books
Hachette Book Group
1290 Avenue of the Americas, New York, NY 10104
www.basicbooks.com

Printed in the United States of America
First Edition: November 2022

Published by Basic Books, an imprint of Perseus Books, LLC, a subsidiary of Hachette Book Group, Inc. The Basic Books name and logo is a trademark of the Hachette Book Group.

The Hachette Speakers Bureau provides a wide range of authors for speaking events. To find out more, go to www.hachettespeakersbureau.com or call (866) 376-6591.

The publisher is not responsible for websites (or their content) that are not owned by the publisher.

Print book interior design by Linda Mark.

Library of Congress Control Number: 2022940721

ISBNs: 9781541601567 (hardcover), 9781541601581 (ebook)

LSC-C

Printing 1, 2022

For Jane

Contents

INTRODUCTION

I N *Nicholas Nickleby*, Charles Dickens tells the tale of a joint stock company. It is, he assures us, of "vast national importance." Its business will contribute to "the wealth, the happiness, the comfort, the liberty, the very existence of a free and great people." Members of Parliament announce their support. Crowds of investors show up to attend its first meeting. There are, in short, great expectations for the United Metropolitan Improved Hot Muffin and Crumpet Baking and Punctual Delivery Company.

"Why the very name will get the shares up to a premium," one of the directors exclaims.

Standing on a stage before a meeting of assembled investors, the directors begin their pitch by denouncing the great evils that beset the current muffin trade. One director tells of a visit he made to the houses of the poor in London. "He had found them destitute of the slightest vestige of a muffin, which there appeared too much reason to believe some of these indigent persons did not taste from year's end to year's end." Another director, "a grievous gentleman of semi-clerical appearance," stands up to detail the sufferings of the so-called muffin boys, the children who walk the streets of London hawking muffins to the public. "It seemed that the unhappy youths were nightly turned out into the wet streets at the most inclement periods of the year, to wander about, in darkness and rain—or it might be hail or snow—for hours together, without shelter, food, or warmth; and let the public never forget upon the latter point, that while the muffins were provided with warm clothing and blankets, the boys were wholly unprovided for, and left to their own miserable resources. (Shame!)" The speeches bring tears to the eyes of the ladies in the crowd.

Fortunately, the directors continue, the United Metropolitan has a plan to solve this melancholy state of affairs. First, the directors promise, they will prohibit, under heavy penalties, all private muffin trading. Second, they will supply the public with muffins of first quality at reduced prices. Finally, they will render the purchase of muffins and crumpets "compulsory upon all classes of the community." The directors announce that a bill to this purpose has been introduced into Parliament.

The directors' words have a profound effect on the crowd. "All the speeches put together did exactly what they were intended to do, and established in the hearers' minds that there was no speculation so promising, or at the same time so praiseworthy, as the United Metropolitan Improved Hot Muffin and Crumpet Baking and Punctual Delivery Company." One director whispers to a colleague that the speeches have caused the value of the company's shares to rise 25 percent. The directors adjourn the assembly to much cheering and acclamation and promptly head to lunch (the cost of which they expense to the company).

The tale of the United Metropolitan Improved Hot Muffin and Crumpet Baking and Punctual Delivery Company presents to us, in a remarkably compact format, the great critiques of the age of capitalism. Unscrupulous managers, corrupt politicians, gullible investors, domineering monopolies—they are all here. And it is clear where Dickens's sympathies lie. One of the company's directors happens to be the novel's primary villain, Ralph Nickleby. But Dickens does not care to expand on philosophy. He is less interested in constructing a grand theory of capitalism than in painting a picture of the people who live inside its walls—the great and the forgotten, the rich and the poor, the owners and the workers. It is no coincidence that, to paint this portrait, he chose to turn his attentions to a corporation. Only by looking inside the corporation, by examining its workings and exposing its methods, could Dickens show the great forces unleashed by capitalism. Dickens knew that the story of capitalism is, in reality, the story of corporations.

THIS BOOK TELLS THE HISTORY OF CORPORATIONS AND THE PEOPLE behind them, from the stockholders who fund them to the executives who manage them to the employees who keep them running. As such, it is a human story, about a diverse group of merchants, bankers, and investors who have over time come to craft the landscape of our modern economy. It is filled with tales of the rich, the powerful, and the ingenious, but also of the conniving, the fraudulent, and the vicious. We will learn about slave traders and robber barons, but also scientists and innovators. We will range from the halls of Roman palaces to the assembly lines of Detroit factories. We will learn about how businesses work and how they fail, about what makes a great leader and what makes a poor one.

If there is one constant in the history of corporations, it is that they have always and ever exerted an outsized influence on world events. In ancient Rome, corporations helped transform the Roman army into the most efficient fighting force known to man. In Renaissance Florence, they oversaw a flourishing of artistic genius that has never been rivaled. More recently, they have ushered in the era of Big Tech, with smartphones and the internet transforming the way we interact with the world. The role of corporations in these developments, of course, has not always been positive. Roman publicans became renowned for their greed and corruption, leading to their eternal association with sinners in the Bible. The Medici Bank in Florence was denounced for engaging in usury, and the Dominican friar Savonarola led bonfires of the vanities to campaign against their vices. Big Tech is under assault on any number of fronts, from its privacy practices to its monopoly positions to its handling of free speech. Sometimes corporations are the hero. Sometimes they are the villain. But they are always on the stage.

This book is divided into eight chapters, each devoted to a single corporation. Corporations may be the basic building block of capitalism. But they have not always looked and acted as they do today. In the Roman Republic, corporations operated within an agrarian economy and dealt exclusively in government contracts for things like road building and tax collecting. In Elizabethan England, corporations catered to a mercantilist economy, devoted themselves to exploration and trading, and regularly engaged in actions that can only be described as piracy. Today, corporations compete in a complex global economy, provide a bewildering array of goods and services, and have access to unprecedented amounts of capital. Over the course of the book, we will explore how this evolution took place.

Before we begin, it may be helpful to set out the terms of the debate. First and foremost, what exactly is a corporation? Today, we often think of corporations as synonymous with business, but in fact they are a particular type of business with its own peculiar form and structure. The idea of the corporation first arose in the Roman Republic, and so it is appropriate that the term *corporation* derives from the Latin word *corpus*, or "body." A corporation, then, is a group of individuals incorporated by law into a single body. What used to be a collection of disparate individuals is now a single entity that can act, and be acted upon, as one. In other languages, the term for a corporation hews closer to the original Roman term for a company, a *societas*. In Italian, for example, a corporation is a *società per azioni*, or "company with shares." This brings us to the second important feature of corporations: the existence of shares and shareholders. The fact that corporations can issue shares to public investors, who give them money in return, allows corporations to tap into the vast oceans of capital owned by the public at large and not just dip into the pockets of the executives running the company. Finally, corporations possess one other characteristic that makes them a particularly attractive vessel for running a business: limited liability. Unlike partnerships, where every partner in the business can be sued if the business fails, the owners of a corporation have no duty to meet the future financial needs of the company. Once the stockholders buy their shares, they can rest assured that their purses are safe from the grasp of creditors, no matter how badly the business goes.

These attributes, when combined, turn corporations into tremendously powerful engines of commerce. In fact, the collection of attributes is so exceptional that William Blackstone, the eighteenth-century English legal scholar, devoted a significant portion of his famous *Commentaries on the Laws of England* to describing them. "The privileges and immunities, the estates and possessions of the corporation, when once vested in them, will be forever vested without any new conveyance to new successions; for all the individual members that have existed from the foundation to the present time, or that shall ever hereafter exist, are but one person in law—a person that never dies: in like manner as the River Thames is still the same river, though the parts which compose it are changing every instant." Sir Edward Coke, another eminent English jurist, put it more simply: corporations are "invisible, immortal."[1]

The development of the corporation paved the way for the creation of an entirely new class of citizen: the capitalist. While there have always been rich people, the corporation provided a new way for the rich to grow richer. Instead of hoarding their wealth or spending it on luxuries and riotous living, the rich could instead invest it in a company. As shareholders in a corporation, they could then sit back and watch their investment grow, day in and day out, all through the labors of others, with little to no input from themselves. This marked a sea change in the nature of business. With a new capitalist class that held shares in companies but had no role in their management, a powerful new force had arisen within the economy, one with its own logic and methods. Capitalists, it turned out, often cared more about dividends and share prices than wages or long-term business success. This did not always work out so well for the companies that they owned. It also created opportunities for a new kind of fraud. By manipulating stock prices, capitalists could amass wealth simply by changing others' perceptions of the value of their companies. One famous shareholder of the East India Company, Sir Josiah Child, was notorious for spreading false rumors that war had broken out in India, causing the company's share price to drop. He would then proceed to buy up entire blocks of shares on the cheap. This kind of market manipulation wreaked havoc on stock markets and the pockets of unsophisticated investors for centuries.

What should we make of the rise of this capitalist system? Adam Smith believed that it was all for the best. In *The Wealth of Nations*, Smith famously argued that an "invisible hand" oversaw the market. The invisible hand ensured that selfish individuals, looking out solely for themselves, ended up promoting the greater good of society as a whole. Precisely how the invisible hand did its work was unclear, but it generally involved some combination of supply and demand: by competing with one another in responding to the demands of consumers, corporations supplied the goods and services that society needed with high quality and at a reasonable price. The idea of the invisible hand of capitalism has since captured the imagination of economists, politicians, and executives around the world. It has worked its way into presidential campaign platforms, government policies, and think tank white papers. We hear echoes of it every day: "Let markets solve the problem." "We need a market-based approach." "We should privatize this." It is what led economist Milton Friedman to conclude that "there is one and only one social responsibility of business—to use its resources and engage in activities designed to increase its profits so long as it stays within the rules of the game." Few economic theories have had such a remarkable effect on the world.[2]

On the other hand, many observers have cast doubt on just how benevolent the invisible hand is and even whether it exists at all. For hundreds of years, people have condemned corporations as a scourge on the world. The complaints are now familiar. Their endless appetite for profit drives them to exploit workers. Their need for raw supplies leads them to ravage the environment. Their underhanded practices harm consumers and drive up prices. The laundry list of bad behaviors could go on, and it has proved ample fodder for critics. Thomas Jefferson wrote that he hoped to "crush in its birth the aristocracy of our monied corporations which dare already to challenge our government to a trial of strength, and to bid defiance to the laws of their country." Karl Marx wrote that corporations were a "a new sort of parasite, in the shape of promoters, speculators and merely nominal directors; a whole system of swindling and cheating with respect to the promotion of companies, issuance of shares and stock speculation." Complaints about individual corporations have tended to be even more colorful. Edmund Burke, writing of the East India Company, concluded that "this cursed Company would, at last, like a viper, be the destruction of the country which fostered it at its bosom." More recently, journalist Matt Taibbi described Goldman Sachs as a "great vampire squid wrapped around the face of humanity, relentlessly jamming its blood funnel into anything that smells like money."[3]

But perhaps the most enduring and devastating criticism of corporations is that they have used their profits to undermine the institutions of democracy itself. They bribe politicians to win government contracts. They hire lobbyists to distort public opinion. They contribute to election campaigns in return for friendly regulation. No one put it better than Teddy Roosevelt. Speaking in 1910 at the John

Brown Memorial Park in Osawatomie, Kansas, he announced that he stood for "the square deal," by which he meant freeing government from "the sinister influence or control of special interests." For Roosevelt, it was no secret who those wielders of sinister influence were.

> Corporate expenditures for political purposes . . . have supplied one of the principal sources of corruption in our political affairs. . . . The true friend of property, the true conservative, is he who insists that property shall be the servant and not the master of the commonwealth; who insists that the creature of man's making shall be the servant and not the master of the man who made it. The citizens of the United States must effectively control the mighty commercial forces which they have called into being.

Roosevelt would be neither the first nor the last leader to worry about the powerful sway that corporations had come to hold over government. William Shakespeare put it more directly in *King Lear*: "Plate sin with gold, and the strong lance of justice hurtless breaks: arm it in rags, a pigmy's straw does pierce it."

It is only natural that corporations are powerful political actors. Democratic governments are supposed to reflect the societies they represent—their interests, their preferences, their ambitions. As corporations have become increasingly integral parts of society, their interests have inevitably gained greater sway in the political arena. If anything, it would have been more shocking if governments had not shifted their policies to respond to the interests of the mammoth corporations within their borders. But the pressing question today is not *if* corporations have changed democracy—they surely have—but *how much* they have done so and in what ways. And to many observers, including a surprising number of corporate insiders who have witnessed firsthand the relentless power of the entities they run, the answers are decidedly negative. What was once created to expand and enrich the republic has instead come to command and impoverish it.

A cynic might look at this situation and shrug. "Of course corporations have grown rich off the suffering of others, and bribed politicians, and corrupted democracy," the cynic might say. "What else would you expect?" But the history of corporations suggests that we should not be so quick to rush to judgment. Time and again, after some new corporate scandal or some new abuse has come to light, society has risen to the challenge and fashioned solutions. After capitalists were found to be oppressing the Roman provinces in collecting taxes for the government, the emperor Augustus shifted tax-collection duties to his own imperial agents. After the East India Company realized that its share structure incentivized infighting among its employees, it created a permanent stock that aligned their incentives better. After the stock market crash of 1929 exposed widespread fraud in the sale of shares to the public, Congress enacted the Securities Act and the Securities Exchange Act to hold capitalists liable for misleading the public. These are astounding changes in the world of capital, and yet we often overlook them. Today, we take for granted that the government, not a corporation, collects our taxes. We take for granted that most corporations have permanent shares, not profits interests based on individual projects. We take for granted that corporations must provide information to their shareholders. But it was not always so.

At the core of this book lies a simple argument. Many believe that corporations are soulless entities devoted single-mindedly to the pursuit of profit above all else. Some go even further, arguing not only that corporations elevate profits above all other considerations but that it is their duty to do so. Both of these groups are wrong. From their very beginnings, corporations have been institutions designed to promote the common good. From ancient Rome to Renaissance Florence to Elizabethan England, corporations have been the workhorses of the republic, tasked with building and maintaining a thriving society. Corporations are public entities with a public purpose, given special rights and privileges precisely because governments believe they will contribute to the greatness of their nations. While they sometimes—perhaps even often—stray from this purpose, their original and abiding justification has always been their ability to promote the good of all.

Adam Smith, the father of capitalism, understood this. In the seldom-read passage of *The Wealth of Nations* in which he articulated his vision of the invisible hand, he was careful to provide an important caveat about capitalism as a cure-all. The invisible hand is not infallible. "By directing [his] industry in such a manner as its produce may be of the greatest value, he intends only his own gain; and he is in this, as in many other cases, led by an invisible hand to promote an end which was no part of his intention," Smith wrote. "Nor is it always the worse for the society that it was no part of it. By pursuing his own interest, he frequently promotes that of the society more effectually than when he really intends to promote it." The section is remarkable for what it does not say. Smith does *not* say that profit-seeking individuals always promote the greater good. He says only that they frequently do. More importantly, he is clear that the profit motive is simply a means to an end, not an end in itself. We allow firms to profit from their efforts because we believe that it will ultimately benefit us all. Firms have a public purpose, in Smith's view, and that is to promote the public good.

The connection between corporations and the public good has historically been much clearer than it is today. In the beginning, corporations had to petition the monarch or the government for a charter. To be granted one, they had to convince the state that their businesses were not just profitable but also of benefit to the state itself. The East India Company promised Queen Elizabeth I in 1600 that it would act "for the honour of this our realm of England, as for the increase of our navigation." The Union Pacific Railroad's charter was granted by Congress in the middle of the Civil War. A transcontinental railroad, the company's backers argued, would bind together a riven nation.

In the last century, we have lost sight of the true spirit of corporate enterprise. We have elevated profit seeking from a means to an end to an end in itself. This shift was driven partially by law: by the twentieth century, corporations no longer had to petition monarchs for charters and instead could be created with the submission of some paperwork to the local authorities. No longer did corporations have to justify their existence. But more importantly, the shift was driven by politics. The existential challenge presented by communism and the Cold War forced Western nations to double down on their belief in the virtues of capitalism. Corporations were no longer seen as flawed but useful structures for channeling human effort, as Adam Smith viewed them, but rather as a defining feature of Western life—one that set us apart from the benighted citizens of the communist bloc. Democracy and capitalism became synonymous. As a result, corporations turned from tools into heroes. They defined us, and, in return, we lionized them.

But this revolution in the history of corporations has spawned dangerous repercussions. Corporations have grown and multiplied, and yet they are rarely asked any more to give public-minded reasons for their decisions. Market morality has given way to market efficiency. If a company is profitable, it must be efficient, and efficiency is the good we are after. This belief pervades not just society but also the leaders of corporations themselves. It has tended to make business leaders less reflective about society's great problems and more intensely focused on extracting profit. It has contributed to the growth of financial capitalism, a species of corporate activity devoted to financial engineering rather than material production. It has also promoted the "move fast and break things" ethos of Silicon Valley, which values rapid technological growth over responsible behavior. And while corporate leaders occasionally pay lip service to their role as guardians of the public interest, with a few notable exceptions they appear less and less convinced of it.

We are now witnessing a moment when corporations and the titans who run them wield an unimaginable amount of wealth and power—more than would have been conceivable at the time of the East India Company. But we have abandoned the founding purpose of the corporation as a tool for crafting a flourishing society. This is a

dangerous moment. Over time, as corporations have evolved, so too
have the ways in which unscrupulous managers have figured out how
to "game the system" to extract wealth from others. What happens in
the next chapter of the global economy depends on whether we can
return to the original intent of the corporation or we have sunk irrevo-
cably into the swamp of profit maximization at all costs.

IN THIS BOOK, I SEEK TO DEPICT THE WORLD OF CORPORATIONS. IT
is a world I have spent my career studying.

After graduating from Harvard Law School, I worked as an associate in the mergers and acquisitions (M&A) group of Sullivan &
Cromwell (S&C). Sullivan & Cromwell is one of Wall Street's most
storied law firms. Its lawyers advised on the construction of the Panama Canal and the creation of U.S. Steel. It counts among its alumni
Supreme Court justices, heads of the Central Intelligence Agency,
and secretaries of state. Today, it advises some of the world's largest
corporations on their most significant transactions. In my time there,
I worked on some of these deals. While I eventually left law firm life
for a career in academia, I will always be grateful for the chance it
gave me to see from the inside how corporations work, what makes
them tick, and what they want.

In fact, the idea for this book first came to me while I was at the
firm. It was around 1 a.m. on a weekday. I was seated in my office on
the thirty-sixth floor, the home of S&C's famed M&A group. The remains of my firm-reimbursed Thai dinner lay strewn across my desk.
A Rothko painting hung on the wall over my head. My officemate
had left for the day, and the office was eerily silent. I was stressed and
tired, and upon reviewing my hastily scrawled to-do list, I realized that
I still had several hours of work to finish before I, too, could head out.
In a pique of something like existential crisis, I pushed back my chair
and walked to the window. I could see the Statue of Liberty shining in
the distance. Below, a long line of black cars stood idling at the curb,

waiting to take associates home. There was a certain sense of magnificence about it all, but also a sense of oppression.

I wondered to myself, what created all this? How did we get here—to an entire generation of smart, conscientious young people, all devoting every waking hour of their day to pursuing the interests of corporations? What did it all mean? This moment of clarity made me understand the need for this book. We need the story of corporations to be told—to put them in their historical context and show how they evolved into what they are, for better and for worse. Their story helps us understand our own stories.

Eventually I left Sullivan & Cromwell and became a law professor. Now I teach classes on topics like corporate law, mergers and acquisitions, and international business. I tell anecdotes about my experience on Wall Street. I advise my students as well as I can about how to navigate these worlds dominated by corporations. But I have never forgotten those bigger ideas lingering under the surface. Every year, in my course on corporate law, I open the first lecture by asking my students a simple question: What is the purpose of a corporation? The overwhelming majority reply that it is to "turn a profit." When pressed, they may clarify that it is to "turn a profit for shareholders." This, as we learn through the semester, is more or less the right answer under modern law: courts have repeatedly held that CEOs have an obligation to protect the interests of shareholders above all others and that shareholders are interested in profits above all else. But, as we will see in this book, it is decidedly wrong from a historical perspective. It would have come as a surprise to Queen Elizabeth I that she was chartering the East India Company to line the pockets of a group of London merchants or to Abraham Lincoln that he was forming the Union Pacific Railroad to enrich a few Boston capitalists. They were after something much grander and more important—the common good of their nations.

This work, I hope, will provide a guidebook of sorts. It will show the ways that corporations evolved over time into the creatures they are today. It will show where they have flourished and where they have faltered. It will show where they have ennobled and where they have corrupted. But most importantly, to return to the wisdom of Dickens, it will explore the complicated, conflicting, and ever-changing role that corporations play in creating and sustaining "the wealth, the happiness, the comfort, the liberty, the very existence of a free and great people."

one

CORPUS ECONOMICUS

I N 215 BC, EMPIRES WERE AT WAR. ROME AND CARTHAGE, THE two great powers of the Mediterranean, were locked in a fierce struggle for survival. The epic conflict spanned from the shores of Spain to the land of Greece to the sands of Tunisia. It swept in the peoples of Gaul, Numidia, Macedon, and Syracuse. The winner would lay claim to vast swathes of Europe, Africa, and Asia. The loser could well be wiped from the face of the earth. It was nothing less than a contest for the future of the Western world.

The war had raged for decades, but now, under the leadership of Hannibal, the Carthaginian general and military genius, Carthage found itself on the verge of victory. In 218 BC, in a risky maneuver, Hannibal had crossed over the Alps into Italy at the head of an enormous army of heavy infantry, cavalry, and elephants. He quickly defeated a succession of Roman armies rushed into the field to meet him. At the Battle of the Trebia and then the Battle of Trasimene, he inflicted lopsided defeats on the Roman Republic, with minimal losses to his own army. And then, in his most shocking victory yet, at the Battle of Cannae, he defeated the largest army that the Roman Republic had ever assembled, a massive force of eighty-six thousand men. Roman losses were enormous, with an estimated seventy-six thousand killed and ten thousand captured. Twenty percent of Rome's men of military age died in a single day of fighting, including eighty of the republic's three hundred senators. Afterward, Hannibal roamed freely through southern Italy, ravishing the countryside, scouring its fields, and raising troops from its towns. Rome's allies, seeing the tides turning in favor of Carthage, defected in droves. Things looked dire for the young republic.

The story of how Rome recovered from these defeats to drive Hannibal from Italy and eventually destroy his army is familiar to any student of ancient history. The Romans adopted the famed "Fabian strategy," avoiding the large, set battles that had so decimated their forces in prior combat and instead engaging only in small skirmishes, prolonging the war and requiring Hannibal and his army to remain in the field and away from home indefinitely. The talented Roman commander Scipio Africanus won major battles in Spain against Carthaginian forces and then, instead of confronting Hannibal in Italy, set sail for Africa, where he threatened the city of Carthage itself. Hannibal, forced to leave Italy to defend his homeland, eventually suffered defeat by Scipio at the Battle of Zama.

Less well known in this affair is the role of capitalists in allowing Rome to keep the war effort alive. In 215 BC, with Hannibal on the loose in Italy, Publius Cornelius Scipio (the father of Scipio Africanus) wrote to the Senate from Spain with bad news. His armies were desperately short of supplies, and he could neither pay nor feed his troops for much longer. If Rome did not send him provisions soon, he wrote, he would lose both his army and all of Spain. But with the Roman treasury nearly empty, the Senate could not afford to provide him what he needed. As a last resort, the Senate made a desperate plea to the people of Rome: if citizens would supply Scipio's troops with clothes, grain, and equipment out of their own pockets, they would be repaid from the Roman treasury when it was replenished. In response, three companies (or *societates*, in the original Latin), consisting of nineteen men in total, came forward and agreed to supply the necessary provisions. In return, they asked only that they be exempted from military duty and that, if they lost their cargoes at sea, either from storms or enemy action, they be reimbursed for the loss (the fact that they did not ask for a similar guarantee for their cargoes on land suggests that the famed Roman roads were well protected). The Senate agreed to their terms.

The companies followed through on their promise. Livy wrote in his *History of Rome*, "As all the supplies were magnanimously contracted for, so they were delivered with great fidelity, and nothing was furnished to the soldiers less generously than if they were being maintained, as formerly, out of an ample treasury." With provisions in hand, Scipio and his brother were able to go on the offensive. They defeated the forces of Hasdrubal, Hannibal's brother, in several pitched battles, a string of victories that convinced "almost all of the people of Spain" to defect from the Carthaginians and ally themselves with the Roman Republic. Livy wrote that the affair served as a testament to the virtue of the Roman citizenry, noting that the private companies that stepped in to supply the army did so not out of a base desire for profit but out of a sense of duty to their country. "This character and love of country," Livy said, "uniformly pervaded all ranks."[1]

But setting aside what the affair says about the character of Roman citizens, the incident also sheds light on another important feature of the Roman world: the power of its economy and its private enterprise. The very fact that a group of just three companies could provide the necessary supplies for the armies of Publius Cornelius Scipio in Spain suggests that these companies were sizeable businesses. They must have had access to capital, grain, clothing, ships, seamen, and much more. They must have been well established in the fabric of Roman society if the Roman Senate thought to offer up the contracts to them. And their intervention changed the course of the war.

It was a remarkable moment in the history of the Roman Republic. The government, teetering on the edge of collapse, had been bailed out by a group of powerful Roman companies. And so, as Livy wrote, for a time during one of the most serious of crises, "the Republic was carried along by private money."[2]

※ ※ ※

TODAY, WE DEFINE a corporation as a business entity that possesses a particular set of traits. It has shareholders. It lasts for an indefinite period. It grants its owners limited liability. It is treated like a person—at least insomuch as it is empowered to transact and be bound on its own account. And, as Supreme Court Justice Anthony Kennedy famously explained in his decision in *Citizens United v. Federal Election Commission*, corporations even have a constitutional right to freedom of speech. Corporations are instantly recognizable by their names—they end in "Inc.," "Corp.," or "Co.," or some variation thereof.

The Roman corporation, though, looked substantially different. It dealt exclusively in government contracts, handling things like building roads, collecting taxes, and supporting the army. It was run by a single social class—the Roman knights. Not all of its owners had their personal assets protected from liability. And it was notoriously warlike. Its executives were often accused of lobbying for new Roman conquests.

But the legacy of the Roman corporation tells us something about why corporations have persisted and why they possess the form they do today. The Roman state and the Roman corporation were close partners in a grander project: building a prosperous and flourishing society. The Roman Republic granted corporations special rights and privileges in return for their services to the republic. The relationship was mutually beneficial. The privileges increased the efficiency and stability of business enterprise, which could, in turn, serve the state more efficiently and reliably.

In *De monarchia*, Dante Alighieri wrote of the Romans, "That holy, pious and glorious people, repressed all greed that is harmful to the community, preferring universal peace and liberty; so much so that they seem to have sacrificed their own advantage in order to secure the general well-being of mankind." Dante, genius that he was, got it wrong here. The Romans, throughout their history, exhibited a consistent and sometimes astonishing appetite for wealth and opulence, on the one hand, and violence and cruelty, on the other. Rome's greatest conqueror, Julius Caesar, once accepted the surrender of a rebellious town in Gaul and proceeded to cut off the hands of every male of military age he found inside. Rome's wealthiest man, Marcus Licinius Crassus, created a private firefighting department that would show up at burning houses and refuse to extinguish the fire until the owner had sold him the house for pennies. Rome's most prominent statesman, Cato the Elder, witnessed the growing prosperity of the neighboring city of Carthage and ever after concluded his speeches, whatever the topic, with the phrase *Carthago delenda est*—Carthage must be destroyed. Dante's belief that Rome had repressed all greed and sacrificed itself for the general well-being of mankind required a supreme act of imagination.[3]

At the same time, Dante's opinion of ancient Rome gets at an important truth—one that is often overlooked. While the Romans may not have eliminated greed or acquisitiveness, they were keenly aware of the importance of mobilizing it for the public good. Indeed, the connection between business and government in the Roman Republic is so close that, at some points in history, the distinction vanishes entirely, as it did during the events of the Second Punic War when, as Livy wrote, the state was only continued through private funds. Business always played an integral role in Roman warfare, both in prosecuting it and, sometimes, in instigating it. Over time, this relationship between private business and public government led Rome to develop elaborate and sophisticated mechanisms for allowing businesses to seek their own profits in a way that also benefited the empire itself. We owe everything to the Romans, from our language, to our government, to our laws. It should come as no surprise, then, that we also owe to them the idea of a corporation.

The role of corporations in the Roman Republic is a subject of some debate. For one, there is always a problem with using modern terms to describe ancient phenomena. Were Roman *societates* the same thing as corporations of the modern era? Certainly not. There were no secretaries of state around to issue certificates of incorporation or extensive business codes regulating securities offerings, shareholder lawsuits, and director duties. But did Roman *societates* bear many of the core features of what we now would call a corporation? It appears so, particularly in the case of a special kind of *societas* called a *societas publicanorum* (more on them in a bit). A second issue relates to the structure and function of Roman business. Some scholars read the evidence we have from Roman writers as suggesting that ancient Rome had a large and active stock market, in which the shares of Roman companies could be traded among the public much like on a modern-day stock exchange. Others disagree, arguing that these scholars have exaggerated the available evidence. This book will not settle these debates, but it is worthwhile to keep in mind that substantial disagreement exists on these and other important facts about the economic life of ancient Rome.[4]

With that noted, we can now turn to what we do know about what Roman enterprise looked like.

FROM ITS MYTHICAL FOUNDING BY THE TWIN BROTHERS ROMULUS and Remus in 753 BC to its transition to an empire under Augustus in 27 BC, ancient Rome never developed the trappings of a large government. This is a striking fact. Despite growing from a small village on the banks of the Tiber to a sprawling world power ruling territories from the plateaus of Spain to the coasts of Syria, from the deserts of the Sahara to the shores of France, the Roman Republic operated with only the smallest of bureaucracies and a mere handful of civil servants. Government was mostly run by the exertions of Roman senators and a few of their designated officials. Without a body of civil administrators devoted to managing the many everyday tasks that the republic increasingly required, a question arose. How could the Roman Republic govern its rapidly expanding imperium? While a definitive answer was never established until the republic was replaced with the empire and its expansive imperial administration, one piece of the puzzle was the growing use of private enterprise to perform the duties of government, particularly through what became known as the *societas publicanorum*.

Societas publicanorum literally means "society of publicans." So who were these publicans? For Christians, the name has a decidedly negative connotation. The Bible mentions publicans numerous times and never in a positive light. The apostle Luke, for example, tells a story of Jesus meeting a publican named Levi and eating a great feast at his house, alongside many other publicans. The Pharisees, seeing Jesus in the company of the publicans, asked him, "Why do ye eat with publicans and sinners?" Jesus replied, "They that are whole need not a physician; but they that are sick. I came not to call the righteous, but sinners to repentance." Publicans and the idea of sin have ever after been closely linked.[5]

But Romans living in the Roman Republic viewed publicans quite differently. The publicans were a respected and even revered class within Roman society for much of the existence of the commonwealth. Their very name suggests their close connection to the state: *publica* means "public," and *res publica*, "public thing" or "republic." The *publicani* themselves were government contractors—that is, private citizens who negotiated with the government to perform public duties. Since there was no large government bureaucracy to do so, the republic depended heavily on publicans to keep the state running.

The publicans emerged very early in the existence of the Roman Republic. Blackstone even claimed that the mythical Roman king Numa Pompilius first created them. But the first historical mention of publicans appears in the work of Dionysius of Halicarnassus, who wrote that in 493 BC the Roman government entered into contracts with private parties for the building of temples to honor the Roman gods Ceres, Liber, and Libera (the so-called Aventine Triad of the deities of agriculture and fertility). Pliny wrote that publicans were responsible for providing horses for the circus, as well as feeding geese on the Capitoline hill. (Feeding geese may not sound like much, but it would have been considered a deeply important and even reverent act in the Roman Republic, for geese had warned the Romans of an impending attack of the Gauls during their sacking of the city in 390 BC.)[6]

By the third century BC, the publicans had become firmly entrenched in the operation of the Roman state. During the Second Punic War, for example, they were sufficiently organized to lobby the Roman government as a group, seeking to extend their contracts for the restoration of temples and the provision of chariot horses. But their business ranged much wider by then. They both provided services and supplies to the public (*opera publica et sarta tecta*) and developed public property like mines and quarries (*ager publicus*). Indeed, if we marvel at the ingenuity of Roman cities, it is largely due to the works of the publicans: they constructed and maintained nearly everything a Roman would have seen on a walk around town, including streets, city walls, temples, markets, basilicas, statues, theaters, aqueducts, public sewers, and the circus. And of course, the military victories of the Roman legions owed much to the publicans, who supplied the Roman army with food, clothes, horses, and equipment even after the terrors of Hannibal.[7]

But the publicans became most famous for a slightly seedier side of their business: collecting taxes. Tax collection was a significant source of revenue for the publicans, and they became closely associated with the practice. Indeed, many translators render the term *publicanus* as simply "tax collector" or "farmer of the revenue." The idea of tax farming is unfamiliar to many today, but it was widely practiced in the ancient world. In Rome, it was an essential (perhaps *the* essential) means of funding the Roman state. As Caesar said, "There were two things which created, protected, and increased sovereignties—soldiers and money—and these two were dependent upon each other." There were many different forms of taxation in the Roman Republic, but as a general matter, the conquered territories bore the brunt of Roman taxes. These taxes could be high. In Sicily and Asia, for example, farmers were required to hand over 10 percent of their agricultural production every year. Whenever a new province was added to Rome's jurisdiction, either through conquest or annexation, it became subject to Rome's tax. But since the Roman Republic did not have a large administrative state, it did not have the capacity to enforce and collect the taxes owed to it, and the problem only grew as the Roman imperium expanded across the continent. The Senate resolved this problem by turning to tax farming. Under this system, instead of collecting the taxes directly, Rome would auction off the right to collect taxes to private enterprises, and then these enterprises would collect the taxes for their own profit.[8]

The process of auctioning off tax-collecting rights was a formalized affair. Auctions were held in the Roman Forum and managed by the Roman censor (a magistrate in charge of the census and, importantly for our purposes, government finances). The auctions were required by law to take place in public, before the people of Rome, in order to make the process open and transparent. Roman censors would set forth the terms and conditions of the contract ahead of time and then offer up the contract for bidding. The heads (or *manceps*) of the various *societates* in attendance would raise their hands if they were willing to pay the steadily increasing auction price. At the end of the auction, the winning company would then be obligated to pay a fixed sum to the Roman treasury (sometimes up front and sometimes in installments over the course of the contract). The enterprise would, in return, have the right to go off to the province and collect taxes for its own profit from the inhabitants. This was a mutually advantageous system for the Roman Republic and the *societates*—although perhaps not so much for the inhabitants of the provinces themselves. The Roman treasury received a guaranteed sum and did not have to go to the trouble of administering its tax system, which it likely did not have the capacity to do in any case, given the minuscule size of its bureaucracy. The *societates* had the possibility of recouping their money many times over if the province proved prosperous and their collection efforts sufficiently vigorous. Over time, the *societates* evolved into highly specialized creatures, with certain entrepreneurs gaining a reputation as repeat players in the auctions.[9]

The publicans quickly became important and wealthy constituents of the Roman Republic. Their accomplishments were widely recounted in public speeches of the time. Marcus Tullius Cicero, for example, frequently lauded their role in maintaining the republic. Defending the public official Gnaeus Plancius from charges of bribery, Cicero noted that Plancius was the son of a prominent equestrian publican. "And who is there who does not know what a great assistance that body of men [that is, the publicans] is to any one in seeking for any honor? For the flower of the Roman knights, the ornament of the state, the great bulwark of the republic is all comprehended in that body." By the time of Cicero, Caesar, and Augustus, the publicans had emerged as a potent economic and political force.[10]

BUT THE PUBLICANS COULD NEVER HAVE RISEN TO THE DIZZYING heights of power and wealth that they achieved in the first century BC without an important development in the structure of their business. It did not take them long to realize that they were much more powerful when they united their forces together than when they acted alone. As individual citizens, they would never have had the wealth necessary to carry on the massive projects of supplying armies and building temples. Separately, they were subject to all the circumstances of human fate—illness, injury, and death—that inhibit our ambitions. They were much more together than they were apart. Similarly, from the perspective of the Roman government, the idea of a society of publicans committed to promoting the state's affairs was appealing. It was a problem when the death of a single publican could interrupt the provision of government services or cut off the flow of government revenue.

And so the idea of a *societas publicanorum* with a special collection of rights and privileges evolved. The resulting *societas* looked strikingly similar to a modern-day corporation. First and foremost, the *societas* was recognized as an entity separate and apart from its owners. This is an important difference from a typical Roman partnership, where the partners could be held responsible for anything that the other partners did. If one partner failed to pay for something on time, the other partner could lose his farm. In a *societas*, on the other hand, the company could negotiate and contract with others on its own behalf and not that of its owners. Because the *societas* was a separate entity from its owners, it could "act like a person," as the *Digest*, the index of Roman law, concluded. This also meant that it could continue in existence even after the death of a member, or *socius*. Second, and relatedly, the *societas* had shares, or *partes*, that represented ownership interests in the company and could be bought either from other shareholders or directly from the company itself. Shares appear to have had fluctuating values as well, with Cicero writing of *partes illo tempore carissimas*, or shares that were at that time very expensive. Third, because many shareholders did not want to participate in the actual management of the company, the *societas* developed a management class devoted to running the business itself. The separation of shareholders from managers created new tensions that called for measures to regulate the relationship between the two groups. In order to ensure that the managers did not abscond with the shareholders' money, for example, managers were required to produce public accounts (or *tabulae*) of the business, setting forth the company's revenues and expenses. Indeed, there appear even to have been shareholder meetings where the managers and the shareholders could discuss the company's affairs together.[11]

The hierarchy of the *societas* ended up looking much like that of a modern corporation too. At the head of the *societas* stood the *manceps*. As mentioned before, the *manceps* was the individual who directly bid on contracts for the *societas*. He was also obligated to provide security for the company's contracts, typically in the form of land that he owned personally; if the company failed to fulfill its obligations, the Roman Republic could seize his land as repayment. The *manceps* was joined by a group of other *socii*, or partners, who provided capital to the company and sometimes, but not always, also offered guarantees in the form of pledged property. The *socii* and the *manceps* together created the company and registered it with the censor. The *socii*, like modern shareholders, did not directly run the affairs of the company and instead turned this over to the *magistri*, who might be compared with the board of directors of a modern corporation. These *magistri* were subject to annual election and were frequently replaced.[12]

This intricate structure allowed the *societates* to grow into sprawling institutions. Their revenues were enormous. One contract for togas, tunics, and horses from the second century BC amounted to around 1.2 million denarii, the equivalent of the total annual pay for ten thousand soldiers. Another contract, for the building of the Marcian aqueduct, came to forty-five million denarii, which would have equaled the wealth of Rome's richest citizen, Marcus Crassus. With operations throughout the Roman world, from the mines of Spain to the lands of Mithridates, the *societates* developed fast and efficient courier systems to communicate across the thousands of miles of territory. Their couriers became so renowned for their speed and reliability that the Roman Republic at times leased them out for their own messages.[13]

Being a corporate executive brought with it many perks. Beyond their wealth, the managers of Rome's corporations also held powerful positions in politics and society and, as a result, were catered to at every turn. People addressed them with the terms *maximi* (excellent), *ornatissimi* (highly honored), *amplissimi* (of high standing), and *primi ordinis* (of first rank). In an ancient version of corporate box seats, in 129 BC, the Roman Senate even passed a law reserving fourteen rows of seats at the games to the Roman *equites* (the class that ran the *societates*).[14]

But the benefits of the Roman *societates* did not accrue solely to the corporate executives. The Roman public partook in the bounties as well, partially through steady increases in state revenue and partially through direct share ownership. The budget of the Roman Republic tells the financial story in broad strokes. In the third century BC, the revenue of the Roman Republic was around four to eight million sestertii a year. By 150 BC, it had risen to fifty to sixty million sestertii. And by 50 BC, the heyday of the *societates*, state revenues had soared to 340 million sestertii a year. The dramatic rise in the state's wealth allowed the Roman Republic to engage in massive public works projects on a scale never before seen—roads, temples, aqueducts, sewers, and, of course, the circuses. The people of Rome also benefited from the *societates* more directly by owning shares in them. In fact, it appears that shares of the *societates* were widely dispersed in Roman society. Polybius wrote, "There is scarcely a soul, one might say, who does not have some interest in these [government] contracts and the profits which are derived from them." Shares of the Roman companies were traded freely among Roman citizens, typically at the Temple of Castor in the Forum. Polybius gives a sense of the breadth of the business: "Through the whole of Italy a vast number of contracts, which it would not be easy to enumerate, are given out by the censors for the construction and repair of public buildings, and besides this there are many things which are farmed, such as navigable rivers, harbors, gardens, mines, lands, in fact everything that forms part of the Roman dominion." Modern commentators, perhaps stretching the available evidence, have concluded that

Rome had a true capital market. Economic historian William Cunningham, in his classic *Essay on Western Civilization*, wrote, "The Forum, with its basilicae, may be regarded as an immense stock exchange where monetary speculation of every kind was continually going on." Another commentator described the scene at the Forum in bustling terms: "Crowds of men bought and sold shares and bonds of tax-farming companies, various goods for cash and on credit, farms and estates in Italy and in the provinces, houses and shops in Rome and elsewhere, ships and storehouses, slaves and cattle."[15]

But as the companies grew in size and power, so too did their potential dangers to the republic. One problem was fraud and corruption. In his *History of Rome*, Livy describes a scam orchestrated by two publicans during the Second Punic War, when the Roman Republic had been forced to rely on private contractors to provide supplies to troops in the field. Two opportunistic publicans who had entered into these contracts realized that there was a loophole in their terms: the agreement provided that if any supplies were lost at sea, the government would reimburse them for the loss, but the government had no way to verify what had been lost except by asking the publicans. Seeing an opportunity, the publicans began taking rickety old vessels, loading them with a few items of the lowest quality, and then intentionally sinking them. The publicans would then go back to the government and claim that they had lost a cargo of great value. Profits ensued. Eventually, the Senate got wind of the treachery and moved to prosecute them. The much-anticipated trial ended in chaos when other publicans assaulted the hearing ground, protesting against the prosecution of "two of their own." The Senate, undaunted, set another date for trial, but this time the two publicans fled into exile rather than face justice.[16]

Fraud was not the only problem with the *societates*, though. They also earned a reputation for cutthroat business practices. In 104 BC, the Romans asked Nicomedes III of Bithynia, a Roman ally, to provide troops for a war against German tribes on the border. Nicomedes replied that he did not have citizens to spare because "most of the Bithynians had been taken away as slaves by the publicans." The Senate, apparently shocked by the revelation, decreed that from that time forward, no citizen of an allied state could be enslaved by the publicans. That it was legal for them to do so before the Senate's decree is, perhaps, the most remarkable part of the story. But in fact, the *societates* enslaved people quite openly and, often, to great profit. The silver mines in New Carthage alone were worked by forty thousand slaves. The life of a slave in these mines was abominable. The Greek historian Diodorus Siculus wrote,

> The men engaged in the mining operations procure unbelievably large revenues for their masters, but through their excavations under the earth both by day and by night they wear out their own bodies, many of them dying because of the exceptional hardships; they are not allowed any relaxation or rest, but are compelled by the beatings of their supervisors to endure these terrible evils and throw away their lives in this wretched manner, although some of them who can endure it suffer their misery for a long time because of their bodily strength or sheer will-power; but they prefer dying to surviving because of the extent of their suffering.[17]

The abuses of the *societates publicanorum* led them to face harsh criticism from observers both ancient and modern. Livy wrote, "Where there was a publican, there was no effective law and no freedom for the subjects." Harvard classicist Ernst Badian wrote that the publicans "were the curse and the scourge of the conquered nations, largely responsible for the detestation of the Roman name among the subjects of Rome, and perhaps even for the downfall of the Roman Republic." Rome was beginning to feel the effects of just how dangerous private enterprise, turned to the wrong purposes, could be.[18]

BADIAN CLAIMED THAT THE ROMAN SOCIETATES WERE "PERHAPS" responsible for the downfall of the Roman Republic. This is an audacious claim. Other factors are more obvious culprits: the conflict between the rich and the poor, the growing power of the military, the overreaching ambitions of Caesar, the fierce suspicions of the Senate. But when one looks closely enough, one can detect the influence of the *societates* in nearly all of these forces.

Tracking the fortunes of the *societates* in the first century BC provides an intimate and sometimes surprising view of the tumultuous years from the fall of the republic to the rise of the empire. A fundamental conflict of Roman life at this time was the clash between the wealthy senators and the poor plebeians. The balance of power between these two groups fluctuated constantly throughout the century. Under the reign of the populist Gracchi brothers, the Senate had diminished in power, as the Gracchi granted new rights to a separate class of *equites* (or knights) as a counterweight to the Senate. One of their most important actions was assigning tax-collection rights in Asia, Rome's richest province, to the *societates publicanorum*. This gave the companies an enormous and enduring source of profits and power, and it tended to reduce the power of the Senate as a result, since senators were prohibited from participating in the *societates*.[19]

Cicero, the famed orator, philosopher, and politician, was particularly good at gaining the goodwill of the *societates* and, throughout his career, benefited from cozying up to them. Cicero himself came from the equestrian class, and many of his early speeches were devoted to advocating in favor of the *societates* before the Senate. During Rome's war against Mithridates of Pontus in 66 BC, on the urging of a group of publicans, he made one of his most famous speeches, "On Pompey's Command," arguing that the skilled general Gnaeus Pompeius Magnus should be given sole control over the war effort. In defense of this position, he pointed to the large investments that the *societates* had made in Asia, investments that would be imperiled if

Mithridates triumphed in the war. And if the *societates* failed, Cicero argued, so too would the Roman Republic:

> The publicans, most honorable and accomplished men, have taken all their resources and all their wealth into that province; and their property and fortunes ought, by themselves, to be an object of your special care. In truth, if we have always considered the revenues as the sinews of the republic, certainly we shall be right if we call that order of men which collects them, the prop and support of all the other orders. . . . It will, therefore, become your humanity to protect a large number of those citizens from misfortune; it will become your wisdom to perceive that the misfortune of many citizens cannot be separated from the misfortune of the republic. . . . In the next place, we, having learnt by disaster, ought to keep in our recollection what Asia and Mithridates taught us at the beginning of the Asiatic war. For we know that then, when many had lost large fortunes in Asia, all credit failed at Rome, from payments being hindered. For it is not possible for many men to lose their property and fortunes in one city, without drawing many along with them into the same vortex of disaster. Preserve the republic from this misfortune; for, believe me (you yourselves see that it is the case), this credit, and this state of the money-market which exists at Rome and in the forum, is bound up with, and is inseparable from, those fortunes which are invested in Asia. Those fortunes cannot fall without credit here being undermined by the same blow and perishing along with them. Consider, then, whether you ought to hesitate to apply yourselves with all zeal to that war, in which the glory of your name, the safety of your allies, your greatest revenues, and the fortunes of numbers of your citizens, will be protected at the same time as the republic.

Cicero saw that the *societates* had become so intertwined with the Roman state that they had become systemically important: if they failed, they would pull many others with them into their "vortex of disaster." The republic simply could not allow this to happen.[20]

At the same time, Cicero was not blind to the abuses of the *societates*. In a letter to his brother providing advice on how to govern a province, he once wrote,

> Now there is one great obstacle to your will and endeavor: the publicans. If we oppose them, we shall alienate from ourselves and from the state a class to which we owe a great deal and which we have brought into alliance with the public interest. On the other hand, if we defer to them all along the line, we shall have to close our eyes to the utter undoing of the people for whose interests, as well as survival, it is our duty to care. . . . Asia must also remember that if she were not in our empire she would have suffered every calamity that foreign war and strife at home can inflict. Since the empire cannot possibly be maintained without taxation, let her not grudge a part of her revenues in exchange for permanent peace and quiet.

Cicero knew that corporations abused the inhabitants of the provinces, but he thought this better than the alternative: not being part of Rome at all. For him, the greatest good was the Roman Empire, and anything that supported the empire was worth enduring. As he wrote to a friend, "You seem curious to know how I manage about the publicans. I dote upon them, defer to them, butter them up with compliments—and arrange so that they harm nobody."[21]

Caesar's two closest allies, Pompey and Crassus, were also intimately linked with the *societates*. Pompey, the renowned general, eventually gained command of the war against Mithridates, at least partially due to Cicero's eloquent speech on his behalf, and proceeded to conquer the kingdoms of Bithynia, Pontus, and Syria. In doing so, he added vast new provinces for the *societates* to do business in. The companies became powerful supporters of Pompey's political career as a result. (So much for Thomas Paine's comment in *The Rights of Man* that "if commerce were permitted to act to the universal extent it is capable, it would extirpate the system of war.") Crassus, famous mostly for his wealth, also represented the interests of the *societates* before the Senate and earned their support. As Oxford historian Charles Oman put it, "By his enormous money-making, and the place to which he had risen in the world of finance, [Crassus] had made himself the king and lord of the whole tribe of publicani." He may have even held shares in the *societates*.[22]

One particular event from 60 BC, the year before Caesar was elected consul, illuminates the powerful influence that the *societates* wielded in the Roman political system in the waning years of the republic. The corporations, overly optimistic about the amount of taxes they could collect from the provinces of Asia Minor, had paid much more in the latest round of auctions than they were able to recoup. As a result, if the contracts were enforced as written, they would face severe financial losses. Crassus resolved to protect their interest and took the matter up before the Senate. Cicero explains the scene in characteristically colorful terms:

> The state of the commonwealth in which we live here is weak and sad and unstable. I suppose you have heard that our friends the knights have pretty well broken with the Senate. To begin with, they were greatly annoyed by the promulgation under a senatorial decree of a bill providing for an investigation into the conduct of jurors guilty of taking bribes. . . . Aware that the equestrian order took it amiss, though they said nothing in public, I administered what I felt to be a highly impressive rebuke to the Senate, speaking with no little weight and fluency in a not very respectable cause. Now along come the knights with another fancy, really almost insupportable—and I have not only borne with it but lent it my eloquence. The publicans who bought the Asiatic taxes from the censors complained in the Senate that they had been led by over-eagerness into making too high an offer and asked for the cancellation of their contract. I

was their foremost supporter, or rather foremost but one, for it was Crassus who egged them on to make such an audacious demand. An invidious business! The demand was disgraceful, a confession of recklessness. But there was the gravest danger of a complete break between the Senate and the knights if it had been turned down altogether. Here again it was I principally who stepped into the breach.

The fate of the Roman Republic, Cicero argued, depended on bailing out the capitalists. The Senate, however, was unconvinced. It declined to accept the demands of the corporations and instead listened to the advice of Cato, the stern moralist, who insisted that the companies be held strictly to the terms of their agreements.[23]

The Senate's decision was a blow to the corporations and almost certainly bore a part in the negotiations of the Triumvirate, the alliance between Caesar, Pompey, and Crassus that led the three powerful men to act in concert to promote their mutual political interests and whose actions would eventually bring down the republic. A year later, in 59 BC, when Caesar became consul, he quickly nullified the Senate's decision and amended the companies' contracts in Asia to bail them out. Although we do not know much about Caesar's motivation for the decision, it is possible that Caesar himself was a shareholder in the *societates* and was acting to protect his own financial interests. In one of his speeches, for example, Cicero makes an intriguing reference to a former tribune having "extorted shares, very valuable at that time, from Caesar and from the publicans." Caesar may also have simply been seeking to curry favor with a powerful constituency.[24]

Many observers have picked up on the connection between corporations and the rise of the Triumvirate. Sociologist Max Weber attributed Caesar's success directly to the influence of the publicans. In *The Agrarian Sociology of Ancient Civilizations*, he traced how the demands of corporations drove the cycle of Roman warfare and its effects on Roman life. "Expansion overseas was capitalist in origin. The aristocracy of office preferred to maintain a cautious foreign policy and avoided interventions. It was the merchants, publicans, and domain leaseholders who prevailed and used Roman power to destroy the ancient trading centers of Carthage, Corinth, and Rhodes—all to serve their own capitalist interests." Weber believed that the key to understanding Roman development during the republic was understanding the "sharp struggle of interests" between the Roman aristocracy, which controlled the Senate, and the Roman bourgeoisie, which controlled the corporations. "The senatorial clans showed themselves to be determined to keep the bourgeoisie—the knights—under control. . . . Nevertheless the result of Rome's conquests was to increase steadily the opportunities for profit, and this meant that the economic power of capitalists constantly increased, for they were essential to the state treasury because they could advance cash and because they had the business training needed to manage public revenues." Weber believed that the ascendance of the publicans marked the "high point" of ancient capitalism. But conflict was inevitable, and after the Senate passed reforms that limited the powers of the corporations, the bourgeoisie looked for support elsewhere, eventually finding it in the Triumvirate. "The result of these changes [that is, the Senate's regulation of the corporations] was that the equestrians were driven to support Caesarism, which thus was able to rely on economic as well as military interests in its conquest of power."[25]

Ironically, while Caesar may have owed his success to the support of the corporations and the capitalist class behind them, he appears to have been quite skeptical of them as an institution. Throughout his career, he displayed a striking sympathy with the people of the provinces, a position directly contrary to the interests of the capitalist publicans. Caesar had first risen to prominence by launching prosecutions of provincial governors. In 77 BC, for example, when Caesar was just twenty-three years old, he charged Gnaeus Cornelius Dolabella, a former consul, with abusing his authority during his time as governor of Macedonia. He lost the case—a widely expected result given

Dolabella's prominent position in society—but won widespread admiration for the eloquence of his speech and the force of his arguments.[26]

When the Triumvirate eventually fell apart and Rome descended into civil war, the corporations began a long decline. During the civil war, they found their properties and assets confiscated by the rival sides. Business disappeared. Afterward, when Caesar emerged victorious, he enacted a series of reforms aimed at limiting the power of corporations. In Asia and Sicily, he did away with some tax farming and handed other tax-collecting duties to local government officials, thus removing them from the hands of the corporations. And where the *societates* maintained their tax-collecting rights, he reduced the amount that they could collect.[27]

The power of the corporations waned even further after the assassination of Caesar on the Ides of March in 44 BC. The emperor Augustus implemented a set of tax reforms that gradually replaced the *societates*, which had collected taxes for private gain, with *procuratores Augusti*, direct agents of the Roman Empire. Other laws were passed to limit the lawful activities that the *societates publicanorum* could undertake. By the second century AD, the *societates* had declined into obsolescence. Government bureaucrats had finally vanquished the private companies.

※ ※ ※

ANCIENT ROME PROVIDES us with a lesson about what corporations are and why they exist.

Let's take the second topic—why corporations exist—first. Roman corporations were created to solve a problem. The Roman Republic had expanded too far, too quickly. It was good at conquering, but it now had to become good at administering. But with no government bureaucracy to speak of, this was hard to imagine happening. Who was going to provide the Roman people with bread and circuses? Who was going to build the bridges and roads? Who was going to equip the armies? Who was going to collect the taxes? The *societates publicanorum* solved the problem. Rather than have the republic invent an administrative state out of thin air, Rome used the money, manpower, and expertise already in the hands of private capitalists to perform the state's key functions. The relationship was mutually beneficial, as the capitalists could not have performed these functions without the support of the state. It was an ingenious solution. The companies proved incredibly adept at organizing and concentrating human effort, and they quickly became ingrained in the fabric of the republic.

In other words, corporations were created to promote the good of the commonwealth.

But what about the first topic—what corporations are. Again, the needs of the republic were paramount in defining how corporations worked. In return for their services, the corporations were granted special privileges and rights not available to other businesses. They had a form of immortality, continuing even after the death of their owners. They had tradable shares, and owners of the shares benefited from limited liability. They were treated as separate people for the purposes of acting and transacting.

If you think about it for a bit, why these attributes developed becomes clear. Long-lived companies were more reliable than short-lived ones, which had the pesky habit of dying at the most inconvenient times. Limited liability and the trading of shares made it easier for the companies to raise money, which could then be used to pay massive sums to the state for tax-collection contracts. Treating corporations as people simplified business in all sorts of ways—suing, being sued, entering into contracts, all of these were easier when there was a single person to deal with rather than dozens or hundreds.

In short, the corporation is based on a single premise: when we unite individuals into a single body, not just abstractly but in the formal mandates of the law, they can accomplish more than they could ever accomplish acting alone. This premise explains both why corporations exist and what they are. We created corporations because we needed them to promote the good of the state. And corporations took the form they did because we believed in the virtues of cooperation.

But the Roman experience also provides us with a cautionary tale. The Roman corporation ended up undermining the Roman Republic. The desire for profit led the *societates* to oppress foreign peoples and clamor for new military conquests. Their appetite for risk-taking caused financial crises at home. Corporate greed corrupted politics. Harnessing the powers of private enterprise for the glory of the state, Rome discovered, was a dangerous task. With the massive restructuring of the state apparatus under the Roman Empire, the *societates* would become irrelevant and eventually disappear entirely.

The idea of the corporation, though, never died out. Roman law proved deeply influential over the coming centuries, and aspects of the corporation appeared in businesses throughout Europe. But the true rebirth of the corporation began over a thousand years later and just a couple hundred miles up the road from Rome. This time, the corporation took an even more powerful form. Rather than collecting money, it started creating it, ushering in a new era of speculation.

two

THE BANK

O N April 26, 1478, Lorenzo de' Medici strode into Florence's Duomo with a cardinal at his side and a crowd of ten thousand eager Florentines behind him. As befitted a man nicknamed "Il Magnifico," or "the Magnificent," the affair was a spectacle of the grandest kind. Lorenzo chose to celebrate the cardinal's visit by bringing him to High Mass in the Duomo, where he could admire Giotto's astonishing Gothic campanile and Brunelleschi's recently completed dome. Afterward, Lorenzo had invited the lords, nobles, and ambassadors in attendance to a lavish banquet at the Medici Palace, where they could peruse the family's renowned collection of artwork and luxury goods from around the world: tapestries, vases, jewels, clocks, exotic cloths, and porcelain from China. Among its treasures were two paintings by Botticelli, three by Giotto, and six by Fra Angelico. Donatello's *David* stood in the courtyard.[1]

Lorenzo was just twenty-nine years old at the time, but he already possessed that peculiar combination of innate talent and intellectual curiosity common to all the great minds of the age, a phenomenon that we now recognize with the term *Renaissance man*. He was a popular ruler, governing the Florentine Republic when it was the most powerful city-state in Italy. He was a wily diplomat, treating with dukes and kings and popes and often getting the better of them. He was a great connoisseur of artwork, patronizing what would become history's greatest collection of artists, including Michelangelo, da Vinci, Botticelli, and Ghirlandaio. He was a talented equestrian and jouster. In his free time, he wrote poetry and studied philosophy.

He also happened to be at the helm of Europe's greatest financial institution, the Medici Bank, founded over eighty years before by his great-grandfather, Giovanni. The bank's sky-high profits and international reach had lifted the family from relative obscurity to the heights of dynastic power. The family provided four popes to the Vatican and two queens to France. In Florence, it oversaw and paid for a flourishing of knowledge, art, literature, and architecture that has never been equaled. In Italy, it ushered in an era of economic and artistic transformation, the effects of which can be seen to this day. And in Europe, it paved the way for nations to emerge from the Middle Ages into a new era of prosperity.

But in a time of warring city-states and ever-shifting alliances, the success of the Medici Bank generated jealousy and resentment. One family in particular, the Pazzi, had become the sworn enemies of the Medici. The Pazzi, an old Florentine family, counted among its ancestors Pazzino de' Pazzi, the first knight to scale the walls of Jerusalem in the First Crusade. The family ran a rival bank that had suffered during the Medicis' ascent. Time and again, it had seen its efforts to regain lost glory stymied by the Medici Bank's seemingly unstoppable business empire. It was common knowledge that the Pazzi bore a grudge against Lorenzo and would be more than happy to see his bank falter.

But unbeknownst to Lorenzo, the Pazzi family had finally convinced powerful allies to join them in a plot to overthrow the Medici. And Lorenzo had just walked into their trap.

※ ※ ※

AT THE FOUNDATION of every banking business lies a formula made up of two variables: a deposit and a loan. A saver deposits money in a bank. The bank promises that, in return, it will pay interest on the deposit. The bank then turns around and loans out the deposit to a borrower who needs cash. The borrower promises, in return, to pay the bank interest on the loan. As long as the amount of interest that the bank receives from the spender is higher than the amount that it pays to the saver, the bank turns a profit.

So far, so good, but there is nothing particularly special about charging more for something than one pays for it. All businesses aspire to do that. The magic of banking stems from what happens as a consequence of this money-shuffling business. In the process of taking deposits and making loans, banks are in fact *creating* new money. When the saver deposits money at the bank, the bank issues a credit to the saver's account. At the same time, the bank loans out the money to a spender and issues a credit to the spender's account as well. There are now two deposits, and, importantly, both of these deposits can be used to pay for things. Voilà! The bank has just created money. As the economist John Kenneth Galbraith has described it, "The process by which banks create money is so simple that the mind is repelled. Where something so important is involved, a deeper mystery seems only decent."[2]

Banking has two important consequences for the world of capitalism. The first is that banks, wherever and whenever they have existed, exert an unusually strong influence on the surrounding economy. Banks decide who receives money and how much. They channel money from those who have it to those who need it. When doing their jobs well, banks facilitate the flow of capital to its best and highest use. Declining industries with dwindling prospects will find it harder and harder to receive loans, while promising new ones will find it easier and easier, as banks seek to redirect money to profitable enterprises.

Economists refer to this as "capital allocation"—finding efficient uses for capital. As British journalist Walter Bagehot put it, "English capital runs as surely and instantly where it is most wanted, and where there is most to be made of it, as water runs to find its level." A functioning banking system has proved the basis of all thriving economies. After all, banks can make or break businesses, industries, and even humans simply by deciding who is worthy of a loan. The business of banking, then, is about much more than just banking. It is about making markets work.[3]

The second consequence of banking is more pernicious. Banking has an inherent flaw in its code. It is, by its very nature, unstable and thus risky. Banks promise to give savers their money back whenever they demand, but at the same time they also loan those deposits out to borrowers. Banks keep some reserves of cash on hand, of course, but nowhere near the total amount of deposits they receive. As a result, if a large number of savers all of a sudden decide they want to reclaim their money, the bank has a problem. It does not have enough reserves on hand to pay them all back. When savers get wind of this, they may become increasingly panicked and rush to the bank in ever greater numbers to withdraw their savings, triggering a liquidity crisis—in other words, a run on the bank. Bank runs have a way of becoming self-fulfilling prophecies. Worry about a bank failing can cause the bank to fail. And what is more, given the first consequence of banking—its intricate interweaving in the broader economy—banking crises have a nasty tendency to ripple outward, bringing panic and crisis everywhere they reach. It is no exaggeration that much of financial regulation of the past century has been about trying to solve this problem of systemic risk.

The rise of banking proved a watershed moment in the history of corporations. It amplified the power of business enterprise at the same time that it inflated the risks. It laid bare just how closely connected corporations had become to the fates of nations. And while banks laid the foundation on which corporations would be built, they were often corporations themselves. No bank better exemplified these tensions than the Medici Bank.

THE MEDICI WERE, BEFORE ANYTHING ELSE, BANKERS (NOT DOCtors, as their name would suggest in Italian). Through their bank they established relations with popes and kings and dukes. Through their bank they set up outposts around the continent to link Europe's emerging markets. And through their bank they made the almost unimaginable fortunes that they then showered on artists and architects to create the world's most beautiful works. In order to understand the foundations of the Renaissance, we must turn to Florentine banking.

Florence's vibrant banking scene arose from the soil of disorder. At the time, the geographical area we today call Italy was a patchwork of feuding cities and kingdoms and, looming over them all, the Vatican. Three major cities—Venice, Genoa, and Florence—controlled international trade but fought constantly over their neighboring territories. Venice and Genoa had established thriving sea-trading routes from their own cities, while Florence entered the trading game after conquering Pisa and its ports in 1406. In Rome, the Vatican ran a sprawling empire of "Papal States" peppered throughout central Italy and constantly sought to enlarge it by any means necessary. Further south, the powerful Kingdom of Naples and Sicily struggled with internecine conflict between the rival houses of Anjou and Aragon.[4]

All of these areas were also recovering from the ravages of the Black Death. The plague had swept through Europe in the midfourteenth century, causing massive upheaval wherever it went. The disease had hit Florence particularly hard. The city suffered multiple waves of infection that ultimately killed approximately two-thirds of its inhabitants. As a result, the city's population had dropped from ninety-five thousand in 1338 to a mere forty thousand by 1427. The terrors of the plague inspired the Florentine poet Boccaccio to write his masterwork, the *Decameron*, which tells the story of a group of men and women fleeing diseased Florence for the countryside. In it, he describes what life in Florence was like during the Black Death: thousands falling sick in a single day, men and women dying in the streets, the odor of putrefying corpses filling the air. Churches were so overwhelmed with dead bodies that they ran out of cemetery space to bury them all and instead simply piled them into enormous trenches, layer over layer. "The whole city was a sepulcher," Boccaccio wrote. The physical and emotional toll on the city was staggering. Indeed, the founding father of the Medici Bank, Giovanni di Bicci de' Medici, lost his own father to the plague in 1363.[5]

Yet Florentines living in the fifteenth century also had reasons to be proud. They could lay claim to Italy's greatest poet, Dante Alighieri, and his masterpiece, the *Divina commedia*, written in 1320. Their economy was thriving, and the golden florin, the city's currency, was in high demand across Europe. And, despite everything its residents had suffered, Florence remained a self-governing republic. This could not be said of many other regions of Italy, like Naples, Sicily, Sardinia, and Piedmont, all of which foreigners had conquered.

Florence's political freedoms were ensured by an elaborate electoral system that contributed to the rise of the Medici. Elections in the city were held every two months by lottery. The guilds—associations of traders and merchants who controlled the city's most important commercial industries—provided a list of all eligible members who were over thirty years of age, and these names would then be written on tickets and placed in eight leather bags by election officials known as *accoppiatori*. Every two months, eight names would be drawn from the bags at random, and the eight citizens so chosen would serve as the priors of the *signoria*, or government, of Florence, along with a chief executive known as the *gonfaloniere della giustizia*, also chosen at random. Together, these new governors would all move into the Palazzo della Signoria in central Florence, where they would live together for the next sixty days and preside over the city's affairs. After their term was up, the whole process would begin again, with new names and new priors. The complex governmental machinery gave significant power to the guilds, which came to exercise decisive influence over both the economic and the political life of the city.

One of the oldest and most powerful guilds was the *Arte del Cambio*, or banking guild. By the fifteenth century, Florence had earned a reputation for its active banking scene: the city was so synonymous with finance that the term *banking* comes from the Florentine practice of having bankers sit at a *banco*, or table, to do business. It helped that the city maintained two parallel currencies, the gold florin and the silver *piccioli*, requiring frequent exchanges between the two at fluctuating exchange rates set by the banks. The guild maintained strict order over the banking business. Members would set up their tables or benches in a small area of town known as Orsanmichele, near the Mercato Nuovo. They identified themselves by their red gowns and large purses, which everyone knew to be filled with florins and other coins. Their tables were covered in green cloth, on top of which sat a ledger where the banker carefully recorded the day's transactions. The guild's rule was so powerful in the city that it even governed the manner in which bankers conducted this business: bankers had to be *sedentes ad tabulam cum tasca, libro et tappeto* ("sitting at a table with a purse, a ledger, and a cloth"). Under the guild's rules, every transaction had to be recorded in the ledger in the presence of the customer, and any member who destroyed or changed his ledger risked immediate expulsion from the guild. For those who followed the rules, money changing was a profitable affair. Many of the city's richest families, such as the Bardi and Peruzzi, descended from banking dynasties.

There is an unavoidable irony in the fact that banking arose in Florence. Rome, the Vatican, and the pope, after all, were just over one hundred miles away. Their religious authority at the time was supreme, and their position on money lending for profit was clear: it was strictly off-limits. Anyone found to be engaged in usury, as money lending was then called, was guilty of a grave sin under canon law. Violators could face serious punishment. The First Lateran Council of 1179 held that usurers could not be given a Christian burial. In the *Inferno*, Dante put usurers alongside sodomites in the seventh circle of hell. The Franciscans called usury "making the coins fornicate," among other memorable characterizations, and the friar Bernardine of Feltre argued that the Black Death was God's way of punishing usurers. The Vatican's concept of usury was also extraordinarily restrictive. Usury didn't just mean charging borrowers excessive interest rates, as the term implies today. Rome defined usury as charging borrowers *any interest at all*. This naturally proved an impediment to banks, which were in the business of loaning money and thus had to go to great lengths to structure their enterprises so that they could make money without running up against canon law.[6]

Perhaps the fear of eternal, fiery punishment forced Florentine bankers to think creatively. Perhaps regulation birthed innovation. Whatever the reason, the Vatican's rules proved no obstacle to the emergence of the world's first great bankers, the Medici.

In 1397, Giovanni di Bicci de' Medici, a mild-mannered thirty-seven-year-old Florentine working in Rome as a bank manager, decided to move his wife and two young children back to the city of his birth to set up his own bank. The family had long ties to the city of Florence—his great-grandfather had once served as *gonfaloniere*, and his grandfather had been an ambassador to Venice—but Giovanni had inherited little from his father and had to make his own way in the world. Upon settling the family in a modest house in Via Larga, he went to work registering his new bank with Florence's banking guild.

Giovanni had chosen an opportune time to set up shop. While Florence had a thriving banking sector, it had recently suffered the loss of two major players, the Bardi and the Peruzzi. These two families had reigned supreme in the fourteenth century but had made the mistake of granting enormous loans to the English king Edward III in the 1340s to fund his military campaigns in the Hundred Years War.

Edward defaulted on the loans in 1345, and the Bardi and the Peruzzi banks went bankrupt as a result. Their liquidation left a void at the center of Florence's banking world that Giovanni di Bicci hoped to fill. Even still, he had competition. According to the records of the banking guild, there were seventy-one banks in Florence in 1399. And in 1460, when the Medici Bank was at the height of its powers, there were still thirty-three banks operating in the city. It was a competitive landscape. But Giovanni knew that if he could beat his rivals, the opportunity for profit was immense. Florence was famed throughout Europe for its financial prowess, and the city's bankers were trusted with handling the most important transactions for the continent's elite.

During his time in Rome, Giovanni had become intimately familiar with canon law on usury, and he used this knowledge in setting up his bank. In fact, in many ways, Giovanni's elaborate efforts not to cross swords with the church drove the development of the Medici Bank as an international powerhouse. One particularly ingenious strategy was the bill of exchange. Giovanni knew that the Vatican defined usury as any loan that required the borrower to pay more than the initial amount borrowed. In Latin, this concept was rendered as *quidquid sorti accedit, usura est* ("whatever exceeds the principal is usury"). So one could not charge any amount over the initial loan sum. But he also knew that usury law only applied to loans — *usura solum in mutuo cadit*, as the Latin text phrased it. Thus, if a transaction was not a loan, it could not be considered usury. Giovanni realized he could use this loophole to his advantage. Instead of loaning someone money to be paid back with interest at a later date, the Medici Bank would give them money and ask that it be repaid somewhere else in a different currency. This made the transaction look like not a loan but an exchange. Giovanni could then manipulate the exchange rate, as well as the repayment date, to ensure that the bank received a reasonable amount of interest for its services. The bank could also charge commissions since this, after all, was not a loan.[7]

The Medici Bank's bills of exchange were not entirely subterfuges; nor, for that matter, were they entirely new. In fact, they served an important purpose in the emerging European economy. Diplomats, churchmen, and pilgrims often requested them before embarking on voyages to fairs, churches, and other prominent destinations across Europe. Travelers of the time were naturally leery of carrying large sums of money in their belts and saddlebags as they crossed the ever-shifting borders of the continent. The Medici Bank's bills of exchange offered them a better alternative. Instead of carrying coin with them, they could get a letter of exchange from the Medici Bank, which would then be payable in the local currency once they arrived at their destination.

Creating this seamless system, however, required a complex set of procedures within the Medici Bank. The *drawer* branch—that is the branch of the bank that received cash from an individual, called a *remitter*—would issue to the remitter a bill of exchange that would specify a long list of details: the identity of the remitter, the amount received (in local currency), the amount to be repaid (in foreign currency), the date and place of future repayment, the identity of the *drawee* (that is, the individual who was responsible for making the repayment, typically the manager of the foreign branch of the Medici Bank), and the identity of the *beneficiary* (the person who would receive the repayment in the foreign location and who was sometimes, but was not always, the same person as the remitter who initially paid for the bill of exchange). This information was all carefully recorded on the drawer branch's books. When the date for repayment came, the beneficiary could present the bill of exchange to the foreign branch manager of the Medici Bank and demand payment in the local currency. The books of all the respective branches would then need to be regularly reconciled to ensure that bills of exchange were being properly accounted for. Filling in the details of bills of exchange required intimate knowledge of travel times, the reliability of foreign merchants, and current exchange rates. Because there were often long delays between the initial payment and the future repayment—the customary time, or usance, for Florence-to-London exchanges, for example, was ninety days—there was substantial risk that exchange rates could fluctuate to the bank's disadvantage in the interim period. What is more, because the balance of trade between various branch locations was not always even—the Bruges branch notoriously received more cash than it sent elsewhere—the bank faced serious rebalancing issues to ensure that all the branches had sufficient capital to operate in their local jurisdictions. The whole process was so intricate that the Medici Bank took to writing lengthy manuals instructing employees on how to structure it. In 1417, one employee of the bank, upon finishing a new draft of the manual, appended a word of advice at the end: "He who deals in exchanges and he who deals in merchandise is always anxious and beset by worries. I will instead give you a recipe for lasagna and macaroni."[8]

The Medici Bank was not content to limit its use of bills of exchange just to international travelers, however. There was a strong and consistent demand for access to ready money in Florence and elsewhere, and people were willing to pay for it. In order to cater to this market, the Medici Bank invented another, even more complicated transaction called the "dry exchange." A dry exchange looked very much like a regular bill of exchange except that, instead of happening abroad, the currency exchange would occur in the same place, and twice over. For example, a borrower might take out a loan from the Medici Bank in florins and promise to repay in English pounds at a later date. Once that later date arrived, he would then enter into another exchange, in which he borrowed English pounds and promised to repay in florins at a later date. In the end, he would just repay the initial florins that he had borrowed in the first place. The involvement of English pounds was entirely superfluous, and, in fact, the foreign currency often never even changed hands at all. The Medici Bank would profit by building in differing exchange rates and commissions to guarantee themselves an appropriate interest rate. But, because this was still technically an exchange—two exchanges, to be precise—and not a loan, it did not break usury laws.[9]

One practical consequence of the bill of exchange was that the Medici Bank, from the very beginning, was deeply interested in foreign affairs. The burgeoning business in exchanging currencies drew the Medici Bank further and further into the waters of international commerce. In order to set exchange rates, the Medici bankers needed to know things about other countries and cities and towns. They had to send employees abroad to learn about business conditions, government policies, and currency values all across Europe. They set up branches in these foreign lands in order to develop relationships with sovereigns and traders. Their foreign branches would provide regular reports back to Florence about conditions in their countries, and these reports were filled with insights about the cultures and economies of other cities.

Another way that the Medici Bank got around the usury problem was by using something called a *deposito a discrezione*, or "discretionary deposit." The discretion here referred to the bank's decision about whether to pay the depositor interest on an initial deposit. This, of course, was a way to pay savers for the benefit of holding their money, but, again, it was important that it not be considered interest due to the usury laws. As a result, the *discrezione* was structured as an optional gift, freely offered by the bank and gratefully accepted by the saver. Since it was a gift, it couldn't be considered usury. This seemed like a neat end run around church doctrine, and bankers and savers alike embraced it. But the problem was that because the *discrezione* was, by definition, discretionary, the Medici Bank could decide not to pay it. This rarely occurred, but when it did, it could be devastating for the saver. In 1489, for example, the Lyons branch of the Medici Bank declined to provide a *discrezione* to Philippe de Commines, a wealthy French diplomat and historian, on his deposit of twenty-five thousand ecus with the bank. After making his initial deposit with the Medici

Bank's Lyons branch, Commines had been arrested and imprisoned for his part in the Orleanist rebellion against French king Charles VIII. He spent years in an iron cage as punishment for his role in the revolt. In 1489, he came to the bank to ask for his money back in order to pay a hefty fine levied against him and get himself out of jail. But by that time the Lyons bank had run into troubles of its own, a combined result of mismanagement and a mounting portfolio of bad debts, and thus the bank could only pay him back his initial deposit, with no *discrezione* at all. Distraught, Commines appealed directly to Lorenzo de' Medici, writing him in a letter that the bank was treating him unfairly. Lorenzo wrote back that he could do nothing. The bank's losses were simply too great.[10]

Needless to say, the complexity of all these transactions—bills of exchange, dry exchanges, *discrezione* deposits, currency fluctuations, branch withdrawals, and many others—required careful documentation. The Medici Bank had to keep track of its assets and liabilities over long periods and across borders if it wanted to grow its business and perpetuate its elaborate anti-usury subterfuges. To do so, the Medici Bank used a system known as double-entry bookkeeping, a brilliant form of accounting that remains in widespread use today. Under the double-entry system, each transaction of the bank led to two entries in the bank's accounts: one credit and one debit. The system helped the bank to prevent sloppy record keeping, as mistakes were easily detectable if one side of the account did not balance with the other. Though the Medici didn't invent double-entry bookkeeping—other Florentine banks of the time also used the method, and there is evidence of its use in Genoa as early as 1340—they perfected the art. The bank's accounting records were so comprehensive that we are still able to reconstruct with pinpoint accuracy the profits and losses made by individual branches in individual years for most of the bank's existence. It is a remarkable testament to the Medici Bank's fine-tuned system of financial engineering.

GIOVANNI KNEW THAT ALL OF HIS COMPLEX SCHEMES AND STRUC-
tures would mean nothing if his bank did not have customers. And
so, from the very beginning, he went to work cultivating them. His
first stop was the church, and he gambled big on it. In the late 1390s,
a young Neapolitan archdeacon named Baldassare Cossa was making a name for himself within the Vatican. Cossa had been born into
an aristocratic but impoverished family on Procida, an island just off
the coast of Naples, near Ischia. In his earlier life, Cossa had been
a pirate, a vocation he shared with his two brothers. But Cossa left
piracy for a brief career in law, which he studied at the University of
Bologna, and then the priesthood. He quickly worked his way up the
ranks of the church using something he had learned in his previous
incarnations: the value of a well-timed threat. He ingratiated himself
with Pope Boniface IX through his uncanny knack for "convincing"
bishops to offer large gifts to the church. His favorite strategy for doing
so was to threaten bishops with reassignment to Muslim lands unless
they paid up. Sometime during this rise to power (we do not know
precisely when), Giovanni di Bicci de' Medici met Cossa, and they
struck up a lively friendship. In 1402, when Cossa needed money to
seal his appointment as a cardinal, Giovanni loaned him ten thousand
florins. While it is impossible to give a precise modern value for this
amount, it would certainly have been considered a sizeable sum: in
1400, a construction worker could expect to earn approximately a florin a week for his labor. In other words, Giovanni's loan would have
been sufficient to employ ten thousand laborers for a week. In 1404,
the Medici Bank's accounts record a loan of 8,937 florins to Cossa,
suggesting continued business between the two. The relationship between Giovanni and Cossa appears to have been a warm one: letters
from the period show Cossa addressing Giovanni as his "most dear
friend." And then, in Giovanni's greatest victory yet, in 1410, the Con-
clave of Bologna elevated Cossa to the papacy. Cossa promptly named
the Medici Bank as the Vatican's formal depositary. The Medici were
now officially God's bankers. The Medici then proceeded to grant

Cossa—now going by the name John XXIII—loans of almost one hundred thousand florins to finance his war to secure his contested claim to the papacy.[11]

From then on, the Medici Bank would claim the Vatican as its biggest client and its most reliable source of income. The bank helped the Vatican gather its tithes and taxes from around Europe, a big business covering vast geographical areas and involving complicated logistics, further encouraging the Medici Bank's international expansion. It also served as the "depositary general" for the Apostolic Chamber, meaning that funds given to the Vatican's treasury would be parked with the Medici Bank. Combined, these businesses were enormous profit centers for the bank. The Medici Bank's Rome branch accounted for well over half of the bank's revenues all the way until 1434. Giovanni assigned employees to set up branches wherever the pope was currently located, moving variously from Constance to Basel to Rome. Indeed, in the bank's records, the Vatican branch is often simply referred to as *i nostri che seguono la corte di Roma* ("ours who follow the court of Rome").[12]

Beyond the church, kings, rulers, and nobles formed another important component of the Medici Bank's clientele. These groups were in more or less constant need of money during the Renaissance to fund their wars, build their castles, and buy their luxury goods, and the Medici Bank proved a reliable source of it. The bank's Geneva branch, for example, counted among its customers the king of France, the duke of Savoy, and the duke of Bourbon. The Milan branch's main customer was Francesco Sforza, the duke of Milan. The London branch made loans to a succession of English kings and nobles. Sometimes this required the Medici Bank to ship large sums of gold and silver around the continent by trusted courier, often hidden in bales of cloth. At other times, the transaction was handled by a bill of exchange. The Medici Bank also catered to the tastes of its wealthy clientele by sending them precious goods like silk, jewelry, and exotic spices. Once the Medici Bank even sent a giraffe as a gift to the duchess of Bourbon, but, much to the bank staff's dismay, it died en route.[13]

Loans to rulers did not come without their risks. Unlike with lowly churchmen, the Medici Bank could exert little leverage if rulers chose not to pay. It was, after all, bad loans made to Edward III that ruined the last major Florentine banks, the Bardi and Peruzzi banks of the fourteenth century. In order to mitigate these risks, Giovanni often asked borrowers to offer some item of value as a security against default. Pope John XXIII gave Giovanni a precious miter. Innocent VIII gave the Medici Bank his tiara. The archduke of Austria gave the bank a nineteen-pound reliquary covered in jewels known as the fleur-de-lys of Burgundy. Securing collateral was not a new practice—Florence was home to a large group of pawnbrokers, typically of Jewish background and thus not subject to usury laws, who regularly engaged in secured loans—but the Medici elevated the practice to new heights. These were the perks of doing business with the great and the powerful during the Renaissance.[14]

But Giovanni's genius was not limited to his careful circumvention of usury or his dutiful cultivation of powerful clients. It also extended to the very structure of the bank itself. The organization of the Medici Bank was a marvel of legal and political acumen. Formally, the Medici Bank was a partnership of leading family members and their associates. But the Medici were acutely aware that, as one of the richest families in Europe, they could easily become the targets of jealous or resentful rulers and merchants. In order to protect themselves, the Medici Bank invented a corporate-like arrangement that might today be best described as a bank holding company. At the center of this arrangement stood the Medici Bank itself, in which members of the Medici family served as partners or owners, sometimes with one or two other parties. But the branches that the Medici

Bank established all around Europe—nine of them in all—were set up as their own separate partnerships (sometimes in the form of *accomandite*, an early form of limited partnership that protected partners from lawsuits). The Medici Bank would typically serve as the majority partner of these branches, while the branch manager would serve as a junior partner. This innovative structure gave the branch managers incentives to work hard—as partners, the branch managers shared in the company's profits and losses and so had a vested interest in the bank's success. It also incentivized the regular workers (or *fattori*)— the Medici, as a general rule, chose managers from the ranks of the *fattori*, and thus the *fattori* had a fair chance of one day "making partner" if they did their job well. Finally, it provided a way for the Medici Bank to benefit from a version of limited liability: if one branch failed, only its own assets could be confiscated, not the assets of the Medici Bank as a whole.[15]

This scheme for distributing risk worked like a charm. It often protected the bank from the claims of jilted clients. In 1455, for example, one Damiano Ruffini of Milan bought nine bales of wool from the London branch of the Medici Bank. The bales, poorly packed, were damaged while in transit to Bruges. When Ruffini tried to sue the Bruges branch of the bank for damages, its branch manager argued in municipal court that the London branch was an entirely different company, one that he was not responsible for. The Bruges court confirmed that Ruffini only had a claim against the *London* branch, not the Bruges one, and sent Ruffini away empty-handed.

The careful separation of power did not, however, mean that the Medici Bank did not exert control over the other branches. It very much did. Giovanni went to elaborate lengths to ensure that the bank's various branches were all working for the benefit of the bank as a whole. To oversee these affairs, the Medici Bank in Florence employed a general manager, who could issue orders and set policies for all the other branches. The general manager would, for example,

look over the accounts and records of each branch and make sure
that it was staying profitable and not issuing ill-advised or excessively
risky loans. Like the CEOs of modern times, the Medici Bank's general managers took on outsized roles in the history of the bank, and
its fortunes depended on their success. Perhaps the most famous was
Giovanni d'Amerigo Benci, known for his deep financial acumen,
who presided over some of the bank's most profitable years in the
1440s and 1450s. His successor, Francesco di Sassetti, on the other
hand, was a dismal failure, and his oversights are often pointed to as
one of the causes of the decline of the bank itself. (Sassetti did, however, manage to enrich himself—at one point, he had a fortune of
fifty-two thousand florins, a house in Florence, three farms, a villa in
Montughi, jewels, a library, and forty-five thousand florins invested in
the Medici Bank.)

Bank employees were carefully monitored and subject to strict
rules of behavior. The bank required branch managers to stay in their
branch's city for the duration of their term, which often lasted four
to five years. (Exceptions were given if they were explicitly called
to Florence to account for their business or if they had to travel to
a short list of essential markets.) Branch managers were prohibited
from making loans to princes—these loans were sensitive businesses
for the bank, and so decisions on them were reserved for the Medici
themselves. Most ordinary citizens were excluded from doing business with the bank at all, as it restricted its client list almost exclusively to the wealthiest and most powerful in society. At the same
time, employees themselves were richly rewarded if they proved trustworthy. Low-level employees were often promoted up the corporate
ladder. Many of them developed close personal friendships with the
Medici family. When one of Cosimo de' Medici's managers, Folco
Portinari, died in 1431, leaving several children without a father, Cosimo brought the children into his own household and raised them
as his own. Perhaps it helped that the Portinari children were distant
descendants of Beatrice, Dante's famed love.[16]

WITH ALL OF THESE PIECES IN PLACE, GIOVANNI CONSTRUCTED one of the most successful companies in history, and the bank generated huge profits for decades. The family amassed an immense personal fortune as a result. During the period from 1397 to 1420, Giovanni himself made a personal profit of 113,865 florins from his bank, an average of 4,950 florins a year. These profits only accelerated in future years. In 1427, tax returns from the Florentine *catasto* reveal him as the second richest man in Florence (behind only Palla Strozzi, another banker and one of Giovanni's personal rivals). In 1457, his son Cosimo de' Medici declared on his tax return that he owned two palaces on Via Larga, several villas in Careggi, Cafaggiolo, and Trebbio, and houses in Pisa and Milan. By 1469, the assets of the Medici were estimated to be worth 228,000 florins. These are astounding sums. A cost-of-living estimate from 1480, for example, found that a worker could comfortably support a wife and four children with an annual income of just 70 florins. In other words, the Medicis' wealth in 1469 could have supported a good-sized family in comfort for a period of over three thousand years.[17]

But the Medici would never have gone down in history as the patrons of Florence if they had simply used their wealth on personal comfort. They are known today not for their banking prowess but for their deep devotion to and spending on the glory of Florence—its art, its architecture, its learning. Throughout the fifteenth century, the Medici family lavished an astonishing amount of money on the artists of Florence, from Michelangelo to da Vinci to Botticelli to Brunelleschi to Fra Angelico to Ghirlandaio. Giovanni hired struggling artists to paint frescoes on the walls of his house and, in 1419, paid Brunelleschi to design and build a new foundling hospital, the Ospedale degli Innocenti. His son Cosimo de' Medici paid the famed scholar Marsilio Ficino to translate Plato's complete works into Latin, for the first time allowing the West to read the philosopher's works in that language. Cosimo, eager to learn more from the wisdom of the ancients, asked his agent in Lubeck to search for a lost work of Livy

rumored to be in a Cistercian monastery—he never found it, but he
did find a rare Pliny with the Dominicans. Lorenzo "Il Magnifico"
brought Michelangelo into his own household and raised him like a
son. The Medicis' commitment to art and learning transformed the
city. Italian poet Poliziano wrote, "Athens has not been destroyed by
the barbarians but has migrated to Florence." For his contributions
to Florence, Cosimo was given the name *pater patriae*, father of the
fatherland.[18]

Outside art, though, the Medici Bank also fundamentally changed
the way that people interacted with money and exchange. In doing
so, it helped shift the European economy away from agricultural feu-
dalism and toward a more modern capitalism based on finance and
trade. The Medici Bank's reliable network of branches across the continent broke down barriers to dealmaking, reassuring merchants that
they could buy and sell goods where they were most needed without
fear of debased or worthless local currencies. Its couriers and fleets
opened up new markets, sending valuable goods—spices, silk, cloth,
wool, satins, gold thread, jewelry, alum, olive oil, citrus fruits—to all
the great cities of Europe. Its early model of an international financial system spurred extraordinary growth over the course of the century. It would prove one of the great economic innovations of the
Renaissance.

IT IS ALWAYS SAFER TO BE A KINGMAKER THAN A KING. THROUGH-
out the first half of the fifteenth century, the Medici took this lesson
to heart. They carefully avoided assuming the trappings of political
power, preferring the steady profits of finance to the vicissitudes
of statecraft. Giovanni, founder of the bank, spent his time on the
daunting task of putting it on firm financial grounds and steered clear
of overt political ambitions. Since the priors in Florence were chosen
by lot, he did at times serve in the government and, once, in 1421, as
gonfaloniere, but his policies typically evinced a devotion to the inter-

ests of the poor—replacing a regressive poll tax with a more progressive property tax, for example, and defeating a proposal to allow nobles into the government of the *signoria*. More often, he simply refused to accept political honors. In 1422, when Pope Martin V offered to make him the count of Monteverde, he politely declined. Politics was not for him. The best picture of Giovanni's character comes from his final words to his children, spoken from his deathbed:

> Do nothing against the wish of the people, and if they wish what they ought not, endeavor to turn them from it by friendly remonstrance rather than by arrogant dictation. Do not make the government-house your workshop, but wait until you are called to it, then show yourselves obedient, and avoid big swelling words. Strive to keep the people at peace, and the strong places well cared for. Engage in no legal complications, for he who impedes the law shall perish by the law. Do not draw public attention on yourselves, yet keep free from blemish as I leave you.[19]

Giovanni di Bicci's son, Cosimo, succeeded his father in 1420 and followed in his footsteps. He was a consummate businessman, presiding over the Medici Bank's greatest and most profitable period until his death in 1464. During these years, the Medici Bank expanded from its offices in Rome, Geneva, Venice, and Naples to cities all across Europe: London, Pisa, Avignon, Bruges, Milan, and Lubeck. Its profits rose substantially, from around 6,500 florins a year from 1397 to 1420, to 12,500 from 1420 to 1435, to 20,000 from 1435 to 1450. Cosimo's combination of commercial acumen and personal virtue made him widely admired in Florence and abroad. In his *History of Florence*, Niccolò Machiavelli wrote that Cosimo was "one of the most prudent of men; of grave and courteous demeanor, extremely liberal and humane, [who] never attempted anything against parties, or against rulers, but was bountiful to all; and by the unwearied generosity of his disposition, made himself partisans of all ranks of the citizens."

The sixteenth-century Italian historian Francesco Guicciardini wrote, "No private citizen since the fall of Rome had enjoyed such a reputation." Cosimo himself chalked his success up to modesty. "There is in gardens a plant which one ought to leave dry although most people water it," Cosimo said. "It is the weed called envy." Cosimo was not, however, averse to occasional lobbying in favor of the bank's business interests. One of his major successes was the legalizing of "dry exchanges," the controversial transactions that looked an awful lot like an interest-bearing loan to many observers but proved tremendously profitable to the bank.[20]

Despite his efforts to steer clear of politics, Cosimo could not entirely avoid the day's controversies. In the early 1430s, Florence went to war with Lucca and Milan for control of the flourishing region of Tuscany. War expenses mounted quickly. At one point, the Florentine government dispatched the famed builder Brunelleschi to attempt to divert the Serchio River from its natural route into the city of Lucca, thereby flooding the occupants. The effort failed when the Lucchesi, catching wind of the plot, demolished the canal and flooded the plain below, forcing Florence's army to retreat. Cosimo used the Medicis' cash to help support these expensive projects, but he never liked the war and eventually withdrew his support for it. The move put him at loggerheads with one of the ruling families of Florence, the Albizzi, who had spearheaded the conflict. Sensing the political winds shifting against him at home, Cosimo began taking precautions to protect the bank's interests. In 1433, he secretly began transferring the Medici Bank's cash to its branches in Rome and Naples, and he stashed a large sum of gold with the Benedictine monks of San Miniato al Monte and the Dominicans of San Marco. Cosimo's instincts were, as usual, prescient. In September 1433, he was summoned for a meeting at the Palazzo della Signoria and, upon arrival, was promptly arrested and confined to a small cell in the bell tower called the Alberghettino, or "little inn." The Albizzi family put him on trial, arguing that he should be executed for seeking to "elevate himself above others." But at his trial in front of the *balia*, a committee of two hundred citizens of Florence, the people refused to condemn him. It didn't hurt that the Medici Bank's most powerful clients interceded on his behalf. Both the Venetian Republic and the Vatican, which maintained close business ties to the Medici, sent delegates to Florence to defend Cosimo. In the end, the *balia* decided simply to exile Cosimo from Florence for a period of ten years, and so Cosimo moved to Venice. Because of Cosimo's foresight in transferring assets out of Florence, though, the Medici Bank's business continued without a hiccup, and a year later the *signoria* invited Cosimo back.[21]

When Cosimo de' Medici died in 1464, though, the bank began to show cracks. The problems began when Piero, nicknamed "the Gouty," succeeded his father. Piero had no banking experience and proceeded to make a number of blunders that would seriously harm the bank's business prospects. One of these decisions was to demand that many borrowers repay their loans immediately. The move temporarily inflated the bank's balance sheet, but it also made borrowers less willing to bring their business to the Medici Bank in the future. Many Florentine businesses, unable to meet their debt burdens, went bankrupt as a result. And despite his professed policy of retrenchment, Piero increasingly involved the bank in risky bets on speculative ventures. During his tenure, the Medici Bank took over tax-collection duties in the Gravelines and loaned money to the turbulent Charles the Bold of Burgundy. Both deals turned out badly. Piero spent most of his time dealing with various crises within the government and turned the Medici Bank's management over to a subordinate, Francesco di Tommaso Sassetti. Sassetti enriched himself but did little to turn around the struggling fortunes of the bank.[22]

When Piero died in 1469, his son, Lorenzo "Il Magnifico," took over (as with royal bloodlines, control of the company typically passed to the eldest son, although this sometimes required that new partnership agreements be concluded). Lorenzo, like his father, was largely uninterested in managing the bank—as Francesco Guicciardini wrote,

Lorenzo "did not have a mind for commerce or private things." Instead, he had other, more elevated interests. He wrote poetry. He studied philosophy. He won first prize at a jousting tournament in the Piazza Santa Croce in 1469, and his poems (including his magnificent ode to youth, "Canzona di Bacco") are still widely read in Italy. The bank's business went untended.[23]

Lorenzo's greatest love was politics. As a youth, he led diplomatic missions across Italy—to the Vatican, Bologna, Venice, and Milan—and developed a liking for the art of diplomacy and statesmanship. When he succeeded his father as the head of the family in 1469, he swiftly moved to consolidate control. In Florence, he abolished the popular councils of the *comune* and the *popolo*, removing one of the few real checks on his power in the city. Outside Florence, he forged an alliance with the Sforza family of Milan and courted the favor of the newly appointed Pope Sixtus IV. "It is hard for the rich to live in Florence," he would say in defense of his political maneuverings, "unless they rule the state." Guicciardini wrote simply that Lorenzo "held the city completely in his will, as if he were a prince waving a baton."[24]

When Lorenzo occasionally turned his eyes back to the bank, things tended to go badly. One of his first initiatives was getting the Medici Bank into the alum trade. Alum was a kind of all-purpose mineral used in dying wool, and Lorenzo believed that large profits were to be found in it. When alum deposits were found near Civitavecchia, in a town known as Tolfa, in 1460, Lorenzo hastily secured the mining rights from the Vatican. But the investment turned into a disaster. Imports of alum by the Ottoman Turks constantly threatened the venture's profits. The discovery of new alum deposits in Ischia forced the Medici Bank into an embarrassing profit-sharing arrangement to prevent further price competition. When the Medici Bank bullied the town of Volterra into handing over rights to a new mine discovered there, the population revolted and Lorenzo sent in the famed mercenary Federico da Montefeltro, the duke of Urbino, to sack the town, further tarnishing Lorenzo's reputation. Tensions with the Vatican in the 1470s led to even severer losses until finally, in 1476, Pope Sixtus IV revoked the Medici Bank's alum contract and handed it over to the rival Pazzi Bank. Lorenzo's bet on alum proved costly.

But as Lorenzo waded deeper and deeper into the intrigues of Europe's warring powers, he could not resist the temptation of using the Medici Bank as a tool for furthering his political aims. He increasingly enlisted the bank's financial networks to aid his friends and harm his enemies. He made loans to borrowers of dubious creditworthiness such as the tempestuous Charles the Bold of Burgundy and withheld them from more dependable ones like the church. His bank suffered, with loans going unpaid and his branches facing steep losses. But the worst was yet to come. This mixing of politics and business, always delicate even in the hands of masters like Giovanni and Cosimo de' Medici, turned into dry powder under Lorenzo's watch, ready to explode at the slightest spark. That spark finally arrived on April 26, 1478.

THE PAZZI CONSPIRACY HAD BEEN A LONG TIME COMING. IN Lorenzo's nearly ten-year tenure at the head of the Medici Bank, he had collected enemies as swiftly as he had works of art. By 1478, the list had grown to include many of the most powerful figures in Italy. Francesco de' Pazzi, who ran the rival Pazzi Bank, had a long-standing grievance against the Medici for overshadowing and outmaneuvering his own bank. The archbishop of Pisa, Francesco Salviati, despised Lorenzo for having opposed his church appointment. The affections of Federico da Montefeltro, the dashing warrior-duke who had once helped Lorenzo put down the Volterra revolt, had recently turned cold. But the most important enemy of all sat on the throne in Rome: Pope Sixtus IV. Lorenzo had initially cultivated good relations with the pope, but after the Medici Bank refused to help fund the pope's purchase of the town of Imola for a family member (Lorenzo wanted it for himself), relations deteriorated swiftly. The Pazzi Bank ended up providing the loan instead, and, soon after, the pope chose to re-place the Medici Bank with the Pazzi Bank as the Vatican's financial advisors. But the Pazzi were not content with this small victory: they wanted to permanently remove the Medici Bank from the Floren-tine banking scene. To do so, they needed to eliminate the Medici family itself.[25]

The final pieces of the plot came together in the spring of 1478. Having secured the support of Archbishop Salviati in Pisa and Fed-erico da Montefeltro in Urbino, the Pazzi paid a visit to Pope Six-tus and informed him of their plans to overthrow the Medici. Like so many Renaissance intriguers, Pope Sixtus was evasive in his response. "I desire the death of no man but only a change of government," he told them, before continuing, "I urgently desire that the government of Florence be removed from Lorenzo, for he is a treacherous scoun-drel who consistently defies us. As soon as he is removed, we may deal as we please with the Republic, which will be highly agreeable with us." Not skipping a beat, he promised to provide the Pazzi with troops to carry out their mission. The message was clear: the pope blessed the plot.

As Lorenzo entered the Duomo to celebrate High Mass on April 26, he was blissfully unaware of the conspiracy swirling around him. He took his seat across from his brother Giuliano near the altar. He was listening to "Agnus Dei" when the violence began. A cry of "Take this, traitor!" rang out in the church. Two hooded figures—one of whom was Francesco de' Pazzi—approached Lorenzo's brother Gi-uliano. Wielding daggers, they stabbed him nineteen times in a fury of violence. Giuliano died on the spot. As this happened, Lorenzo turned to find two priests bearing down on him with knives drawn. He received a glancing blow to the neck before leaping over the choir to get away. His close friend and fellow banker Franceschino Nori rushed to stop the attackers but was killed. Nori's intervention gave Lorenzo a few precious seconds to make it to the sacristy, where he barricaded himself behind the bronze doors.[26]

Meanwhile, outside the Duomo, the second part of the conspiracy was unfolding. Other members of the attack, including senior Pazzi family members, led a group of hired soldiers through the streets on horseback, hoping their cries of "Freedom" would rally Florentines to help them overthrow the Medici family. The plan backfired. Florentines, enraged by the assault on their city's ruling family, responded back with cries of *"Palle, palle"* (referring to the signature red balls on the Medici family's coat of arms). The mob attacked and killed the Pazzi conspirators, along with their hired crossbowmen. They then dragged Francesco de' Pazzi and Archbishop Salviati to the Palazzo Vecchio and hanged them.

Once Lorenzo realized that the attack had been rebuffed, he emerged from his refuge in the sacristy with vengeance on his mind. The ensuing weeks would prove the bloodiest of his reign. He ordered all Pazzi family members and accomplices hunted down and murdered. Some were hanged from the windows of the Palazzo della Signoria. Others were thrown from the top floors of the palace. The head of the Pazzi family, Jacopo de' Pazzi, was tortured, hanged, thrown into a ditch, and then dragged through the streets to finally rest at the door of the Palazzo Pazzi, the Pazzi family's palace, where his head was used as a door knocker. Before it was over, every adult Pazzi male was dead with the exception of Guglielmo de' Pazzi, who was fortunate enough to be Lorenzo's brother-in-law and thus escaped punishment. Female Pazzi were forbidden from marrying. The city commissioned Botticelli to paint a fresco depicting the events on the wall of the Palazzo Vecchio as a reminder of what happened to people who opposed the Medici. The enormous fresco—now lost—depicted in gory detail the hanged bodies of the conspirators.

While Lorenzo exacted a swift and brutal revenge against the Pazzi family, the Pazzi conspiracy succeeded in another way: it led to the ruin of the Medici Bank. Lorenzo's violence against the Pazzi alienated his allies and enraged his opponents. After confiscating the Pazzi Bank's assets, the Florentine *signoria* wrote a letter to Pope Sixtus, calling him "Judas in the seat of Peter." The pope responded by ex-communicating Lorenzo and confiscating the Medici Bank's assets in Rome and Naples, including all the remaining alum in the Medici Bank's warehouses. The Vatican and Naples then jointly declared war on Florence. With a weakened bank and a desperate need for cash, Lorenzo began looting money directly from the Florentine treasury, seventy-five thousand florins in all. In the ensuing years, Lorenzo would turn increasingly paranoid and dictatorial. He appointed an emergency committee, the Ten of War, with nearly limitless control over the city, and he had the government grant him a bodyguard of twelve armed men. For the remainder of his life, he devoted himself to politics and diplomacy to the exclusion of all else. The business of the Medici Bank went neglected, its finances steadily deteriorating.[27]

In the waning years of the fifteenth century, the Medici Bank tottered on its last legs. Debts had mounted. Branches had closed. Business had dwindled. In 1492, "Il Magnifico" himself passed away, leaving the Medici family much diminished. The final nail in the coffin came in 1494 when King Charles VIII of France invaded Tuscany and Lorenzo's son Piero ignominiously surrendered to his demands. Angry Florentines revolted and exiled the Medici from the city. The new government confiscated the Medici Bank's assets, and the bank disappeared from existence, never to return.

The Medici Bank's days at the center of the Renaissance were finally over. Soon after, Florence would fall under the thrall of a very different master, Girolamo Savonarola, the fanatical Dominican friar who railed against the vices of the rich and led bonfires of the vanities in Florence's piazzas, burning sinful luxury objects such as books, mirrors, musical instruments, and paintings. But the legacy of the Medici Bank continues to this day. Its innovative financial products, originally created to circumvent the Vatican's harsh usury laws, transformed the European economy. Its hub-and-spoke business structure provided an early model for bank holding companies, and its sophisticated accounting methods remain in use around the globe. And of course, the deep devotion of Giovanni di Bicci, Cosimo, and Lorenzo de' Medici to the pursuit of art and architecture allowed Michelangelo, Donatello, da Vinci, and Botticelli to flourish, creating the greatest burst of artistic brilliance and genius the world has ever witnessed.

※ ※ ※

ONE OF THE more intriguing lessons from the story of the Medici Bank is how it constructed a sophisticated, modern financial system out of nothing. Renaissance Florence was a world of fractured and ever-shifting governments, of war and plague and intrigue. The rule of law was nonexistent. Banking was a terrible sin. And yet, somehow, the Medici created not just a bank but a continent-spanning powerhouse that did business with the great and powerful on equal (and sometimes more than equal) footing. The bank endured for almost a century, earning its founders untold wealth and creating for its city unparalleled beauty. The world needed a bank. The Medici provided it.

The Medici Bank also generated new ideas about corporate structure. Rather than organizing itself as a single entity, located, managed, and owned in Florence, it set up an early form of bank holding structure: the Medici Bank in Florence was the principal entity, but other separate entities were formed across the continent. These separate branches had their own names, administrators, and accounting books—and had to report regularly to the bank holding company in Florence. The structure helped incentivize local managers to operate independently and in the interests of their business, as they were part owners of their own branches. It also helped protect the entire corporate structure from risks, such as the possibility that losses at one bank might bring down the others.

But the failures of the Medici Bank also provide some useful lessons about the dangers of finance. We like to think that financial institutions make decisions for the right reasons—that they give loans only to the most deserving borrowers and allocate capital in the most efficient manner possible. But, as a practical matter, banks don't make decisions. Humans do. Humans are capable of great acts of kindness and generosity, but they are also capable of acts of cruelty, incompetence, and simple laziness—sometimes all at the same time (see Lorenzo "Il Magnifico"). The result is that banks do not always act as perfectly rational economic institutions. They are subject to biases. They make mistakes. They take risks. These inefficiencies create real consequences, not just for banks themselves but also for society. We may no longer have to worry about the pope sending an army to overthrow our government if Wall Street misbehaves, but neither can we be complacent about the inner workings of our financial system. There is nothing inevitable about market efficiency.

The rise of banking was a watershed moment in the history of business, but it lacked an important ingredient. The Medici Bank patched together its corporate form out of duct tape and glue, relying on a canny sense of political winds and the balance of power. But the big bang moment for corporations—when they transformed from rudimentary organizations into society's most powerful actors—would come a little over a century later in Elizabethan England. The joint stock company would unleash the elemental force of stocks on the universe.

three

THE STOCK

I N AUGUST 1613, JOHN JOURDAIN SAILED TO THE ISLAND OF Java in high spirits. The chief merchant of the East India Company had led his crew on a successful six-month journey to the Spice Islands to secure a precious cargo of cloves. He was looking forward to reuniting with his colleagues, who had stayed in Bantam to repair their ships and trade with the locals, but when his ship entered the bay, he and his crew were met with an eerie sight.[1]

The company's flagship, *Trade's Increase*, the greatest English merchant vessel of its era—so large it had failed to launch from its dock four years before—was moored near the shore without a single soul on board. Jourdain called out to the ship and had one of his men fire his gun in the air, but there was still no response. He scanned the beachline and noticed there was no one on the beach either. He began to worry about an ambush from the locals and prepared his men for combat. Just then a rowboat appeared in the distance heading toward them. Jourdain recognized the four men on board as fellow

East India Company traders, but they were not their normal hale and hearty selves. They looked as if they had seen a ghost.[2]

They climbed aboard and told Jourdain that a disease had come to Bantam, killing many of the English and leaving the rest weakened. They were the only four healthy enough to greet the merchant and warned him not to come on land. Jourdain remained skeptical: How bad must it be for not a single person to signal him from the shore? He pressed them further, and eventually one of the visitors pulled Jourdain aside and whispered the truth. "The men do not greatly care for your coming aland," he said, "and are determined not to receive you as principal merchant."[3]

During his six months at sea, a war had indeed broken out, but not with the Javanese. A civil war had erupted over a novel financial concept called a "stock." In the early 1600s, when traders like Jourdain were searching for exotic products like cloves and pepper and nutmeg, the East India Company was still decades away from emerging as "the grandest society of merchants in the Universe" and many more years away from inspiring the works of Adam Smith and Karl Marx, and having its tea dumped at Griffin's Wharf during the Boston Tea Party in 1773. Instead, the East India Company was simply a small society of London merchants desperately seeking to carve out a niche for themselves in the expanding world of global trade. It had been founded on New Year's Eve of 1600, chartered by Queen Elizabeth I, and its first voyages had been profitable, but not overwhelmingly so. Yet the East India Company did have one great advantage over many other businesses: it was a "joint stock company." Joint stock companies, a new concept in English law, proved particularly well suited to the grand voyages of the Age of Discovery. In short, they allowed businesses to sell stock in their companies to investors, who would pay in cash up front in return for a slice of future profits down the line. This was convenient for trading companies, which had high up-front costs (equipping and manning merchant vessels was expensive) and would only turn profits, if ever, several months or years later, after their ships had had time to sail halfway around the world and back again. The joint stock company seemed poised to usher in a new era of global commerce.

There was just one problem: it wasn't clear how the stocks would work. Would stockholders have a right to *all* future profits of the company or just some of them? Would they have a say in how the company was run, or would they simply receive dividends? These sorts of questions were unsettled at the time, and different companies adopted different approaches. In the case of the East India Company, the managers had settled on a system of "separate voyages," in which stockholders would subscribe for a single voyage consisting of several ships that would sail out together. The arrangement helped stockholders limit their risk; the profits from one or all of the ships in their voyage would be paid in a year or so, depending on how swiftly the ships sailed. But the structure created an unexpected problem: traders from different voyages started fighting with each other. Because traders within the same company were compensated based on the success of their own voyage, not on the success of other ones, they had no incentive to cooperate. In fact, they often undercut each other, negotiating side deals with foreign merchants that favored their own voyage or feeding bad information to lead new voyagers astray. As John Jourdain saw firsthand, these tensions sometimes exploded into violence.

During Jourdain's absence, the East India Company merchants had split into rival gangs, with members of the Sixth Voyage setting up a trading post in the upper part of town, and those of the Eighth Voyage doing the same in the lower. Both gangs asserted that they had a right to the contents of the company's warehouses and the profits they would bring when shipped home to London. When Jourdain came ashore, he negotiated peace between the two factions, though not without a brief skirmish, with swords, guns, and halberds drawn, between the two sides. Fortunately no one was hurt, and in the course of the next two weeks, everyone came to an agreement. But Jourdain and his colleagues had recognized one thing: their form of investment holding needed to be improved.[4]

In 1614, the East India Company abandoned the separate-voyages system and adopted a joint stock that gave shareholders ownership of the company itself, not just a portion of it. The change facilitated a dramatic rise in the fortunes of the East India Company, which would soon become the richest and most powerful corporation the globe had ever seen, reigning supreme over global trade for the next two centuries. It also paved the way for a remarkable flourishing of London's financial markets—in the coming decades, a bustling stock exchange opened up along Exchange Alley, coffeehouses started listing share prices for the public to see, and an entire industry of stockjobbers, brokers, and bankers emerged to serve England's investors. And it was all because of stories like John Jourdain's, of intrepid adventurers seeking their fortunes thousands of miles away from their homelands, making mistakes, battling with fear and greed, and learning what worked and what didn't in the dawning age of capitalism.

爨 爨 爨

TODAY, STOCKS ARE so important to our lives that it is hard to even imagine a world in which they didn't exist. Every day, newspapers and cable news channels avidly report on the ups and downs of the Dow Jones, on initial public offerings and exchange-traded funds, on booms and busts. Thousands of investment bankers and hedge fund managers around the world head to their offices to buy and sell stocks for a living. Workers invest their hard-earned salaries in pension funds and stock markets in the faith that stocks will one day fund a comfortable retirement. Our hopes and dreams are deeply invested in the idea of the stock.

At their heart, though, stocks are a simple concept, one developed by and for the corporation. A stock represents a share of ownership. If a corporation has one hundred shares, and you own fifty of them, then you own 50 percent of the company. This means that you have one half of whatever it is that owners are entitled to. While the rights and duties of shareholders are complicated legal issues—entire treatises are devoted to the subject—we can think about stocks as granting holders two basic buckets of rights. In the first bucket are the economic rights, which give holders of shares an interest in the company's profits. In the second bucket are the voting rights, which give holders a say in how the company is run. This all seems very humdrum and ordinary.

But stocks have one great merit and one great flaw. The merit is that they grant their holders limited liability. This is a marvelous power. You own a company, but you are not responsible for what it does. If Apple makes a phone that catches fire, its shareholders don't have to reimburse the victims. If Apple is found to have violated privacy laws, the shareholders don't have to pay the fines. If Apple doesn't pay back its lenders, the shareholders don't have to make them whole. From the perspective of a capitalist looking to put his money to work, it is hard to beat stocks. You get none of the risk and all of the upside.

Or at least, most of the upside. The great flaw of the joint stock system is that it severs the link between ownership and management. Shareholders have nominal ownership of the company, but a group of sometimes conflicted directors have day-to-day control over it. I said above that shareholders have a say in how their corporations are run. That isn't entirely correct. They have a say in some matters but far from all of them. In fact, the only matter they have a regular say in is the election of directors, which happens just once a year. Once the election has occurred and the directors have been appointed, the shareholders then sit back and twiddle their thumbs until the next election, with little control over the actual direction of their company. In fact, in this way, corporate democracy bears a strong resemblance to *actual* democracy. While we like to talk about democracy as government by the people, modern democracy in practice is government by elected representatives chosen periodically by citizens. In the same way, while we like to talk about shareholders as the owners of a corporation, modern shareholding is actually largely passive, entailing reliance on the decisions of professional directors whom most shareholders have never met and may not even know exist. Shareholders may own a company, but for the most part, they have very little to do with it.

That does not mean, however, that shareholders are uninterested in stocks. To the contrary, people pay so much attention to stocks that a theory has emerged to describe the effects of this collective obsession: the efficient markets theory. The efficient markets theory asserts that all information available about a company is built into its stock price. This is an astounding idea. Not just some information, not just most information, but all information, of all kinds, is somehow instantaneously gathered and beamed into the stock price of a company as soon as it emerges. Apple earned higher profits this year than last? Already incorporated. It's planning to release a bigger, more powerful iPhone in September? Already incorporated. Tim Cook has a headache this morning and is not responding to his emails? Already incorporated. One of the most important ramifications of the efficient markets theory is that no investor can accurately predict where stock prices will go in the future. By definition, any information that the investor has is information and, thus, like all other information, has already been taken into account in the stock price. The efficient capital markets hypothesis has its critics — some argue that not all information is incorporated into stock prices, others poke holes in how quickly the information is incorporated, and still others argue that stock prices fluctuate based on other factors, such as hopes and fears and biases, that have nothing to do with rational information diffusion — but the very fact that the theory exists, and has widespread acceptance among financial scholars, is a testament to the power of stocks in our imagination. Stock exchanges are the all-seeing, all-knowing watchers of capitalism.

The consequences of the stock have been momentous and yet not necessarily predictable. It is easy to think that our system of stocks and stock exchanges was inevitable, one required by our commitment to capitalism. But experience, not logic, led us here. The best way to understand how we arrived where we are is to look at the fate of one of the original joint stock companies, a company that perhaps had a greater impact on global affairs than any other, a company that governed nations. Let us turn to the East India Company.

THE STORY OF HOW A SMALL BAND OF MERCHANTS FROM PHILPOT Lane in London transformed itself into "the grandest society of merchants in the Universe" is perhaps the most remarkable one in the history of corporations. From 1600 to 1874, when it was finally dissolved, the East India Company became deeply integrated in the lives of people around the globe. It was the company's tea that made England a country of tea drinkers and that the Sons of Liberty dumped into Boston Harbor during the Boston Tea Party. It was the company's opium that led to the Opium Wars in China. It was the company's stock that dominated the booms and busts of the emerging London stock exchange and the company's coffee that was served at the coffeehouses sprouting up nearby in Exchange Alley. It was the company's soldiers who conquered Bengal and led to company rule over India for over one hundred years. The company's affairs—and scandals—inspired the writings of such diverse thinkers as Adam Smith, Karl Marx, and Napoléon Bonaparte. It would be hard to improve on Edmund Burke's assessment of the company's vertiginous rise: "The Constitution of the Company began in commerce and ended in empire."[5]

The history of the East India Company officially began on New Year's Eve of 1600, when Queen Elizabeth I granted a charter to the "Company of Merchants of London Trading into the East Indies," but the company's roots lie much further back, in the dawn of the Age of Exploration. In 1498, the Portuguese explorer Vasco da Gama navigated around the Cape of Good Hope at the southern tip of Africa and arrived on the shores of India, where he announced that he came "in search of Christians and spices." The journey marked the beginning of a new era in European history, when explorers navigated the globe in search of the riches they presumed to be found across the seas. For the next century, the Portuguese would dominate trade with the East, bringing such exotic commodities as pepper, nutmeg, and clove to European markets.[6]

English merchants knew that the spice trade was lucrative, but just how lucrative remained obscure until a lucky break in 1587 shed new light on the Portuguese monopoly. In that year, Sir Francis Drake, England's government-backed pirate, was out raiding the Spanish coastline in an effort to slow down the construction of the Spanish Armada of King Philip II. In May, Drake raided the Bay of Cádiz and destroyed a large portion of the fleet, a feat that he called "singeing the beard of the King of Spain." Before returning to England, though, Drake decided to follow up on rumors he had heard about a richly laden Portuguese galleon named the *São Filipe* that was returning from India. It had reportedly wintered in Mozambique before recently embarking for Lisbon. Despite his stores being low and his crew exhausted, Drake decided to chance it and began cruising near the Azores in search of the ship. In a stroke of good fortune, Drake spotted the *São Filipe* just as he passed the coast of São Miguel Island, and he easily chased it down and captured it. He then sailed the captured ship back to Plymouth to catalog its contents. We still have the astounding list of the ship's cargo: calicos, quilts, taffetas, silk, indigo, pepper, cinnamon, cloves, mace, china, saltpeter, beeswax, nutmeg, and ebony. Inside a casket were more wonders: gold chains and bracelets, diamonds, rubies, crystal girdles, pearl rings, and bloodstones. Drake personally took the casket, with its precious cargo, to "deliver unto her Majesty with his own hands." In all, the *São Filipe* haul was worth £108,049, an astronomical sum equivalent to around $25 million today.[7]

Drake's discovery sent shock waves through London's merchant class. As scholar and historian Richard Hakluyt wrote, "The taking of this carrack wrought two extraordinary effects in England: first, that it taught others that carracks were no such bugs that they might be taken . . . ; and secondly, in acquainting the English nation more generally with the particularities of the exceeding riches and wealth of the East Indies; whereby themselves and their neighbours of Holland have been encouraged, being men as skillful in navigation, and of no less courage than the Portugals, to share with them in the East Indies."[8]

Armed with knowledge of the profits to be made in the East Indies, a group of merchants in London banded together and requested a charter for a new company, the Company of Merchants of London Trading into the East Indies, from Queen Elizabeth I. At the time, corporations could only be created by petitioning the crown (or, occasionally, the Parliament) for a charter: it was not a right to form a corporation; it was a privilege. The queen granted their request on the final day of 1600, making the 218 merchants "one Body Corporate and Politick, in Deed and in Name" and, importantly, giving them a monopoly over all trade between England and the East Indies. The breadth of this privilege was remarkable. The charter gave the company the sole right to "traffick and use the trade of merchandise . . . into and from the said East-Indies, in the countries and parts of Asia and Africa, and into and from all the islands, ports, havens; cities, creeks, towns and places of Asia and Africa, and America, or any of them, beyond the Cape of Bona Esperanza to the Straights of Magellan." In other words, the East India Company had exclusive rights to trade with any peoples located anywhere east of the Cape of Good Hope at the southern tip of Africa and west of the Strait of Magellan at the southern tip of South America. At the stroke of a pen, just over two hundred men in London had acquired control of a trading territory that covered a majority of the earth.

In return for this massive privilege, the charter was clear about what the company was expected to do: it was to contribute to the greatness of England. The charter stated that the queen was granting the merchants their rights "for the honour of this our realm of England, as for the increase of our navigation, and advancement of trade of merchandize." The ties between the East India Company and the

English nation even extended to the company's branding. The East India Company chose for its corporate seal an image of two golden lions holding a shield decorated with three ships flying the English flag, along with the words *Deo ducente nil nocet* — "Where God leads, nothing can harm us." This explicit connection between corporation and crown led William Blackstone to write in his *Commentaries* that corporations were created "for the advantage of the public."[9]

The founders of the East India Company themselves were a diverse lot. There was Thomas Smythe, a merchant who had made a fortune in the silk and velvet trade before turning to politics as the sheriff of London, who served as the company's first governor (his house on Philpot Lane served as the informal headquarters of the company in its first years). There was John Watts, a wealthy shipowner who had fought against the Spanish Armada and whom the Spanish ambassador to England once described as "the greatest pirate that has ever been in this kingdom." There was Edward Michelborne, a soldier and adventurer who desperately hoped to be appointed commander of the East India Company's first voyage to the East and, when those hopes were disappointed, set up a competing corporation and was expelled from the East India Company, "disfranchised out of the freedom and privileges of this fellowship, and utterly disabled from taking any benefit or profit thereby." Sundry other merchants and traders with similarly speckled pasts populated the list of founders.[10]

It didn't take long for the fledgling capitalists to get started exploring their newly "acquired" territories. On February 13, 1601, just over a month after receiving its charter, the company launched its first voyage to the East Indies, aiming in particular for Indonesia and its purportedly ample sources of pepper. The adventures of this maiden voyage of the East India Company read like something out of a Jonathan Swift novel. The fleet consisted of four ships, the *Hector*, the *Susan*, the *Ascension*, and the *Red Dragon* (rechristened after its initial name, the *Scourge of Malice*, was deemed too bellicose for a trading company). Upon these ships were loaded 480 men and no less than thirty-eight cannons. The leader of the voyage, Thomas Lancaster, had had the foresight to bring bottles of lemon juice on board the *Red Dragon* to fend off scurvy, but the other ships failed to follow his good example. As a result, by the time the fleet reached the Cape of Good Hope, over one hundred sailors had died, and a great many others were sick.

In need of rest and refreshment, the men anchored in the bay of Saldanha, where they encountered a tribe of locals with whom they attempted to trade for provisions. We only have the British story of the encounter, and so the recounting is one-sided and, like many of the accounts of the time, shrouded in ignorance and prejudice. It may well have been a group of Khoekhoen, a pastoralist society that had lived in the region for centuries. "The people of this place are all of a tawnie colour, of a reasonable stature, swift of foot, and much given to pick and steal," one East India Company sailor wrote. "Their speech is wholly uttered through the throat, and they click with their tongues in such sort, that in seven weeks which we remained here in this place, the sharpest wit among us could not learn one word of their language." Eventually, the traders found a solution to the problem: Lancaster "spake to them in the cattle's language, which was never changed at the confusion of Babel, which was 'moath' for oxen and kine, and 'baa' for sheep, which language the people understood very well without any interpreter." After several pleasant weeks at Saldanha, the merchants sailed on, eventually arriving in Aceh, in Indonesia, on June 5, 1602, sixteen months after leaving England.[11]

The ruler of Aceh, Ala-uddin Shah, met them with a parade of elephants, trumpets, and drums, followed by a sumptuous feast and, to top it all off, a tiger fight. While on the island, the company bought pepper, cloves, mace, and nutmeg and set up "factories" (or trading outposts) on Java and the Spice Islands. When they learned that a Portuguese ship loaded with textiles from India was nearby, the company sailed out to capture it. Ala-uddin Shah, hearing of the affair, requested that the company bring him back a "fair Portugal maiden," but Lancaster demurred, telling Ala-uddin Shah diplomatically that "there was none so worthy that merited to be so presented." After a tumultuous trip back to England (the *Red Dragon* lost its rudder and nearly sank in a fierce storm off the Cape of Good Hope), the last ships finally arrived home on September 11, 1603—two years and six months from when they had first departed. They had paid a steep price for the voyage. Of the original 480 men, 182 had died during the round trip. But the profits were great as well. In aggregate, investors in the voyage received a 300 percent return on their investment.[12]

The East India Company was off to an auspicious start. The company would send many more voyages and more ships to the East Indies in the years to come, and the company's fortunes would rise. The *Red Dragon* would feature in many of these trips, at one point serving as the stage for the first-known performance of Shakespeare's *Hamlet*— in 1607 off the shores of Sierra Leone—and going on five trips in total before being sunk in 1619 by the Dutch. Overall, the trade with the East Indies was quite profitable. Spices could be bought for a pittance abroad and resold at many times the original price in London. Ten pounds of nutmeg in the Banda Islands cost less than half a penny and ten pounds of mace less than five pence. In England, they could be sold for £1.60 and £16, respectively, a return of 32,000 percent. Early investors consistently earned high returns. Between 1601 and 1612, returns on capital were 155 percent. Cloves from the third voyage made profits of over 200 percent. Between 1613 and 1616, company returns were 87 percent.[13]

But the company's spice trade was always hamstrung by the presence of an even larger and more vicious competitor: the Dutch East India Company. The Dutch had arrived in the East Indies before the British—an early Dutch voyage arrived in 1596—and they fiercely protected their turf, excluding the British East India Company from the islands and hindering its trade at every turn. The Dutch East India Company's approach to trade was unapologetically militant. In 1614, one of its managers, Jan Pieterszoon Coen, wrote to the company's board in the Netherlands, describing his theory of how the business should be run. "We cannot carry on trade without war, nor war without trade," he summarized. The British East India Company was not prepared for this type of no-holds-barred competition, and it regularly lost out to the Dutch. The final blow to the East India Company's spice trade came in 1623, when a Japanese ronin (or masterless samurai) employed by the Dutch East India Company in Ambon, in modern-day Indonesia, informed the Dutch that British traders were conspiring to seize the Dutch company's fortress there. The Dutch proceeded to arrest, torture, and execute ten British East India Company employees. The Ambon massacre sounded a wake-up call to the East India Company's board, which reluctantly concluded that the company had little recourse against the attack and no hope at all of ever wresting control of the spice trade from the Dutch.[14]

Undaunted, the East India Company pivoted to a new region that appeared potentially even more profitable than the Spice Islands: India. The Mughal Empire had developed a massive textile industry there, producing the world's highest-quality silks, calicos, and cotton. The Mughal emperors were also more than willing to trade with foreign enterprises. The company soon established factories all along the coast, in Surat, Calicut, Bombay, Madras, Masulipatam, and Calcutta. By the 1620s, the company was exporting some 220,000 pieces of cloth a year from Surat to England. By 1684, they were exporting 1.76 million.[15]

The sudden influx of products from India led to wide-ranging changes within England, from language to fashion to politics. Indian words began to enter the lexicon: *bandana, calico, chintz, dungaree,* and *seersucker* all derived from the Indian words for these products. Indian calicos proved so popular that even the queen took to wearing them. Daniel Defoe, author of the novel *Robinson Crusoe* and a keen-eyed observer of English culture, commented on the changes he saw taking place in his country. "These people's obsessions with products from India has now reached the painted calicos, which were formerly used for quilted blankets and the clothing of lower class children," Defoe wrote. "Today they are even used by our finer women. The power of fashion is so great that we see persons of rank wearing Indian clothes even though only the maids were allowed to use them before." John Blanch wrote that the Indian fashions were "impossible to be withstood by a feminine power" and urged Englishmen to "redeem our female sex from the government of the Indians." As these comments suggest, not everyone appreciated the East India Company's efforts. Some of the harshest critiques came from the English wool industry, whose workers worried that the company's imports of high-quality Indian textiles threatened their livelihoods. Weavers, spinners, dyers, and shepherds united in accusing the company of undercutting them and destroying domestic jobs. Political pressure grew throughout the latter half of the century until, in 1696, the House of Commons proposed a bill prohibiting companies from importing any more silk or calico from India. When the bill failed in the House of Lords, thousands of angry London weavers marched to Westminster to protest. Along the way, they broke down the door of the East India House and sacked the residence of the company's deputy governor. British soldiers had to be called in to protect the houses of other East India Company executives. In the end, the weavers had their way: in 1700, Parliament enacted a new Calico Act, banning calico imports into the country.[16]

IN THE COURSE OF ITS RAPID EXPANSION, THE EAST INDIA COMpany rediscovered many of the features of corporate life pioneered by the *societates publicanorum* in ancient Rome and the Medici Bank in Renaissance Florence. Its far-flung commercial empire, spanning the greater part of the globe, was run by a small group of men operating out of a single building in London and thus required a system of checks and balances that ensured that employees around the world vigorously pursued the company's interests. It had a board of directors that met regularly in the company's London headquarters, the East

India House. It had local managers and civil servants located in major foreign outposts to oversee the company's sprawling operations. It developed an extensive record-keeping system in which managers were required to maintain detailed ledgers of the contents of warehouses and the terms of contracts. This was a remarkable level of efficiency for a business operating in the seventeenth century.

But one of the most important innovations of the East India Company was the idea of a stock. The East India Company was not the first joint stock company in England (others date back to as early as the 1550s), but it was certainly the most successful. The joint stock company had three key advantages over the more common partnership: investors had limited liability and thus could not be sued for any losses that the company incurred; stocks could be freely traded among the public and thus could attract capital from a wider array of people; and the company had a stable source of capital and thus could take a longer-term view of its business prospects. All of these attributes were essential for the East India Company, which required massive amounts of up-front capital to supply and equip ships to sail to the East Indies and might not receive returns for two years or more. As the merchants explained in their initial petition to the queen, "A trade so far remote cannot be managed but by a joint and united stock."[17]

While the idea of a "joint stock" was attractive to the East India Company, figuring out exactly how it should work in practice took some time. The learning process was a rough-and-tumble affair. The story of John Jourdain and his rebellious colleagues was one example. Another revolved around how to manage the relationship between shareholders and managers. Shareholders formally owned the company (a fact made evident by the name they were originally given in the company: the "Court of Proprietors"), but, as a general matter, they were not involved in the running of it. Instead, management was delegated to a group of directors or "committees" (known not as the board of directors but rather as the "Court of Committees"). This brought with it an inherent tension. The managers made day-to-day decisions, but the lion's share of the profits from these decisions went to the shareholders. How could the shareholders ensure that managers did their jobs diligently and managed their money dutifully, and how could managers ensure that they were properly compensated for their work?

In the beginning, this conflict led to some quirky arrangements. Shareholders had the right to elect the directors, but only if they held above a certain amount of stock, generally at least £500. Each qualified shareholder only had one vote, regardless of whether he held £500, £1,000, £10,000, or more of the company's stock. As one might have expected, this rule led to a certain amount of gamesmanship by stockholders, who would sometimes "split" their stock into £500 portions and then have those portions owned by friends, family members, or colleagues and thus multiply their voting power. The Court of Committees, on the other hand, whose members were elected by the shareholders and managed the company's affairs, consisted of twenty-four directors chosen from a select group of the richest shareholders (in order to be a candidate for a directorship, a shareholder had to own at least £2,000 in stock). Once elected, the directors would choose a governor (in effect, the chairman of the board). As the East India Company grew, the directors became tremendously influential, not just in the company but in British society more widely. Their powers of patronage and policy could decide families' fortunes, and they often used them to favor friends, colleagues, and relations. In order to protect against entrenchment, directors could only hold their positions for four consecutive years, after which they would have to step down for at least a year.

This arrangement, unusual though it was, worked reasonably well at quelling the worst apprehensions of shareholders, and the board of the East India Company ran a remarkably orderly ship. It held weekly meetings, typically every Wednesday in the new East India House on Leadenhall Street. Meetings were presided over by the chairman, who in turn assigned important tasks to small groups of directors, whose portfolios might include correspondence, treasury, warehouses, or accounts.

Once the directors had settled on a particular business strategy, they would then send letters to their overseas subsidiaries with orders, specifying things like what to buy and at what price. Each trading post, or "factory," had its own president whose responsibility it was to execute these orders. How governors went about meeting the demands of the directors was left largely to their own discretion, though, and governors could amass large personal fortunes as a result. Elihu Yale served as president of the Madras factory from 1687 to 1692 and, during his time there, engaged in a number of questionable transactions that redounded more to his own benefit than the company's. He may have participated in the slave trade; he certainly used the company's funds for private speculation. The company eventually removed him from his post, but by then his fortune had already been made. He returned to London a very rich man. In 1718, he ended up donating a set of books to a recently established university in New Haven, which would soon be renamed Yale in his honor.

To minimize misbehavior abroad, the East India Company required foreign posts to keep careful written records of every occurrence of note. The president of each factory would typically form a council of six to nine members, generally senior factors (more or less equivalent to upper management), which would meet regularly to discuss business. In Madras, the council met punctually every Wednesday at 6 a.m., before the stifling heat of the tropical city set in. The council's resolutions would be recorded and placed in the company register, called "the Diary and Consultations Books," which the board of directors in London would periodically review. These books were an invaluable source of information for the central headquarters, as well as for anyone interested in learning about life abroad. Correspondents did not hold their punches. A letter from the London board in 1718 rebuked the Madras council for spending too much on alcohol at the "public table" where company officials ate: "This is an extravagancy that every one of you ought to blush at the thought of, to give nine pagodas a dozen for Burton ale. If you must have liquors at such prices, pray gratify your palates at your own, not our, expense." Another letter, from the board of directors to the Bengal council, criticized the council's poor record-keeping skills:

> The General Books for these many years have been swelled to an enormous size by the multiplicity of useless heads. This, together with the liberties you have taken of creating innumerable entries for the private convenience of individuals, have rendered them intricate and confused. And as your books have been generally basely copied, entries frequently erased, postings omitted, with other unpardonable irregularities, the person found culpable in any of these instances, together with him who signs as an examiner, shall assuredly feel our resentment. . . . Your Consultations for these several years past wrote in such a vile manner as not to be legible in many places. Indexes often omitted; the Registers, as already noticed, either not punctually kept up or transmitted us; in short, the business in every branch at your settlement has been conducted in such a loose and negligent manner as to reflect shame on those in trust with our affairs. You, our Governor and Council, must set the example of order, method and application. The junior servants shall be taught obedience and kept strictly to their duty; the negligent admonished, and where admonition fails, suspend them the service until our pleasure is known.[18]

But monitoring the behavior of employees thousands of miles away was not an easy task, and all sorts of vice and debauchery sprang up— to the detriment of local populations and company managers alike. The chaplain at Fort St. George wrote a letter to the board of directors in 1676, complaining of the riotous behavior of East India Company employees and pleading for help. "Your heads would be fountains of water, and eyes rivers of tears, did you really know how much God is dishonoured, his name blasphemed, religion reproached amongst the gentiles, by the vicious lives of many of your servants," the chaplain wrote. He vigorously entreated them to take more care with the quality of employee they sent abroad, as the ones he saw engaged in the most abominable practices.

> There come hither some thousand murderers, some men stealers, some popish, some come under notion of single persons and unmarried, who yet have their wives in England, and here have been married to others, with whom they have lived in adultery; and some on the other hand have come over as married persons, of whom there are strange suspicions they were never married. . . . There are also some of the writers who by their lives are not a little scandalous to the Christian religion, so sinful in their drunkenness that some of them play at cards and dice for wine that they may drink, and afterwards throwing the dice which shall pay all, and sometimes who shall drink all, by which some are forced to drink until they be worse than beasts. Others pride themselves in making others drink till they be insensible, and then strip them naked and in that posture cause them to be carried through the streets to their dwelling place.[19]

In order to improve behavior in the ranks, the company instituted a strict hierarchy in its foreign offices, with gradually increasing salaries and responsibilities and promotions dependent on good comportment. New hires were made "writers" (effectively, clerks), a position they would remain in for five years, after which they could be promoted to factor. After three years, factors would be promoted to merchants. If they were very lucky, merchants might be named to the president's council or even made president. In 1764, the company even created a sort of code of ethics, banning the receipt of gifts above a certain value.[20]

Over time, the East India Company's emphasis on hierarchy and organization proved a potent stimulus to growth. The business of the company steadily expanded until eventually it encompassed seemingly every trade that existed in the world. Originally focused on spices like pepper, cinnamon, and nutmeg, the East India Company then started trading in Indian textiles, from seersucker to silk to calico, changing the styles and fashions of England forever. Soon after, it moved into tea and, by the 1750s, was importing three million pounds of tea leaves a year. (Thomas Twining, the famed tea merchant, worked for the company at one point.) Then it moved into saltpeter (an important component of gunpowder) and coffee. It also engaged in slave trading, sending an estimated three thousand enslaved people to destinations from Goa to St. Helena. This array of activities led the company to set up a network of offices across the globe. The first factories were in Java and the Spice Islands. By the early 1700s, the company had bases all along the coast of India. It sent representatives to Japan, China, Singapore, Basra (in modern-day Iraq), Gombroon (in modern-day Iran), and Mocha. It was a global powerhouse.[21]

CLOSER TO HOME, THE EAST INDIA COMPANY DROVE THE DEVELopment of one of London's defining institutions: the stock exchange. Joint stock companies were defined by their capacity to access the capital markets—that is, the money of other people. In order to do that, they needed a way to reliably find buyers of their stock. The stock exchange turned out to be the solution. In the early years of the East India Company, the purchase of shares took place at the Royal Exchange, an imposing stone building on Cornhill Street devoted to commerce and trade. But it soon became clear that stockbrokers—the class of intermediaries that had sprung up to connect willing sellers of stock with willing buyers—disrupted the Royal Exchange with their boisterous behavior, and so the business moved outside to the streets of Exchange Alley. Exchange Alley also happened to be amply supplied with coffeehouses, a favorite of stockbrokers who enjoyed the jolt provided by caffeine and the buzz provided by alcohol (coffeehouses did not serve only coffee at the time). Coffeehouses soon turned into bustling gathering places, where Londoners could stop to enjoy a cup of coffee and linger to read the newspaper and discuss the day's business affairs. One coffeehouse in particular, Jonathan's Coffee House, earned a reputation as the center of London's burgeoning capital markets, and by 1698 stock prices were regularly posted there. London's days at the center of international finance had begun.[22]

The rise of the stock exchange brought along another, less welcome phenomenon: stock manipulation. One of the worst offenders was Josiah Child, who guided the East India Company from the 1670s to the 1690s as a director, chairman, and the company's largest shareholder. Child had previously founded the Royal African Company and led the company's slave trade. As a director of the East India Company, he became known as a severe taskmaster. A letter of rebuke to the Madras office gives a sense of his style of leadership: "The great trouble we labour under is that you cannot get out of your old forms, and your cavilling way of writing or perverting, or misconstruing, procrastinating, or neglecting our plain and direct orders to you as if you were not subordinate but a coordinate power with us." At the same time that he was heaping abuse on his inferiors, he was also perfecting the art of manipulating his own shareholders. Daniel Defoe explained his strategy of false rumors and secretive buying sprees:

> If we may believe the report of those who remember the machines and contrivances of that original of stock-jobbing, Sir Josiah Child, there are those who tell us letters have been ordered, by private management, to be written from the East Indies, with an account of the loss of ships which have been arrived there, and the arrival of ships lost; of war with the Great Mogul, when they have been in perfect tranquillity; and of peace with the Great Mogul, when he was come down against the factory of Bengal with one hundred thousand men; — just as it was thought proper to calculate those rumors for the raising and falling of the stock, and when it was for his purpose to buy cheap, or sell dear.[23]

By the end of the century, government bureaucrats became so concerned with rampant insider trading and manipulation on stock exchanges that they issued a damning report on the "present state of our trade," which, they concluded, was very poor indeed, and all because of the invention of the stock. The Commissioners of Trade wrote in the 1696 report,

> The pernicious art of stock-jobbing hath, of late, so wholly perverted the end and design of companies and corporations, created for the introducing, or carrying on, of manufactures to the private profit of the first projectors, that the privileges granted to them have, commonly, been made no other use of, by the first procurers and subscribers, but to sell again with advantage, to ignorant men, drawn in by the reputation, falsely raised, and artfully spread, concerning the thriving state of their stock. Thus the first undertakers, getting quit of the company, by selling their shares for much more than they are really worth, to men allured by the noise of great profit, the management of that trade and stock comes to fall into unskillful hands; whereby the manufactures, intended to be promoted by such grants, and put into the management of companies for their better improvement, come, from very promising beginnings, to dwindle away to nothing.

The birth of the stock exchange had changed the nature of corporations. Rather than devoting themselves to the honor and prosperity of the nation, corporations had transformed into backroom gambling houses, venues for the skilled and the conniving to enrich themselves off the ignorant and the naive. And there were no casino managers to ensure the game was played fairly.[24]

A CORPORATION WITH GLOBAL REACH, BOTTOMLESS CAPITAL, AND minimal oversight was bound to overreach. The only question was where its grasping arm would extend. Politics turned out to be its arena of choice. As the East India Company grew, it began to treat the British government more like a trading partner, to be bought off, ignored, or actively undercut, than like a sovereign. Josiah Child, again, stands out as an exemplar. In the late 1600s, Child engaged in rampant bribery to win political favor in England. Members of Parliament were eager participants in the joint stock companies of the day, and so Child knew he had a hook. Horace Walpole would later say, "From the Alley to the House is like a path of ants." So when Child was elected governor of the East India Company in 1681, he knew what to do: he promptly made a gift to Charles II of ten thousand guineas. He repeated the gift for the next seven years. When the company's charter was up for renewal, he bribed politicians to ensure they would vote in his favor, leading one investigator to observe, "Companies have bodies, but it is said they have no souls; if no souls, no consciences." Child was so disdainful of government regulation that, at times, he explicitly instructed employees to violate it. After Parliament passed a resolution giving all companies equal rights to trade in the East Indies, thereby eliminating the East India Company's monopoly, he wrote to company officials in India to ignore it: they should follow his orders, "not the laws of England, which were a heap of nonsense, compiled by a few ignorant country gentlemen who hardly knew how to make laws for the good government of their own private families, much less for the regulating of companies and foreign commerce."[25]

But Child's greatest legacy was his transformation of the East India Company from a group of merchants, focused on trade and money, into a company-state, focused on war and power. While violence had always been inextricably linked with the company's business—its ships bristled with guns, and its maiden voyage captured a Portuguese trading ship—the East India Company's directors had long sought to avoid actual war. Indeed, this was official company policy. Under the so-called Roe Doctrine, established by Sir Thomas Roe, one of the company's early ambassadors, the company specifically instructed employees to refrain from engaging in military encounters abroad. "Let this be received as a rule, that if you will profit, seek it at sea, and in quiet trade, for without controversy it is an error to affect garrisons and land wars in India," Roe wrote. "War and traffic are incompatible." As late as 1681, the company's directors were writing to employees in India, "All war is so contrary to our constitution, as well as our interest, that we cannot too often inculcate to you our aversion thereunto."[26]

Under Child, all this changed. His primary business strategy, if you can call it that, was for the East India Company to establish military control over Bengal at all costs. Once it had done so, he believed, the company could finally get out from under the foot of local rulers and foreign companies. Explaining his goals to the president of Fort St. George, he wrote that the East India Company must transform itself from a "parcel of mere trading merchants" into a "formidable martial government in India." His aim was to create "such a politie of civil and military power, and create and secure such a large revenue, as well may be the foundation of a large, well grounded, sure English dominion in India for all time to come."[27]

To this purpose, in 1686, Child sent a force of warships and infantry to Bengal to launch a naval war against the Mughal Empire. Child's War, as it would come to be known, was an abject disaster. His nineteen warships with two hundred cannons and six hundred soldiers were not nearly enough to defeat a Mughal Empire with an estimated four-million-man army. The Mughal emperor promptly captured the company's factories at Hughli, Patna, Kasimbazar, Masulipatnam, and Vizagapatam and besieged the factory at Bombay. Cutting its losses, the company reversed course and sought a pardon from the Mughal emperor, begging him to restore its trading rights. As historian William Wilson Hunter would sum up the affair, "Of this vast programme, conceived in ludicrous ignorance of the geographical distances and with astounding disregard of the opposing forces, not a single item was carried out."[28]

But once placed in the minds of the directors in London, the idea of political control over a continent would never die out. The 1700s witnessed a slow growth of the East India Company's military presence in India, and by 1742 it maintained a force of some twelve hundred soldiers at its base in Madras. The ascendant military power of the company, along with the steady decline in the Mughal Empire, slowly shifted the balance of power in the country. By 1756, when a new ruler started agitating against the company, the company had an army to fight back.[29]

The center of the conflict lay in Bengal, the hub of the East India Company's business in India. The region produced the muslin and calico fabrics that were much valued back in England and, by 1720, accounted for over half of the East India Company's imports. Relations between the company and the government of Bengal, never especially cordial, turned hostile in 1756 when Siraj-ud-Daula was anointed the new nawab (or ruler) of Bengal. Siraj, grandson of the previous nawab, had already earned a reputation for cruelty. Contemporaries accused him of such heinous acts as abducting Hindu women while they were bathing in the Ganges, ramming ferry boats just to frighten the passengers who couldn't swim, and personally executing disfavored ministers. Worryingly for the East India Company, he also had a bone to pick with the European companies that had set up a string of factories along the coast. Siraj believed the foreign companies were abusing their privileges in his country, and he took it as his personal mission to expel them. He certainly had ample resources at his disposal to do so. After coming to power, he undertook a survey of his wealth and found that it came to 680 million rupees, roughly equivalent to $13 billion today. English newspapers called him "Sir Roger Dowler," a corruption of his Indian name and a reference to his immense riches.[30]

Within two months of coming to power, Siraj struck his first blow, attacking and easily overrunning the East India Company's fort at Calcutta in June 1756. The defense of the fort was so poorly organized that one soldier would later say of the company's commander, "Touching the military capacity of our commandant, I am a stranger. I can only say, that we were unhappy in his keeping it to himself, if he had any; as neither I, nor I believe anybody else, was witness to any part of his conduct, that spoke or bore the appearance of his being the commanding military officer in the garrison." The capture of Calcutta was a major loss for the company, as the town stood at the very center of its trading business. The Calcutta factory handled over 60 percent of the company's exports from Asia, and news of its sacking caused the company's share price to plummet, erasing £2.25 million in value, more than half the company's share capital. But the event lived in infamy forever after in company lore because of what came next. After capturing the fort, the Bengali troops forced the 146 East India Company employees they had captured into a tiny dungeon, known as the Black Hole, measuring just fourteen by eighteen feet. Crammed together so tightly that the jailer could barely close the door, with little air from the dungeon's two windows, which were crisscrossed with thick iron bars that cut off the flow of oxygen, the prisoners soon began to succumb to suffocation and heat exhaustion. They cried out desperately for relief but were met with silence. When Siraj came to let them out the next morning at 6 a.m., he found a sepulcher. Only 23 had survived the night; the other 123 lay dead on the floor.[31]

Robert Clive, the company's deputy governor at Fort St. David on the Coromandel Coast, learned of the fall of Calcutta and quickly prepared a counteroffensive. It is perhaps worthwhile to point out that Clive's actions did not emanate from carefully laid plans formulated by the East India Company's board of directors, which, after all, was situated in London, thousands of miles away. Given the difficulty of communicating between Bengal and London (it could take as much as a year for a letter to arrive in London and then another year for the response to arrive back in Bengal), such detailed instructions would have been impossible. Perhaps more surprisingly, the majority of the company's board believed that conquest was not in the company's interest. As company secretary Robert James told the House of Commons in 1767, "The general tenor of the Company's orders were not to act offensively. We don't want conquest and power; it is commercial interest only we look for." Indeed, for most of the conflict, the directors were entirely unaware of what was happening. As James recounted, the war "grew insensibly from one trouble to another—we could form no judgment of their progress."[32]

Instead, Clive made most of the important decisions for himself, sometimes with general directions from the company's local committee at Fort St. George far to the south. Clive and his army retook Calcutta and then, after a series of failed negotiations with Siraj, defeated the nawab's army amid a mango grove at the Battle of Plassey. The defection of one of Siraj's closest generals in the middle of the battle aided Clive's cause. The victory left the East India Company with absolute control over Bengal, and Clive personally walked the newly installed nawab (the traitorous general, it turned out) to his throne. The victory also greatly enriched the company's economic fortunes. The East India Company raided Bengal's treasury of gold and silver and sent it in a fleet of over one hundred boats down the Ganges to Calcutta—the total value estimated to be around £2.5 million (or around $300 million in today's value). Clive took £234,000 (or $28 million today) for himself. He also gifted £24,000 to each of the company's committee members. He would later write that, as a result of the Battle of Plassey, the East India Company had become "the most opulent company in the world."[33]

Clive's triumph over the nawab of Bengal in 1757 ushered in a new era for the East India Company. Political control over the region granted the company entirely new avenues for profit making. In 1765, the Mughal emperor granted the East India Company a *diwani* (a right to collect taxes) over Bengal, effectively recognizing its authority over the region. Clive estimated that the *diwani* would bring the company tax revenues of 25 million rupees, or around £3.5 million, a year. For comparison's sake, before 1765, all of the company's exports from Asia combined amounted to around £1 million a year. This represented a massive increase in the company's size. Recognizing that news of the *diwani* would cause the company's stock price to skyrocket once it reached London, Clive hastily sent a letter to his agent telling him to buy up company stock. Writing in code in order to ensure secrecy, he instructed his agent, "Whatever money I may have in the public funds or anywhere else, and as much as can be borrowed in my name, I desire may be, without loss of a minute, invested in East India stock. You will speak to my attorneys on this point. Let them know I am anxious to have my money so disposed of, and press them to hasten the affair as much as possible." The stock price doubled over the course of the next eight months, delivering Clive a handsome profit.[34]

But the military victory also brought with it deep changes in the way the East India Company saw itself. What had been an economic institution slowly turned into a governmental one. It levied taxes. It raised armies. It declared war. Edmund Burke, describing the situation of the company, concluded, "The East India Company in Asia is a state in the disguise of a merchant." Another commentator, referring to the company's official name, the "United Company of Merchants of England Trading to the East Indies," pointed out that the men of the East India Company were neither merchants nor trading with India. They were, instead, an empire, focused on collecting taxes, administered by civil servants, and supported by a private army.

Almost immediately, the East India Company's experiment as a company-state started to show cracks. Eager to extract revenue from Bengal, it raised taxes on an already impoverished populace. Finding that Bengali weavers were not producing textiles quickly enough, its managers punished them severely, with fines, imprisonment, and floggings distressingly common. Labor conditions became so bad in the silk industry that some workers took to cutting off their own thumbs to prevent being forced to continue. The company's disregard of water supplies and crop production, as well as its hoarding of grain, contributed to a terrible famine in 1770. "All through the stifling summer of 1770, the people went on dying," wrote historian William Hunter. "The husbandmen sold their cattle . . . ; they devoured their seed-grain; they sold their sons and daughters, till at length no buyer of children could be found; they ate the leaves of trees and the grass of the field; and in June 1770 [a company official] affirmed that the living were feeding on the dead. Day and night a torrent of famished and disease-stricken wretches poured into the great cities." The famine caused the deaths of between two and ten million Bengalis.[35]

Outside India, the East India Company threw its weight around to get special treatment for its products, often with disastrous results. In 1773, the company, finding itself with a backlog of tea in its London warehouses, convinced the British Parliament to pass the Tea Act, granting it the right to ship tea directly to North America without paying export duties. Local Boston merchants, fearful of being undercut by the cheap East India Company tea, helped organize a revolt, the culmination of which witnessed Bostonians dressing up as Mohawk warriors, boarding English ships, and tossing the despised East India Company's tea into the water. The Boston Tea Party marked a key turning point in relations between America and Britain, and the East India Company's corporate rapaciousness became a rallying cry in the American Revolution. John Dickinson, writing under the pseudonym Rusticus, wrote that the company's conduct in Asia had given "ample proof how little they regard the law of nations, the rights, liberties, or lives of men." "They have levied war, excited rebellions, dethroned lawful princes, and sacrificed millions for the sake of gain. The revenues of mighty kingdoms have centered in their coffers. And these not being sufficient to glut their avarice, they have, by the most unparalleled barbarities, extortions and monopolies, stripped the miserable inhabitants of their property and reduced whole provinces to indigence and ruin." And now they were turning their eyes to America. "The monopoly of tea is, I dare say, but a small part of the plan they have formed to strip us of our property," Dickinson concluded.[36]

The East India Company also attracted the attention of two philosophers developing new theories about nations and economies. Adam Smith, the father of modern capitalism, famously wrote in *The Wealth of Nations* that an "invisible hand" leads individuals pursuing their self-interest in a free market to simultaneously and unintentionally promote the interest of society more broadly. But in a somewhat less well known section of his treatise, Smith cast doubt on the ability of corporations to do the same. The capitalists who own stock in corporations, according to Smith, are "an order of men, whose interest is never exactly the same with that of the public, who have generally an interest to deceive and even to oppress the public, and who accordingly have, upon many occasions, both deceived and oppressed it." Smith then launched into a remarkable screed against the East India Company, which he believed to be irremediably flawed. Managers ordered entire fields destroyed just because they "foresaw that extraordinary profit was likely to be made" by induced scarcity. Employees were "more disposed to support with rigorous severity their own interest, against that of the country which they govern." The English nation had suffered, paying "not only for all the extraordinary profits which the company may have made . . . but for all the extraordinary waste which the fraud and abuse inseparable from the management of the affairs of so great a company must necessarily have occasioned." So had India. "It is a very singular government," Smith observed, "in which every member of the administration wishes to get out of the country, and consequently to have done with the government, as soon as he can, and to whose interest, the day after he has left it, and carried his whole fortune with him, it is perfectly indifferent though the whole country was swallowed up by an earthquake." In conclusion, Smith wrote that the East India Company and all companies like it were "nuisances in every respect; always more or less inconvenient to the countries in which they are established, and destructive to those which have the misfortune to fall under their government."[37]

Karl Marx, whose theory of communism would emerge as the primary alternative to Adam Smith's capitalism, was, for perhaps the first time in his life, in complete agreement with Smith. In 1853, in an essay in the *New York Tribune*, Marx wrote, "The Company of English merchant adventurers . . . conquered India to make money out of it." The results had been nothing less than catastrophic. "It is settled beyond all doubt," Marx said, "that there is in India a permanent financial deficit, a regular over-supply of wars, and no supply at all of public works, an abominable system of taxation, and a no less abominable state of justice and law, that these five items constitute, as it were, the five points of the East Indian Charter." To Marx, these evils were not the result of bad apples in the company or mismanagement by its executives. They were the inevitable result of the structure of stocks themselves. "On looking deeper into the framework of this anomalous government, we find at its bottom a third power, more supreme than either the Board [of Control] or the Court [of Directors], more irresponsible, and more concealed from and guarded against the superintendence of public opinion." "Who is the master at Leadenhall St.?" Marx asked, referring to the East India House. "Two thousand persons, elderly ladies and valetudinarian gentlemen, possessing Indian stock, having no other interest in India except to be paid their dividends out of Indian revenue." For Marx, there was something rotten at the very core of the stock.[38]

Eventually, the British Parliament came to much the same conclusion. A financial crash in 1769 led the East India Company to the brink of bankruptcy, and the company requested a bailout from the government. The government issued a loan but in return forced the company to limit dividend payouts and to create a new council in Calcutta controlled by Parliament. In 1783, the company again ran into financial straits, and the board again wrote to Parliament for aid. Parliament once again provided a bailout but this time took full control of the company. The India Act created a government-controlled Board of Control for the company that would have full powers to direct the company's civil and military affairs abroad. The British government also reserved the right to remove executives in India. While the East India Company would nominally continue its business for another seventy years (until the Indian Mutiny in 1857 led the British government to fully nationalize the company), its era as a private corporation was for the most part at an end. It had become an arm of the British government.

The East India Company unleashed the primal energy of the stock to transform itself from a small corporation of traders into a full-fledged empire. It was an awe-inspiring achievement, but also a troubling one. What had started as a venture to profit from overseas trade turned into a machine that promoted itself, sometimes to the detriment of the country that founded it. These tensions grew over time and ended in violence. As Edmund Burke warned, "This cursed Company would, at last, like a viper, be the destruction of the country which fostered it at its bosom." But the East India Company had also shown the power that corporations could wield in the world. The joint stock company and its progeny would come to dominate capitalism and commerce for the next several centuries. It would foster the colonization of the New World. It would usher in the Industrial Revolution. And it would fuel the spread and growth of the American economy. Its dominance would soon take on an air of inevitability.

※ ※ ※

THE STOCK AND the exchange are the two ingredients of every capitalist system. The stock allows corporations to raise capital from the public. The exchange allows the public to profit from their stock. As the East India Company discovered to its great delight, this combination is an explosive one. Investors give money to promising companies, and the companies put the money to work on new ventures. When the ventures pay off, the investors make money, which they can then reinvest back into promising companies. Profit. Rinse. Repeat. The only limits are the ambition of executives and the pockets of the public.

But the stock and the exchange also created new problems for corporations. Stock severed the already tenuous link between the owners of companies and their managers. Shareholders owned corporations, but they had little to no say over what those corporations did. Corporate directors might line their own pockets, or raise their own salaries, or pay themselves giant bonuses, all at the shareholders' expense, with little accountability or even likelihood of being caught. There were, of course, ways to reduce these conflicts. Companies could give managers some stock in the company to help align their incentives with those of other shareholders. They could hire accountants to check the books for fraud or mismanagement. They could hire directors with reputations for rectitude and honesty. But these were just stopgaps. They might reduce the symptoms, but they didn't get at the root cause of the problem.

The stock exchange also brought a revolutionary change to the spirit of the corporation. With the rise of stock exchanges and the widespread trading of shares, shareholders steadily became more detached from the companies they owned. They often cared more about the price of shares than they did about the companies those shares were attached to—arguably, their demands for higher stock prices led corporations to engage in ever more cutthroat practices to eke out greater profits. It turned out that stock prices were also susceptible to all sorts of strange behaviors. They were fickle things. They boomed. They busted. They bubbled. They burst. Rumor and gossip ran rampant. As a result, the stock exchange became little more than a guessing game. But traders weren't trying to guess what a corporation would do next. They were trying to guess what other traders were guessing. Capitalism became a game within a game. The stock exchange brought the corporation into stormy new waters, where it was lifted up and tossed down, pulled to and fro, in violent and unexpected ways, all by the fickle will of the market.

The rise of shareholders and stock exchanges provided even more incentives for corporations to run profitable businesses. Dispersed shareholders might not have known or cared much about what a corporation was doing on a typical day, but they were keenly aware of how much money it was making at the end of the year. They felt it in their pocketbooks. And over time, as corporations learned how to adapt to this new world of shareholder capitalism, they found there was one tried-and-true way to turn a profit.

four

THE MONOPOLY

O N JULY 1, 1862, ABRAHAM LINCOLN HAD MUCH ON HIS MIND. Confederate general Robert E. Lee was in the midst of his famous Seven Days Battles, inflicting heavy losses on the Union's vaunted Army of the Potomac. Union general George McClellan was telegraphing Lincoln, asking for reinforcements ("If we had a million of men, we could not get them to you in time," Lincoln telegraphed back, before writing to the states asking them for three hundred thousand more troops for the war). Lincoln had just signed a bill outlawing slavery in the territories. Two months later, he would issue the Emancipation Proclamation freeing all enslaved people in the Confederacy. The Civil War was in full tilt, and Americans were dying by the thousands in vicious, bloody battles in orchards and fields and valleys across the country.[1]

Amid these weighty matters, Lincoln might have been forgiven for overlooking a bill that had just arrived on his desk from Congress. The Act to Aid in the Construction of a Railroad and Telegraph Line from the Missouri River to the Pacific Ocean, and to Secure to the Government the Use of the Same for Postal, Military, and Other Purposes was lengthy and complicated. Its twenty sections ran to ten pages and included dense provisions filled with discussions of meridians and longitudes and interest rates. It might not, on its face, have seemed particularly important in comparison with the other issues on Lincoln's mind that day. But Lincoln knew better. This law, he believed, was essential to the future of the country. At long last, a transcontinental railroad would be built.

Railroads had always been a cause dear to Lincoln's heart. Before launching his career in politics, he had been a railroad lawyer, arguing on behalf of railroad companies and their interests in Illinois. In one of his most famous cases, he won a lawsuit protecting railroads that had laid bridges across rivers from being sued by the steamships that kept running into them. In defending railroads, Lincoln was not just out for a quick payday. He believed they were the future and had great "public utility" for America. They could lift up poor and remote communities, providing them with new ways to travel to and to trade and communicate with other regions of the country. Campaigning for the Illinois House of Representatives in 1832, Lincoln took up the cause of railroads with particular tenacity, saying, "No other improvement that reason will justify us in hoping for can equal in utility the rail road."

A transcontinental railroad had even grander potential. Lincoln thought a railroad running from coast to coast was essential to holding the fragile states together. In fact, he had helped spearhead the bill now on his desk. As railroad executive Grenville M. Dodge would write, "Lincoln advocated its passage and building, not only as a military necessity, but as a means of holding the Pacific Coast to the Union." Lincoln would later tell Cornelius Bushnell, another railroad executive, to hurry up and finish the railroad so that he could take a ride on it when he retired from the presidency at the end of his term. "It would be the proudest thing of his life" that he had signed the bill authorizing its construction."[2]

To Lincoln, the railroad would be integral to the fabric of the nation, weaving the country together both physically and spiritually. Lincoln knew that the bill on his table was just as important as the ebbs and flows of battle. So his strategy for getting the railroad built might come as something of a surprise. The Pacific Railroad Act did not authorize the government to go out and start laying tracks. It did not create a federal railroad department to oversee the work. This would not be a government project at all. Instead, the bill created the Union Pacific Railroad Company, "a body corporate and politic" that was "authorized and empowered to lay out, locate, construct, furnish, maintain, and enjoy a continuous railroad" from Iowa to California. Other provisions of the bill addressed the capital stock of the company, the election of directors, and the conduct of board meetings. It also authorized the Central Pacific Railroad Company, a corporation already formed in California, to build in the other direction, eastward from the Pacific coast. The transcontinental railroad, Lincoln decided, would be built by corporations.

Lincoln was deeply interested in the progress of the transcontinental railroad and kept abreast of developments throughout the remainder of his life. On January 20, 1865, just three months before his assassination, Lincoln, seeing that the Union Pacific was languishing in its construction of the railroad, met with Congressman Oakes Ames to discuss the situation. "Ames, take hold of this," Lincoln told him, "and if the subsidies provided are not enough to build the road, ask double and you shall have it. That road must be built, and you are the only man to do it; and you take hold of it yourself. By building the road, you will become the remembered man of your generation."[3]

Lincoln was wrong that Oakes Ames would be the remembered man of his generation. Lincoln himself would earn that honor. But his words were telling. He believed in the importance of the railroad to his vulnerable nation. And he chose to entrust it to the care of a corporation. A railroad, and a company, would tie the commonwealth together.[4]

※ ※ ※

ON THE LONG list of terrible things that corporations do, creating a monopoly invariably appears at the top. Monopolies are the bugaboos of all economists. When a single company grows so big and so powerful that it becomes the only business operating in its field, prices rise, investment stagnates, and quality suffers. Consumers are left to the whims of unaccountable corporations, and governments stand powerless to help.

Ironically, though, for a concept that is so universally derided, monopoly power is something of a Holy Grail for corporations themselves. They all quest after it. At the heart of capitalism, after all, is the spirit of competition. A principal tenet of economics holds that vigorous competition among businesses—to create a better product, to sell it more cheaply, to deliver it faster, to make it more convenient—will lead to a better world for all. But, of course, companies are not competing for the sake of competing. They are competing to win. Their goal is to create products that are better than their competitors', to sell them for less, to deliver them more quickly. If they do that, then a tantalizing prize awaits them. They will take all the market, sell all the products, and, eventually, put their competitors out of business. And of course, once they possess the object of their quest, they get to level out of the competition game. There are no competitors left to challenge them.

This is, to put it mildly, something of a problem for theorists of capitalism. How can we have a system that is based on competition, when the end result of that competition is the elimination of it? It would be as if the National Basketball Association (NBA) created a system where, if the Lakers beat the Celtics in a playoff series, the Celtics would be not just eliminated from the playoffs but removed permanently from the NBA. If the Lakers went on to win the NBA finals, they would get to remove all the other teams from the NBA. From then on, fans would have the privilege of watching the Lakers scrimmage among themselves—at a significantly higher ticket price. Needless to say, this would not be an attractive version of basketball.

Of course, you might say that even if a corporation does beat its existing competitors, it still has to compete against potential new entrants into the market. If it doesn't keep providing a good product at a low price, better companies will start going after its market share. In the NBA example, you might say that there is nothing stopping those other teams that had been banished from the league from going off and creating their own leagues and competing for viewership with the reigning Lakers. But what if there *were* something stopping them? What if the NBA raised insurmountable barriers preventing other basketball leagues from arising? Perhaps the NBA could enter into contracts with television stations prohibiting them from televising other leagues' games. Perhaps they could drastically cut ticket prices, even to unsustainable rates, for just long enough to put smaller, less deep-pocketed leagues out of business.

Monopolies are a major concern, not just for consumers but for society. Corporations, by their very nature, are constantly seeking to concentrate market power. Once they have acquired dominant market power, corporations have a range of strategies for maintaining it, often at the expense of the public. No story better tells how monopolies form and what happens when they do than that of the transcontinental railroad.

THE MID-NINETEENTH CENTURY WAS A TIME OF TREMENDOUS transformation in the United States. In a very real sense, Americans were busy building a nation and also desperately seeking to keep it from falling apart. New states were joining the Union at a rapid clip, and the borders of the nation were expanding. Between 1830 and 1860, nine states joined the Union, including Michigan, Florida, and Iowa. In 1846, the United States reached a settlement with Great Britain on the long-simmering dispute over the boundary between Oregon and

British North America, finally setting the line at the 49th parallel. In 1848, after the Mexican-American War, the United States acquired undisputed possession of Texas, California, Arizona, Nevada, and Utah. By 1850, it possessed sovereignty over all of the territory that now makes up the contiguous United States.

But expansion brought with it difficult questions about the direction of the country. Some of these questions were practical: How could settlers move to the new territories? How could mail be carried regularly there? How could the army protect these vast lands? But other questions were moral and went to the very root of American identity. One of the fiercest debates of the time was the status of slavery in the newly acquired territories. Slave states in the South wished to open up these territories to slavery, while free states in the North did not. At issue was not just the economies of the individual states but the balance of power within the country more broadly. The influx of new states, with their train of new senators and congressmen, could easily tip control of the national legislature in favor of either slave or free states. The Compromise of 1850 had sought to resolve this dispute by admitting California as a free state, allowing New Mexico and Utah to decide for themselves whether to become slave or free states, and creating a new Fugitive Slave Act, requiring free states to return people escaping from slavery to their enslavers. But while the compromise dampened tensions in the short term, it only postponed a full reckoning.

In this context of hope and despair, the idea of a transcontinental railroad took root. Its boosters believed it would solve both the practical and the moral problems bedeviling the nation. It is important to remember just how difficult and treacherous traveling was in the nineteenth century. Getting from the East to the West Coast was an enormous undertaking. The expedition of Lewis and Clark took three years and yielded the disappointing news that no navigable rivers ran coast to coast. Travelers had only two options for crossing the continent: by land or by sea. Neither was easy. The overland route required travelers to make the perilous crossing of the Rocky Mountains, sift through the deserts of the Great Basin, and then, in a final push, trek over the Sierra Nevada. The sea route, on the other hand, took travelers around the tip of South America and the notoriously stormy Cape Horn and required six months and eighteen thousand miles of travel. There was also a hybrid approach, involving a sea route to Panama, an overland route across the isthmus of Panama, and then a second sea route to California, but the Panamanian leg was feared for its fever and still took thirty-five days. And yet, despite all this, Americans were moving West with astonishing rapidity, driven by greed, desperation, or simply hope for something new. The discovery of gold in Coloma, California, in 1848 led to a rush of immigration that continued for decades. In 1840, California had 8,000 nonindigenous residents; by 1850, it had 120,000; by 1860, 379,994. The legendary Oregon Trail earned a place in the national imagination. All of this intensified demand for a rail link connecting West and East.

A railroad seemed to provide a perfect solution. The introduction of steam-powered locomotives had made railroads efficient, fast, and convenient, and railroad building was in the beginning stages of an enormous boom. In 1834, a mere 762 miles of railroad tracks had been laid in the United States; by 1844, there were 4,311; by 1854, the total was 15,675. The technology was fast improving as well. In the 1830s, Robert Stevens, an American inventor and railroad executive, developed strong, reliable all-iron rails to replace the wooden rails prevalent at the time. Trains grew in size and power and added steam whistles and engine brakes for increased safety. Bridge technology improved to allow railroads to cross rivers and gorges. When cattle were discovered to be one of the main hazards for railroads (as they tended to wander onto the tracks without heeding the trains bearing down on them, often causing them to derail), plow-shaped "cowcatchers" were added to the fronts of locomotives to clear the way. It was said that a well-designed cowcatcher could launch a two-thousand-pound ox thirty feet in the air.[5]

In a time of deep division, the transcontinental railroad was an area of rare national agreement. Both the Republican and Democratic parties endorsed it, and the idea was popular with the public. It was just a question of how, where, and when the railroad would, or could, be built. In 1859, journalist Horace Greeley brought renewed interest to the subject after he traveled to California and recounted his voyage in *An Overland Journey from New York to San Francisco.*

> Men and brethren! Let us resolve to have a railroad to the Pacific —
> to have it soon. It will add more to the strength and wealth of our
> country than would the acquisition of a dozen Cubas. It will prove
> a bond of union not easily broken, and a new spring to our national
> industry, prosperity and wealth. It will call new manufactures into
> existence, and increase the demand for the products of those already
> existing. It will open new vistas to national and to individual aspi-
> ration, and crush out filibusterism by giving a new and wholesome
> direction to the public mind.

At the same time, he warned about the immense difficulty of building such a railroad. Workers would need to lay track over hundreds of miles of inhospitable territory. "I thought I had seen barrenness before, [but] famine sits enthroned, and waves his scepter over a dominion expressly made for him."[6]

But even an idea as universally acclaimed as the transcontinental railroad became bogged down in the muck of political controversy. The core disagreement was where the railroad should run. The southern states wanted a route from New Orleans through Texas to San Diego, arguing that this path would mean crossing fewer mountains and encountering less snow during the winter. Northern states preferred a northern route, starting from Chicago. Other interests wanted to split the difference and go through the middle of the country. In 1853, Congress commissioned a survey of potential routes, appropriating $150,000 for the purpose. Jefferson Davis, the Mississippian who at the time served as secretary of war but would later be chosen as president of the Confederacy, headed up the commission and sent out teams of surveyors to explore potential routes as far south as Mexico and as far north as Canada. The commission's conclusions carried immense importance, as the route of the railroad would determine the fates of towns, cities, and states. Davis's eventual report on the findings of the commission ran to eleven volumes, filled with maps, illustrations, and descriptions of the regions explored. In conclusion, he firmly recommended the southern path. His conclusion, though, was dead on arrival: northern interests would not let such a railroad be built.

By the time of the 1860 presidential campaign that brought Lincoln to power, Congress was clearly too divided to ever reach an agreement on the transcontinental railroad. And yet both parties still professed to support it. Both the Republicans and the Democrats included a plank in their platforms devoted to the railroad. The Democratic version read, "One of the necessities of the age, in a military, commercial, and postal point of view, is speedy communications between the Atlantic and Pacific States; and the Democratic party pledge such Constitutional Government aid as will insure the construction of a Railroad to the Pacific coast, at the earliest practicable period." So while the parties would never find consensus on the route, if one could manage to gain full control of Congress, it just might be able to ram its preferred path through.

THAT MOMENT FINALLY ARRIVED DURING THE CIVIL WAR. WHEN the southern states seceded from the Union, their representatives withdrew from Congress, clearing the one impediment to northern states passing bills through the legislature. Congress promptly acted, sending the Pacific Railroad Act to Lincoln in the final days of June 1862.

The precise terms of the act proved deeply consequential to the future of the railroad, so it is worthwhile examining them in some detail. The act managed to be both nitpickingly specific and head-scratchingly ambiguous. A few things were straightforward; many others were not. It was clear that a Union Pacific Railroad Company was to be created, which would build the railroad west from the Missouri River, and that the Central Pacific Railroad Company, which already existed, would build the railroad east from Sacramento. But the act did not specify where on the Missouri River the Union Pacific was to begin or where the Union Pacific and Central Pacific railroads would meet, questions that would lead to controversy.

In return for their efforts to construct the railroad, the two corporations would be rewarded richly in land and government loans. Each railroad would be granted a right of way of two hundred feet on either side of the tracks it laid, as well as alternating strips of land extending ten miles wide from the railroad in a checkerboard pattern, amounting to sixty-four hundred acres for each mile of track laid. The more railroad the companies built, the more land they would receive. These grants would add up quickly on a railroad that ended up running 1,912 miles (it did not need to run the full width of the United States because the eastern United States already had extensive railroad connections). In addition to the land grants, the two companies would also receive government bonds based on the amount of track laid, with amounts varying according to the difficulty of the terrain. On the plains, where laying track was (relatively) simple, they would get $16,000 per mile built. On the plateau between the Rockies and the Sierra Nevada, where construction was more difficult, they would get $32,000 per mile. In the mountains, where construction was nearly impossible, they would get $48,000 per mile. These bonds were, like all bonds, loans, and thus eventually had to be paid back with interest. But the act failed to specify when interest was due, which also proved a major controversy in later years.

To ensure that the railroad companies did not do shoddy work, both the land grants and the bonds would only be issued after government commissioners inspected forty-mile sections of track to make sure they came up to standard—the criteria for which, like much else, were at once specific and ambiguous. On the specific side was the provenance of the iron used in the railway: "The rails and all the other iron used in the construction and equipment of said road [must] be American manufacture of the best quality." This provision was included at the request of Congressman Thaddeus Stevens, who also happened to own a foundry in Pennsylvania and wanted the railroads to purchase iron from it (though his hopes were largely dashed by Confederate forces, which burned down his ironworks before the Battle of Gettysburg in 1863). Yet the act failed to specify the gauge (or width between the rails) to be used. This was an important omission, as there was no common railway gauge in the 1860s; instead, every railway used its own. The Erie Railroad used a gauge of six feet; the Missouri Pacific, five feet, six inches; the Sacramento Valley Railroad, five feet, three and a half inches; and the New York Central, four feet, eight and a half inches. Recognizing the problem, the act provided that for the Pacific Railroad "the track upon the entire line of railroad . . . shall be of uniform width, to be determined by the President of the United States." Lincoln eventually held a full cabinet meeting on the topic and set it at five feet, a decision overturned by Congress, which passed a law in 1863 setting it at five feet, eight and a half inches, laying the groundwork for that gauge to emerge as the national "standard gauge."

Why did Congress hand over authority for the transcontinental railroad to corporations? The answer was twofold: First, it was thought that corporations would be more efficient than the government at undertaking such a massive project. Corporations could harness and channel the self-interest of a diverse array of forces, from capitalists to business executives to engineers, in a way that government officers never could. And second, there was a fear of expanding the powers of the federal government beyond their proper limits. As James Buchanan said in 1859 in his annual message to the nation,

It would be inexpedient for the government to undertake this great work by agents of its own appointment and under its direct and exclusive control. This would increase the patronage of the executive to a dangerous extent, and would foster a system of jobbing and corruption which no vigilance on the part of federal officials could prevent. The construction of this road ought, therefore, to be intrusted to incorporated companies or other agencies, who would exercise that active and vigilant supervision over it which can be inspired alone by a sense of corporate and individual interest.

Buchanan's distrust of the federal government—and corresponding confidence in the corporation—was consistent with the Democratic Party's platform at the time, which emphasized the constitutional limitations of the federal government and the priority of private industry in directing the economy.[7]

The Pacific Railroad Act was a grand bet on the virtue of corporations. Horace Greeley celebrated it by writing on April 15, 1863, "The Pacific Railroad is, therefore, not only the grandest and noblest enterprise of our age, but is morally certain to prove the most beneficent and the most remunerative." In order to achieve it, though, the federal government decided to create a monopoly (or a duopoly, depending on one's perspective). Only the Union Pacific had the right to build westward from Omaha; only the Central Pacific had the right to build eastward from California. Now the monopolies would get started.[8]

THE CONSTRUCTION OF A RAILROAD ACROSS THOUSANDS OF MILES of some of the most desolate, inaccessible, and treacherous terrain in the world required political savvy, financial sophistication, and, most importantly, engineering genius. In the beginning, the Union Pacific had none of these. It needed to figure out how to physically build a railroad over such immense and inhospitable territories—as well as how to pay for it. These problems were both hard and interconnected:

it was hard to raise money to build the railroad without a plan for surmounting the engineering problems, but it was hard to do the work
needed to surmount the engineering problems without money.

On the financial side, things got off to a rocky start. The Pacific
Railroad Act called for a board of commissioners—made up of railroad investors, bankers, and politicians—to meet to decide on the
organization and management of the Union Pacific Railroad Company. The board met in Chicago two months after the passage of the
bill, on September 2, 1862, but the meeting was poorly attended—
fewer than half the commissioners deigned to show up. When the
commissioners chose Samuel Curtis, a general in the Union Army,
as chairman of the corporation, he proclaimed his opinion that the
Union Pacific could not possibly survive. "Notwithstanding the grant
[of the Pacific Railroad Act] is liberal," he said, "it may still be in-
sufficient." Not exactly inspiring words from the inaugural leader of
the company. Nevertheless, the commissioners agreed to open stock
subscription books in cities across the country and start raising money
by advertising the stock sales in national newspapers.[9]

The stock sales, too, proved a pitiful affair. The goal had been
to sell at least two thousand of the company's one hundred thousand authorized shares at a price of $1,000 each, which would yield
the amount that the act required before a permanent board of directors could start running the corporation. But four months after the
sales had begun, a mere eleven investors had come forward, buying
a grand total of forty-five shares. They were not even close to meeting their goal. The lone bright spot was that Brigham Young, head
of the Mormon Church in Utah, had agreed to buy five shares. He
wanted the railroad to run through the newly founded Salt Lake City
and hoped that by buying shares, he would have some influence in
the route. He would eventually be disappointed in this. Young would
nonetheless prove to be an avid supporter of the Union Pacific in
later years, even helping to build a substantial portion of the railroad
when it eventually arrived in Utah. But the company would need

much more than the support of one man if it was to start building the railroad in earnest.

Out of this crisis arose Thomas Durant, a Machiavellian genius of railroad finance. "Doc" Durant had been born in Massachusetts in 1820 and studied medicine as a young man, but afterward went into business, joining his uncle's import-export firm, dabbling in stock speculation, and then settling into a prosperous career as a railroad executive. He was short-tempered, manipulative, and sometimes downright unethical, but he had an eye for grand business schemes, and he never hesitated to grasp a good opportunity when he saw one. In 1863, he saw one in the Union Pacific, which was floundering but, in his eyes, presented an attractive investment. He bought fifty shares for himself and then promoted the company to his network of wealthy capitalist friends in Boston, New York, and Philadelphia. Many met him with skepticism. "If you attempt to build a railway across the desert and over the Rocky Mountains, the world will call you a lunatic," one of his colleagues said. But Durant, sure in his convictions, persevered. At times he resorted to fronting the investors their initial investment just to ensure that they bought the stock. He also reassured them that he had schemes already underway to improve the company's financial prospects. Recognizing that a major problem for raising money was that the railway act had not been sufficiently generous in its terms, he began lobbying Congress to revise it. At the same time, he started researching routes for the railroad that might surface hidden value, and he hired a geologist to search for mineral deposits along the route.[10]

Durant's efforts paid off. By September 1863, he had managed to cobble together a group of investors willing to buy two thousand shares, meaning that the Union Pacific could now finally hold its stockholder meeting to elect a board of directors, appoint officers, and begin construction. At the meeting, former treasury secretary General John Dix was appointed president of the Union Pacific. It was something of a figurehead role. The real leader was Durant, who, as anticipated, had been elected vice president. Durant immediately set to work implementing his grand plan. The first step was settling on the "eastern terminus" where the Union Pacific Railroad would begin. Durant had a personal interest in the question, as he owned another railroad, the Mississippi & Missouri, that was to run to Council Bluffs, Iowa, and would therefore benefit if a transcontinental railroad ended there.

Durant telegraphed his head engineer that he wanted more surveys to provide him with ammunition to convince President Lincoln to select Council Bluffs as the eastern terminus of the railroad. The impatient tone of the message would become typical of Durant as a railroad executive. "Want preliminary surveys at once to make location of starting point," he wrote. "Delay is ruinous. Everything depends on you." But again, it was effective. On November 17, two days before delivering the Gettysburg Address, Lincoln issued an executive order establishing Council Bluffs as the terminus. With his preferred terminus now established, Durant telegraphed his head engineer again, ordering him to break ground on the railroad. "You are behind time for so important an enterprise. Break ground on Wednesday."[11]

Durant's lobbying in Congress also paid dividends. In 1864, Congress passed a new Pacific Railroad Act, improving the terms offered to the railroad corporations. The land grants were doubled, from 6,400 to 12,800 acres per mile of railroad built. The companies were also given the right to issue their own first-mortgage bonds, providing them a new way to raise capital. And, in a great coup for Durant, the companies were given rights to any coal, iron, and minerals found in their land grants, a right not included in the first version of the bill. Durant's geologist had found coal and iron in the Black Hills, and Durant believed that they would prove a mine of wealth for the company in the future. Durant smoothed the way for passage of the act by brazenly handing out Union Pacific bonds to powerful politicians. Joseph P. Stewart, a lobbyist whom Durant had hired, gave out $250,000 in Union Pacific bonds in connection with the bill, including $20,000 to Charles T. Sherman, the brother of General William Tecumseh

Sherman, and $20,000 to Clark Bell, the New York lawyer who drafted the act.

The Union Pacific now had in place a favorable law, substantial capital, and a group of powerful executives. Construction could now begin. This would prove just as difficult as many had expected. Nearly every step of the initial construction was a logistical nightmare. Settling on a route was still a major problem. The railroad engineers wanted to lay as straight a route as possible to their final destination, but of course they didn't know their final destination because it hadn't been determined yet. Trains of the time could not ascend or descend an incline of much more than 2 percent, so the engineers wanted, where possible, to avoid hills, ridges, and ravines. But trains also couldn't go around sharp curves, so they needed to avoid these obstacles by some distance. At the same time, steam engines required water, so they needed to be close to rivers. But crossing rivers was hard, and so they also wanted a route that avoided meandering rivers that zigged and zagged too much, requiring multiple crossings. Everyone wanted a route close to buffalo so that builders had an ample source of food. But they also wanted to avoid straying too close to the lands of Native American tribes, many of which viewed the railroad with suspicion or outright hostility. Since there were essentially no established cities along any potential route, the teams had to bring all their supplies with them—floating them down the Missouri River or carting them by wagon for hundreds of miles. And the Union Pacific still had it easy compared to the Central Pacific, which had to cross the daunting peaks of the Sierra Nevada.[12]

All of these problems, as well as the internal squabbles they generated, slowed down construction considerably. By the beginning of 1866, two and a half years after the passage of the Pacific Railroad Act, the Union Pacific had laid only forty miles of track, a woefully short distance. It had become increasingly clear that Durant, for all his financial acumen, simply did not have the knowledge necessary to build a railroad. He needed an engineer deeply versed in the nitty-gritty of surveying, grading, and laying railroad track. One, and only one, man in his mind was capable of doing the job, but he happened to be off fighting a war.

Grenville M. Dodge is something of a legendary figure in the history of the transcontinental railroad. Dodge was a Massachusetts-born engineer who had early on in his career devoted himself to the emerging railroad industry, working for railroad companies in Illinois, Mississippi, and Missouri. He had long dreamed of building a railroad across the continent and spent much of his twenties exploring potential routes. He had always had an eye for detail, and his years in the industry had taught him much about what made for a good railroad. Out of these years of research and experience, he had drawn a map, detailing all the particular needs of a transcontinental railroad. As he described it, his map "gave the fords and where water and wood could be found" and was "the first map of the country giving such information." He had come to the conclusion, shared by Durant, that Council Bluffs was the ideal eastern terminus of the railroad, given its easy river access and the natural grade of the Platte River valley. In 1859, he had even met Abraham Lincoln in Council Bluffs, when Lincoln was in town to inspect real estate. At a party at the Pacific House held in honor of Lincoln's visit, Dodge and Lincoln sat down together on the stoop to talk after dinner. Lincoln had heard of Dodge's passion for the transcontinental railroad and asked for his advice. "Dodge, what's the best route for a Pacific railroad to the West?" Lincoln asked. Without blinking, Dodge replied, "From this town out the Platte valley." "Why do you think so?" Lincoln asked. The conversation went on at length, until, as Dodge described it, Lincoln "by his kindly ways soon drew from me all I knew of the country west, and the results of my reconnaissances. As the saying is, he completely 'shelled my woods,' getting all the secrets that were later to go to my employers."[13]

Durant knew that Dodge was the man the Union Pacific needed, but when the Pacific Railroad Act was passed in 1862, Dodge was busy fighting in the Union Army. Notwithstanding this, Durant repeatedly propositioned him to come work for the company. Dodge repeatedly declined. His railroad expertise was proving invaluable to the Union Army, as he built and repaired railroads everywhere he went, earning a sterling reputation among the highest ranks of the army: General Ulysses S. Grant wrote extensively about Dodge in his memoirs, calling him an "exceedingly efficient officer" and an "experienced railroad builder." In 1865, though, the seemingly interminable war finally came to an end. Durant and the Union Pacific finally had the last piece of the puzzle: a master engineer. Dodge joined the Union Pacific as chief engineer in May 1866.[14]

WHEN DODGE CAME ON THE SCENE, THE FORTUNES OF THE UNION Pacific took a sharp turn for the better. He quickly set to work reorganizing the company's workforce and instilling employees with some of the discipline he had learned in the army. He hired former soldiers from the war, believing them to be more disciplined workers, and assigned them to separate teams, with surveyors, graders, track layers, and others each focused on their individual tasks. He was deeply devoted to building the best railroad he could, finances be damned, and his single-minded focus on finding the best route and laying track accordingly turned the company around. One of his best decisions was to hire the Casement brothers, Jack and Daniel, to oversee the construction teams. Jack stood just over five feet tall, but he loomed large over the end of the track, strutting around in a Cossack hat and carrying a long bullwhip. Soon the Union Pacific crew had turned into a well-oiled machine.

The scene was magnificently organized. As a correspondent for the *Philadelphia Bulletin* described it,

On they came. A light car, drawn by a single horse, gallops up to the front with its load of rails. Two men seize the end of a rail and start forward, the rest of the gang taking hold by twos, until it is clear of the car. They come forward at a run. At the word of command the rail is dropped in its place, right side up with care, while the same process goes on at the other side of the car. Less than thirty seconds to a rail for each gang, and so four rails go down to the minute. Quick work, you say; but the fellows on the Union Pacific are tremendously in earnest. The moment the car is empty, it is tipped over on the side of the track to let the next loaded car pass it, and then it is tipped back again, and it is a sight to see it go flying back for another load, propelled by a horse at full gallop at the end of sixty or eighty feet of rope, ridden by a young Jehu, who drives furiously. Close behind the first gang come the gaugers, spikers, and bolters, and a lively time they make of it. It is a grand anvil chorus that those sturdy sledges are playing across the plains. It is in triple time, three strokes to the spike. There are ten spikes to a rail, four hundred rails to a mile, eighteen hundred miles to San Francisco. Twenty-one million times are those sledges to be swung, twenty-one million times to come down with their sharp punctuation, before the great work of modern America is complete! . . . Sherman, with his victorious legions, sweeping from Atlanta to Savannah, was a spectacle less glorious than this army of men, marching on foot from Omaha to Sacramento, subduing unknown wildernesses, scaling unknown mountains, surmounting untried obstacles, and binding across the broad breast of America the iron emblem of modern progress and civilization.[15]

With Dodge and the Casement brothers on the front lines, the Union Pacific started moving fast. In April 1866, before Dodge started, the company had laid just sixty-three miles of railroad in the three and half years of its existence, but by June 4 of that year, it had reached one hundred miles of road. By late July, it had reached Grand Island, with 153 miles of track laid. And in an important milestone, it reached the hundredth meridian on October 6, 1866, having laid 247 miles of track. To celebrate the occasion, Durant organized an excursion of senators, congressmen, investors, and newspaper reporters on the line. He took them out on the railroad in the plush Pullman Palace Sleeping Cars that George Pullman had made famous. The visitors had the option of going out to watch the Casements' team lay track, visiting a prairie dog colony, or going out hunting for buffalo and antelope. One morning during the trip, a group of Pawnee warriors came thundering through their camp in war paint, whooping and hollering. The terrified guests cowered in their tents until it became clear that Durant had staged the attack. The Pawnee warriors then performed a war dance and a mock battle, including a fake scalping.[16]

But as the Union Pacific pushed deeper into the wilderness and away from established cities, it increasingly intruded upon the territory of Native American tribes that fiercely opposed the invasion. By the time the railroad had reached Fort Sedgwick in Colorado Territory, Union Pacific employees were facing regular attacks by Native American war parties. The warriors tore up tracks, assaulted workers, and stole supplies. Dodge began ordering his men to carry rifles and organized them along military lines, ready to form ranks at the earliest sign of trouble. The trouble got so bad that the Union Pacific started squelching news of attacks in order to prevent terrified workers from quitting in droves.

One of the most serious attacks occurred in August 1867, near Plum Creek in Nebraska. At the time, General George Armstrong Custer was heading a military expedition against Native American tribes for control of the Great Plains. A group of Cheyenne warriors led by Chief Turkey Leg fled Custer's army and, for the first time, happened upon a train. They had never seen one before and watched it curiously from a ridge. One of the warriors, Porcupine, described the experience of watching the train: "Far off it was very small, but it kept coming and growing larger all the time, puffing out smoke and steam, and as it came on we said to each other that it looked like a white man's pipe when he was smoking." After inspecting the "metal road" and discussing what to do about it, they decided to attack the next train that came. They placed a large branch on the rails and set a fire next to it, and then the group settled down to see what would happen. After sundown, a Union Pacific handcar came down the track. "Presently the sound grew loud," Porcupine continued, "and through the darkness we could see a small thing coming with something on it that moved up and down. When the men on the car saw the fire and the Indians, they worked so as to run by them quickly, but when the car struck the stick, it jumped high into the air. The men on it got up from where they had fallen and ran away, but were soon overtaken and killed." Seeing that a large train might simply break through the wood, the Cheyennes then bent the iron rail of the railroad and, a few hours later, derailed a full-size train, which they proceeded to loot.[17]

Remarkably, one of the Union Pacific men on the handcar survived the attack to tell about it. Englishman William Thompson, a telegraph repairer, had been sent out that night with five other employees to find a break along the Union Pacific line. When they came to the branches laid across the track, the Cheyenne jumped up from the grass all around and fired on them. Thompson fled on foot.

An Indian on a pony singled me out, and galloped up to me. After coming to within ten feet of me he fired, the bullet passed through my right arm; but seeing me still run, he rushed up and clubbed me down with his rifle. He then took out his knife, stabbed me in the neck, and making a twirl round his fingers with my hair, he commenced sawing and hacking away at my scalp. Though the pain was awful, and I felt dizzy and sick, I knew enough to keep quiet. After what seemed to be half an hour, he gave the last finishing cut to the scalp on my left temple, and as it still hung a little, he gave it a jerk. I just thought then that I could have screamed my life out. I can't describe it to you. It just felt as if the whole head was taken right off. The Indian then mounted and galloped away, but as he went he dropped my scalp within a few feet of me, which I managed to get and hide.

Thompson would later crawl away under cover of night to the Willow Island station, where he was found by a rescue party. He brought his scalp in a pail of water, "somewhat resembling a drowned rat," to a doctor, hoping that he would be able to reattach it to his head. When the operation failed, he donated the scalp to the Council Bluffs Public Library, where for many years visitors could see it displayed in a jar of alcohol.[18]

With hostilities continuing to increase, in 1867 Andrew Johnson created an Indian Peace Commission to hold conferences with various Native American tribes. A meeting held at North Platte with the Sioux and Cheyenne aimed at preventing further violence and safeguarding the railroad. Language problems, holdouts, and misunderstandings, however, bedeviled the negotiations. The resulting agreements did little to stem attacks. Instead, the Union Pacific increasingly went about its work with military protection, assigning troops to guard its engineers and workers. Meanwhile, the railroad brought with it increasing numbers of settlers and disrupted buffalo migrations. Worse times were to come for Native American tribes. As General John Pope wrote,

The Indian, in truth, has no longer a country. His lands are everywhere pervaded by white men; his means of subsistence destroyed, and the homes of his tribe violently taken away from him; himself and his family reduced to starvation, or to the necessity of warring to the death upon the white man, whose inevitable and destructive progress threatens the total extermination of his race. The first demand of the Indian is that the white man shall not come into his country; shall not kill or drive off the game upon which his subsistence depends; and shall not dispossess him of his lands. How can we

promise this . . . unless we prohibit emigration and settlement? . . .
The end is sure, and dreadful to contemplate.[19]

As the Union Pacific made its way across Wyoming and into
Utah in 1869, its work sped up. Throughout the process, it had been
keeping a wary eye on the progress of the Central Pacific, then rac-
ing to meet it from California. In the summer of 1867, the Central
Pacific had blasted its way through the Sierra Nevada, its most daunting obstacle and, from then on, had made steady progress. And since
the Pacific Railroad Act compensated the two railroads based on the
number of miles of track they laid, and the number of miles between
them was finite and swiftly dwindling, every mile laid by the Central
Pacific meant money snatched from the Union Pacific's pockets. It
was near-perfect competition. This created strong incentives to move
fast and also surfaced long-dormant conflicts between Dodge the engineer and Durant the financier. Durant's messages grew increasingly
urgent as the finish line approached. His telegraphs of the time read
like temperamental bursts of raw ire: "Important the track should be
laid faster, can't you lay one mile per day," he wrote, and then, "What
is the matter that you can't lay track faster."[20]

Dodge, meanwhile, believed that the focus on speed to the detriment of all else threatened the workmanship of the road. In order
to keep up with Durant's expectations, corners would have to be cut,
precautions overlooked, and the men overworked. It was a recipe for
disaster. In 1868, he wrote to Union Pacific president Oliver Ames,
complaining about Durant's orders: "Nothing is being done on repairs
and the order of the vice president is to skim and skip everything for
the purpose of getting track down, and your temporary bridges will
now hardly stand to get trains over them, and winter will close in on
you with nothing done. Your immense subsidy will be spent in dividends, and what few men you have among you who have a name or

reputation will be, in the eyes of the country, disgraced." Dodge felt
redeemed when, in a tense meeting with Durant and General Grant
in July 1868, Grant, recently chosen as the Republican candidate for
president of the United States, told Durant that he wanted Dodge
leading the work on the transcontinental railroad. Grant had seen
Dodge's work during the Civil War and knew that he could get the job
done better than anyone. "The government expects this railroad to be
finished, the government expects the railroad company to meet its obligations, and the government expects General Dodge to remain with
the road as its Chief Engineer until it is completed." The message was
clear: Durant could not get rid of Dodge without incurring the wrath
of the future president of the United States.[21]

And so, in 1869, the Union Pacific tracks finally arrived in Utah.
By this point, its teams were well-oiled machines. Whereas, in the
early years, they would have been lucky to lay a single mile of track
in a full day's work, by the time they arrived in Utah, they were
laying five, six, sometimes seven miles a day. The Central Pacific,
spurred by competitive spirit, outdid them, laying a record ten miles
and fifty-six feet of track on April 28, 1869. But despite the fact that
both railroads were well into Utah by the spring of 1869, Congress
still had not settled on their meeting point—the railroads didn't
know where they were supposed to go. For weeks, the two railroads
had graders working within feet of each other, oftentimes in parallel, sometimes crossing. At times, the workers heckled each other,
and in one perhaps apocryphal incident, a group of Chinese workers
for the Central Pacific even set off an unannounced explosion on
their line that buried a group of Irish workers for the Union Pacific.
Finally, at a contentious meeting on the evening of April 8, 1869,
that ran into the early hours of the next morning, Dodge met with
the Central Pacific's powerful vice president, Collis Huntington, in
Washington, DC, and the two hammered out an agreement: the two
railroads would meet at Promontory Summit, just to the north of the
Great Salt Lake. Soon after, the Union Pacific stopped grading west

of Promontory Summit, and the Central Pacific stopped grading east of it (but not before the two railroads had graded over two hundred miles of overlapping track).[22]

On May 10, 1869, just under seven years since Lincoln had signed the Pacific Railroad Act into law, the moment of union finally arrived. The two railroads had laid tracks all the way up to Promontory Summit, and all that was left was to drive the last spike connecting the roads. A large crowd gathered to mark the occasion — Dodge, Durant, and the Casement brothers were there to represent the Union Pacific; Leland Stanford arrived from California to represent the Central Pacific. Workers, photographers, journalists, soldiers, visiting dignitaries, and even a band gathered around to witness the meeting of the lines. A Union Pacific locomotive and a Central Pacific one drew up along their respective lines to meet, nose to nose. A special golden spike was made for the occasion, the last spike that would be driven in, which would unite the transcontinental railroad. The two sides squabbled a bit over who would drive it: the Central Pacific argued that it should be Stanford because the Central Pacific had broken ground on its line first; Dodge argued that it should be Durant because the Union Pacific's line was longer. In the end, both drove spikes, and, according to some accounts, both swung and missed. Undeterred, Stanford and Durant telegraphed a joint message to President Grant: "Sir, we have the honor to report that the last rail is laid, the last spike is driven. The Pacific Railroad is finished."[23]

THE TRANSCONTINENTAL RAILROAD WAS AN AWE-INSPIRING achievement. It ran 1,912 miles across the most inhospitable and inaccessible territories of the nation, across deserts, mountains, and rivers. The poet Walt Whitman captured the spirit of national celebration in his poem "The Passage to India": "Singing my days, Singing the great achievements of the present, Singing the strong light works of engineers, Our modern wonders, (the antique ponderous Seven

outvied,) . . . I see over my own continent the Pacific Railroad, surmounting every barrier, I see continual trains of cars winding along
the Platte, carrying freight and passengers, I hear the locomotives
rushing and roaring, and the shrill steam-whistle, I hear the echoes
reverberate through the grandest scenery in the world."

But amid the jubilation, there was still a business to be run. The
Union Pacific had shown only expenses to date. Now, it had to show
profits. The Union Pacific could offer an undeniably unique and valuable product. During the Gold Rush, before the railroad had been
built, getting from the East Coast to the West could take upward of
six months and cost hundreds of dollars. After the completion of the
railroad, travelers could make the journey in less than a week and at a
price of just sixty-five dollars. Shipping became cheaper, as did mail.
The Union Pacific also introduced innovations to make travel simpler
and more comfortable. In 1868, it reached an agreement with George
Pullman to provide sleeper cars for the railroad. In 1869, it added a
"Hotel Train" that included not just sleepers but also a dining room,
a drawing room, and saloon cars, meaning the train wouldn't have to
stop for meals along the route. The New York–San Francisco route
would now take just five and a half days. It proved immensely popular:
in 1870, the railroad carried some 150,000 passengers. Railroads published schedules, and, as a result, the United States introduced time
zones rather than having localities choose their own times.[24]

Passengers meant settlers. Even before it was finished, the Union
Pacific had been creating towns everywhere it went. The "Hell on
Wheels" tent cities, which popped up at the end of the rails to cater
to workers' sometimes less-than-savory tastes, had quickly gained notoriety throughout the country. Most of these cities disappeared once
the railroad had moved on, but some had staying power. Laramie,
Wyoming, first planned and laid out by Grenville Dodge's surveyors,
would become famous for gunfights, the outlaw Steve Long, and his
Bucket of Blood saloon. The journalist Henry Morton Stanley, now

most remembered for finding Dr. David Livingstone on the shores of Lake Tanganyika, was perhaps even more shocked by his discovery of the surreal dreamscape of the Hell on Wheels:

> I walked on till I came to a dance-house, bearing the euphonious title of "King of the Hills," gorgeously decorated and brilliantly lighted. Coming suddenly from the dimly lighted street to the kerosene-lighted restaurant, I was almost blinded by the glare and stunned by the clatter. The ground floor was as crowded as it could well be, and all were talking loud and fast, and mostly every one seemed bent on debauchery and dissipation. The women appeared to be the most reckless, and the men seemed nothing loth to enter a whirlpool of sin. . . . Watch-fires gleam over the sea-like expanse of ground outside of the city, while inside soldiers, herdsmen, teamsters, women, railroad men, are dancing, singing or gambling. I verily believe that there are men here who would murder a fellow-creature for five dollars. . . . Not a day passes but a dead body is found somewhere in the vicinity with pockets rifled of their contents.

But not all the settlements were filled with vice. Larger, permanent cities emerged along the route, particularly where the railroads placed their supply depots. Reno in Nevada and Cheyenne and Evanston in Wyoming all were founded as railroad towns. Vast swathes of the country, previously inaccessible, were suddenly a short trip from either coast.[25]

The Union Pacific also had a strong financial interest in settlers moving west. It had been compensated for its work through vast government grants of land—the Union Pacific's haul came to 11,401,176 acres in state and federal grants, an area slightly larger than West Virginia. It now needed to sell these acres, and so it published advertisements in newspapers and magazines promising cheap land and boundless opportunity. The railroad was aided in this effort by its old ally, Horace Greeley, who exhorted, "Go West, young man, go West."[26]

Actually going west on the railroad, though, was not the most pleasant experience. Despite efforts to make the trains more comfortable, passenger complaints abounded. One group of unlucky passengers took a trip along the Union Pacific line in 1869 and were so scarred by the experience that they wrote an open letter to the *Chicago Tribune* denouncing the company. "We can but believe that human life will be very insecure, and the road simply an elongated human slaughterhouse, in place of the safe, substantial, and well-built road which the public had good reason to expect from the munificent appropriation made by Congress," they wrote. They saved their worst imprecations for a different practice of the company: baggage fees. "Evidently to annoy, they obliged us to take a caboose car, hitched on to a freight train stationed at least one fourth of a mile from the depot, where we were crowded together like cattle, and to which they obliged the passengers—men, women and children—to walk and transport their own baggage, after charging extra for all over twenty-five pounds of baggage, and even weighing blankets and overcoats."[27]

Despite the discomfort, the railroad proved a great spur to trade and commerce. As Ralph Waldo Emerson put it, "Railroad iron is a magician's rod, in its power to evoke the sleeping energies of land and water." The railroad helped ferry crops and minerals east from California and manufactured goods west from the East Coast. And the effects were not limited to just the direct east-west route of the initial railroad. Branch railroads were constructed all along the route, from Denver to Salt Lake City to Eureka, Nevada. In 1880, $50 million in goods were transported by the railroad—around $100 billion in today's value. Freight turned into the majority of the company's business, with passenger fares and mail transportation accounting for most of the rest. It was the beginning of a national market, the greatest the world had ever known.[28]

THE TRIUMPH OF THE UNION PACIFIC AND ITS COMPLETION OF the transcontinental railroad were not unalloyed by criticism. Almost from the moment of its victory, controversies began to emerge. Charles Francis Adams, one of the railroad's foremost critics and, ironically, one of its last presidents, said in 1869 that the Pacific Railroad "will one day be the richest and most powerful corporation in the world; it will probably also be the most corrupt." He was right on both accounts.[29]

The seeds of the Credit Mobilier scandal that nearly toppled the company were laid from the day the Union Pacific was born. The scandal turned on the tricky economics of building a railroad, particularly one the length and cost of the transcontinental. Building railroads took money: for supplies, workers, and services. Most of these things had to be paid for up front. But railroads only started making money much later, when people started using them and paying for freight and travel. So how were companies to bridge the gap? Of course, the traditional way to fund a corporation was to sell stocks or bonds. But stocks in the Union Pacific were a risky investment and, as the first effort to peddle them showed, a difficult sell—after all, who knew when the corporation's directors would decide to issue dividends? They might also have taken out loans or sold bonds: these provided the buyers with a bit more certainty, because bonds typically owed regular interest, but given the riskiness of the entire endeavor, bonds, too, were a hard sell.

One of Durant's friends, the appropriately named George Francis Train, hit on a solution. On a visit to France, he had learned of a strategy used by French railroads to get cash quickly. The leaders and major stockholders of the railroad would form a separate construction company that could provide services to the railroad and get paid immediately in the form of railroad stocks and bonds, which they could then either sell on the market or use as collateral for bank loans. What is more, since the same people controlled both the construction company and the railroad company, the construction company could inflate its actual costs and bill the railroad company at exorbitant rates, with no risk that the railroad would push back. Durant liked the idea. Train and Durant bought a derelict corporation, the Pennsylvania Fiscal Agency, whose broad statement of purpose in its charter authorized it to engage in "the purchase and sale of railroad bonds and other securities, and to make advances of money and credit to railroads." As the French version of this scheme was called the Credit Mobilier, Train and Durant renamed the Pennsylvania Fiscal Agency the Credit Mobilier of America. Durant became president, and Train was made a director. Many of the major shareholders of the Union Pacific were rewarded with shares in the new Credit Mobilier as well. In order to prevent Congress from investigating its affairs, Credit Mobilier transferred a large block of shares to Oakes Ames, a Massachusetts congressman, for him to "put . . . where they will do the most good to us." Shareholders in the Credit Mobilier made out like bandits: in 1868, Credit Mobilier issued dividends in securities and cash amounting to around $3,500 for every $1,000 invested—this while the Union Pacific had still not completed its railroad and was more or less drowning in debt.[30]

This all worked magnificently until, in 1872, the *Sun* got a hold of the story and published it in its pages. The resulting backlash was quick and fierce, with both Congress and the Department of Justice opening investigations into the affair. Charles Francis Adams, then head of the Massachusetts Railroad Commission, explained to the American public just how brazen the conspiracy had been. The Credit Mobilier has "got into its hands all the unissued stock, the proceeds of the bonds sold, the government bonds, and the earnings of the road—in fact, all its available assets." Enormous profits of 40 percent a month had been paid out to its owners, who included a ring of the rich and powerful in Washington, New York, and Chicago. "In Washington they vote the subsidies, in New York they receive them, upon the Plains they expend them, and in the Credit Mobilier they divide them." More than thirty politicians ended up being implicated in Credit Mobilier's business, and Congress censured Oakes Ames for his role in it. The real harm, though, was reputational: the Union Pacific was no longer the shining idol of American industry that it once was.[31]

WHILE THE CREDIT MOBILIER SCANDAL WAS DEEPLY EMBARRASS-ing for the Union Pacific and its executives, it ultimately ended in a whimper. No one was jailed. The conspirators were given the lightest slaps on the wrist. A different sort of problem, though, would bring farther-reaching consequences to the company and the nation.

The problem of monopoly had long roots. Adam Smith himself had condemned what he called the "oppressive monopolies" of his day, including the East India Company. And railroads, it turned out, were excellent candidates for monopolization. They had very high fixed costs (laying railroad was tremendously expensive) but low operating costs (once built, railroads were relatively inexpensive to maintain). The high barriers to entry meant that incumbent railroads tended to have few, if any, competitors. As a practical matter, this meant that consumers had to pay whatever price the local railroad offered or be shut out of the business entirely. The wealthy capitalists of the late nineteenth century understood that this was a formula for high profit. Titans of industry like Andrew Carnegie, Cornelius Vanderbilt, and J. P. Morgan all piled into the railroad business, earning themselves reputations as schemers and connivers at the same time that they earned large dividends. The robber barons were railroaders.

By universal acclamation, the worst robber baron of all was a man named Jay Gould. Gould had earned notoriety in the late 1860s for his role in the so-called Erie Wars, in which he and his associate Daniel Drew duped Cornelius Vanderbilt into purchasing boatloads of essentially worthless "watered" shares in the Erie Railroad. When Vanderbilt found out about the scheme and convinced a judge to issue a warrant for Gould's and Drew's arrest, the duo escaped from

Manhattan by boat and fled to Jersey City, where they sheltered in
a hotel and posted cannons on the waterfront to prevent any assault.
Gould and Drew ended up winning the war when a bribe-induced
New York legislature validated their actions. A few years later, Gould
was arrested for kidnapping Lord Gordon-Gordon, who, ironically, had
swindled Gould. It was not for nothing that some described Gould as
a "pasty-faced little weasel." He was something of a Uriah Heep–type
figure of the age—introverted, sharp, and scheming.[32]

So when rumors started circulating in 1874 that Gould was buying shares of the Union Pacific, the railroad world shuddered. Executives, stockholders, and the public at large all wondered what he had
in mind. Some thought it spelled ruin for the company. A banker in
Buffalo remarked that Gould and his ring would "steal all its available
money and run up a large floating debt." Former Union Pacific president Oliver Ames took a more positive view of things: "There seems
to be a general impression that Gould has from 100 to 125,000 shares
of stock in his control—I feel that he will not use his power adverse to
the interests of the road." It took some time for Gould's real strategy to
become clear, though.[33]

Years later, when asked by a *World* reporter why he had become
interested in the Union Pacific, Gould would explain it in the simplest
of terms: "There is nothing strange or mysterious about it. I knew it
[i.e., the Union Pacific] very intimately when I was a child, and I have
merely returned to my first love." This may well have been true, but
there were also other, less romantic reasons for his acquisition. The first
was that Horace F. Clark, son-in-law of Cornelius Vanderbilt and a railroad executive himself, had toured the railroad in May 1873 and came
back deeply impressed. Clark told Gould about the trip, and Gould,
seeing an opportunity, placed an order to buy any Union Pacific shares
for sale at less than thirty-five dollars. Clark died shortly thereafter, and
Clark's own sizeable stake in the company was dumped on the market.
As a result, Gould's standing offer scooped up more stock than he had
anticipated. By February 21, 1874, he had 132,000 shares and had

become the company's largest shareholder. Gould wasted no time in consolidating control. He met with his friend and sometime partner Sidney Dillon and agreed to install Dillon as president of the Union Pacific, while Gould would stay behind the scenes as a director. It was clear to everyone, though, that Dillon was just a figurehead. As Charles Francis Adams said of the arrangement, "Mr. Dillon never consulted anyone except Mr. Gould, and Mr. Gould was in the custom of giving orders without consulting Mr. Dillon at all." Gould assiduously courted the favor of Grenville Dodge, who had resigned from his position as chief engineer but remained an influential director in the company, reassuring him that he intended to do right by the company, that his goal was to "make it a big thing."[34]

Gould surely did intend to make the Union Pacific "a big thing," but perhaps not in the way that Dodge believed. Gould's primary goal was to eliminate the Union Pacific's competitors using any means necessary. One of his first targets was the Pacific Mail Steamship Company, a New York corporation that specialized in shipping cargo across the continent by sea via the Panama route. The existence of the Pacific Mail was a major thorn in the side of the Union Pacific, providing shippers with an alternative to the railroad route across the country and severely limiting the company's ability to raise its prices. "It is outrageous that we have to carry out California business at so low rates," Gould would say when he saw the prices the Union Pacific was charging for freight. So in late 1874, Gould set to work. He spread rumors that the Pacific Mail had been engaged in fraud and bribery, allegations that led to a congressional investigation and the eventual resignation of the Pacific Mail's president (the rumors had some truth to them). The news drove the Pacific Mail's stock to all-time lows. Gould pounced, buying up the stock at the depressed price and acquiring control of the company. Following the script he had used to such effect with the Union Pacific, he placed himself on the board and installed Dillon as president. With the competitor eliminated, the Union Pacific then raised the rates on the railroad, a move that, according to Gould, "ought to add ten per cent to our stock and will help all our securities."[35]

Having eliminated his competitors on the sea, Gould turned to his competitors on land—the other railroads. While there was only one transcontinental railroad, ruling out direct competitors for coast-to-coast freight, many smaller regional railroads competed on other routes. Often these railroads would secretly offer favorable prices to large shippers in return for using their road rather than a competitor's. The resulting rate wars, Gould believed, were undermining the entire industry's long-term profitability, and he sought to eliminate them. First, he set his eyes on the Kansas Pacific Railway, a company running an east-west line across Kansas that roughly paralleled the more northern route of the Union Pacific. In 1875, Gould and his associates acquired a majority of the Kansas Pacific Railway's shares. As he explained to Oliver Ames in November 1875, "You and I together have over a majority, which makes it easy to manage and lay out a definite policy without consulting any body else." In the next few years, he would proceed to acquire control of many more railroads, including the Wabash Railroad, the Central Branch Union Pacific, the Texas and Pacific Railway, and the Missouri Pacific. And in his coup de grâce, he managed to negotiate a contentious merger between the Kansas Pacific, the Denver Pacific, and the Union Pacific, creating the largest railroad network in the world. On January 14, 1880, the directors of the Union Pacific came to Gould's house in the evening to negotiate the terms. Gould, who had sold a significant portion of his shares in the Union Pacific by this point but retained shares in the other companies, held out for better terms against his erstwhile colleagues. The negotiations lasted until midnight, bogged down by disagreements over the respective value of each company's shares, but finally an agreement was struck, bringing to life a new and significantly larger Union Pacific Railway Company that now controlled twenty-three hundred miles of railroad. Gould made a hefty profit on the transaction. One railroad executive estimated that Gould had "cleared more than ten millions of dollars by the operation."[36]

Throughout his reign at the Union Pacific, Gould displayed a shocking disregard for anything other than profits. Learning of the massacre of George Custer's army at Little Bighorn, where more than two hundred troops had been killed, Gould coldly replied, "The ultimate result will be to annihilate the Indians and open up the Big Horn and Black Hills to development and settlement, and in this way greatly benefit us." When the federal government began withholding payment for freight charges in response to the Union Pacific's refusal to make interest payments on its debt to the government, he responded by suing the federal government in court, a shortsighted and vindictive lawsuit that dragged on for years with no resolution.[37]

Gould's aggressive tactics with the Union Pacific started to raise doubts about whether the railroad was earning its profits at the expense of society. As his railroads built new lines, local governments felt they had no choice but to accept Gould's terms, no matter how steep the price, out of fear that he might bypass their locales. Journalist Henry George wrote in 1883 that "a railroad company approaches a small town as a highwayman approaches his victim. The threat 'If you do not accede to our terms we will leave your town two or three miles to one side!' is as efficacious as the 'stand and deliver,' when backed by a cocked pistol. For the threat of the railroad company is not merely to deprive the town of the benefits which the railroad might give; it is to put it in a far worse position than if no railroad had been built."[38]

Some of the most vocal opponents of railroads were farmers. Farmers had bought land, grown crops, and raised herds on the belief that railroads could provide them with a fast and cheap way to transport their produce to market. But as the railroads consolidated into the hands of a few mammoth conglomerates, rates began an inexorable rise. Farmers complained that they had little leverage to push back.

Out of this rage arose the powerful Grange movement, a loosely organized group of corn growers, cotton farmers, and wheat ranchers that, in 1875, claimed as many as 860,000 members—one out of every ten American farmers. Their explicit aim was to fight the railroads, and they often did so by calling on the rhetoric of free competition. A resolution from the Illinois Farmers' Convention of 1873, for example, read, "The railways of the world, except in those countries where they have been held under the strict regulation and supervision of the government, have proved themselves arbitrary, extortionate, and as opposed to free institutions and free commerce between states as were the feudal barons of the middle ages." In the 1870s, Grange legislatures were elected in several states, including Iowa, Wisconsin, and Illinois. The legislatures then passed laws setting maximum rates that railways could charge for passengers and freight. In 1875, Nebraska adopted a new constitution with a provision for regulating railroads. Gould, alarmed by the growing public backlash, wrote to an associate that he should "lay the pipes for its defeat." His efforts were unsuccessful, though, and the constitution came into force as written.[39]

But the states could only do so much to rein in the Union Pacific's practices. Under the so-called Dormant Commerce Clause of the US Constitution, states could not discriminate against interstate commerce by protecting local companies against out-of-state interests, and so their hands were tied in how much they could regulate railroad behavior. It seemed to many that the railroad corporations had grown so large, so fast, that society simply did not have means to control them any longer. As railroad reformer Charles Francis Adams wrote, "Practically, state lines are done away with by corporations created by states. The machinery of civilization has entirely outgrown the system of government under which it was organized, and has neutralized many of the fundamental laws which regulate the control and disposition of property." In the late 1800s, the federal government struck back. In 1887, Congress passed the Interstate Commerce Act, a comprehensive law governing railroads. It created a commission to monitor railroad practices and forbid their worst abuses, such as pooling (the practice of sharing profits between rival railroads, one common way of ensuring that railroads did not compete with one another) and price discrimination (the practice of charging different shippers different prices for the same service, a strategy that tended to hurt farmers and other small businesses).[40]

The depredations of the railroads also led to wider interest in addressing the looming problem of monopoly power, and in 1890 the country passed its first antimonopoly law. John Sherman, speaking in defense of his Antitrust Act, denounced the "kingly prerogative" of monopolies, proclaiming them "injurious to the public" and stating that "the individuals engaged in [them] should be punished as criminals." He was careful to point out that his attack on monopolies was not an attack on corporations themselves. "Experience has shown that they are the most useful agencies of modern civilization. They have enabled individuals to unite to undertake great enterprises only attempted in former times by powerful governments." But unscrupulous corporations had invented a new and dangerous form of business, the monopoly, that subverted the true spirit of the corporation. "Such a combination is far more dangerous than any heretofore invented. . . . If we will not endure a king as a political power, we should not endure a king over the production, transportation, and sale of any of the necessaries of life. If we would not submit to an emperor, we should not submit to an autocrat of trade." The Sherman Antitrust Act remains today the principal antimonopoly law in the United States.[41]

But by the time these laws were passed, Gould was long gone from the Union Pacific. He had made his money and then departed. Gould's investment, as always, turned out to be quite profitable for him. By 1878, Gould owned, directly or indirectly, 200,000 of the company's 475,000 shares. In 1879, he sold 173,000 shares at a profit of $47 per share, plus dividends of $20 per share, for a total profit of $10.5 million. Soon after the merger went through, Gould sold his stock in the merged company.[42]

BY 1884, CONGRESS HAD HAD ENOUGH OF THE UNION PACIFIC'S underhanded ways. In return for not passing punitive legislation against the railroad, Congress demanded that the company appoint a new president, Charles Francis Adams Jr. Adams was a natural pick. He was a longtime critic of the Union Pacific—and, in fact, had predicted at the company's inception that it would prove to be the most corrupt corporation in the world. He had also served as a railroad regulator. Congress believed that he was the perfect man to clean up the Union Pacific's act. When Adams joined, Dillon stepped down as president, and Gould (who had recently bought a large block of the company's shares and been elected to the board) resigned his directorship. Adams's inauguration promised to mark a new era in the corporation's history.

But Adams inherited a deeply troubled company. It was heavily in debt. It faced severe labor problems, with workers striking in protest of proposed wage cuts. Local politicians and the public alike viewed it with skepticism. Adams did what he could to reverse these things, but most of his efforts proved too little, too late. To improve the labor problem, he proposed to create a retirement pension for employees and to fund schools for educating their children. "From those thus educated, the higher positions in the company would thereafter be filled," Adams said. "The morale of the service would gradually be raised, and the morale of a railroad is, if properly viewed, no less important than the morale of an army or navy." Adams also argued that a railroad's workers should be "allowed a voice in its management." "It will be impossible to establish perfectly good faith and the highest morale in the service of the companies until the problem of giving this voice to employees, and giving it effectively, is solved. It can be solved in but one way: that is, by representation." But when he proposed to create a council of employee representatives, elected by the employees, to negotiate directly with railroad management, other executives derisively shot him down, arguing that employees would "become careless if they understood that the head of the department in which they are working did not have full power to dismiss them for neglect of duty, or other good and sufficient cause." Conflicts among workers only grew under his watch. In 1885, tensions between white and Chinese miners at the company's Rock Springs mine exploded into violence, with white miners attacking the Chinese workers with clubs, shovels, picks, and guns. Twenty-eight Chinese workers were killed, and the rest fled into the hills. Work only restarted after the US military physically escorted the Chinese back to town.[43]

Adams, who thought of himself as more an intellectual than a businessman, took to calling his time as president of the Union Pacific "this everlasting rowing against wind and tide." His heart was in a different project, a two-volume biography of the lawyer and abolitionist Richard Henry Dana, which he finished in 1890. In any case, he could not solve the Union Pacific's woes. By 1893, the Union Pacific had outstanding $11.5 million in collateral trust notes and $5.2 million in maturing sinking fund bonds, two bond types popular with railroads at the time; the first was secured by other bonds or securities, and the second required the corporation to set aside certain profits to redeem them. The Union Pacific had no chance of paying such a massive debt load. And then, in May, the Panic of 1893 struck the final blow. A series of bank runs and commodity crashes led to a drastic reduction in commerce, and railroads, already overstretched by years of building and expansion, faced a reckoning. "Bottom dropped out of west bound transcontinental business," wrote the Union Pacific's new president, Silas Clark. In the first six months of 1893, the Union Pacific's net revenue dropped $800,000 from the previous year, and the decline only accelerated from there. In July and August, it was down $2 million. In all, the Union Pacific's gross earnings for the year would decline by $8 million, or around 17 percent. The corporation was already teetering on the edge of bankruptcy, and the economic downturn pushed it over. In October 1893, the company filed for receivership. In this, it was not alone. Railroads were collapsing all around the United States. In all, 153 railroad companies went bankrupt during the ensuing depression, representing more than a third of the country's total railway mileage. It was the beginning of the end of the railroad age. Soon, a new mode of transportation would be all the rage, one that promised even greater freedom to its users.[44]

The Union Pacific represented something entirely new in the history of corporations. It was born in the crucible of the Civil War, envisioned as an institution to unite a riven country. The remarkable accomplishments of its engineers over the next decade caught the imagination of the nation as they hacked a route across thousands of miles of desert, plains, and mountains. The transcontinental railroad demonstrated the enormous creative power of the corporation in all its majesty. But in its greatest achievement also lay the seeds of its defeat. Robber barons hell-bent on turning the corporation into a monopoly that could extract the highest possible prices from citizens, farmers, and businessmen soon turned a company that was once a national champion into a national villain. Over the coming decades, the United States would grapple with how to deal with these dangerous trusts threatening to undermine the country, leading eventually to the passing of the landmark antitrust laws giving the government powers to break up monopolies. But the danger of monopolies, once surfaced, would never disappear from the landscape of capitalism.

※ ※ ※

CONTRARY TO POPULAR opinion, monopolies are not illegal. And no matter how much we like to bash them in theory, in practice, we are surrounded by them. Amazon, Facebook, and Google all have monopolies in one area or another. (They would vigorously deny these claims. But let's be honest, how many people really use Bing?) If we don't like monopolies, why do we not simply prohibit them?

If you looked at the language of the Sherman Antitrust Act, you would be forgiven for thinking that we, in fact, *had* prohibited them.

Section 2 of the act, which is still valid law in the United States, provides that "*every person who shall monopolize*, or attempt to monopolize, or combine or conspire with any other person or persons, to monopolize *any part of the trade or commerce among the several States*, or with foreign nations, *shall be deemed guilty of a felony*." The language is remarkable for its clarity. Anyone who monopolizes a trade is guilty of a felony. All monopolies, one might conclude, are illegal. And, in fact, during the first two decades of the twentieth century, the United States brought dozens of antitrust claims accusing companies of restraining and monopolizing trade, culminating in the landmark decision of the Supreme Court in 1911 ordering that Standard Oil, the world's largest oil company, be broken up.

But over the course of the century, antitrust law and practice have slowly walked back the seemingly absolute prohibition on monopolies. The foundations for this development were, ironically, laid by the Supreme Court in its decision in *Standard Oil Co. of New Jersey v. United States*. In that case, the Supreme Court endorsed a reading of the Sherman Antitrust Act that significantly limited its scope. Instead of interpreting the act to prohibit *all* monopolies and restraints on trade, the court concluded that, under a so-called rule of reason, the act only prohibited *unreasonable* monopolies and restraints on trade. In time, more and more restraints on trade were deemed reasonable.

Today, antitrust bears only the slightest resemblance to its Gilded Age origins. Consider, for example, how the late justice Antonin Scalia described monopolies in 2003 in *Verizon v. Trinko*. "It is settled law that [a Sherman Act] offense requires, in addition to the possession of monopoly power in the relevant market, the willful acquisition or maintenance of that power as distinguished from growth or development as a consequence of a superior product, business acumen, or historic accident. The mere possession of monopoly power, and the concomitant charging of monopoly prices, is not only not unlawful; it is an important element of the free-market system." Notice the change of tone. Not only are monopolies not illegal; they are now an important element of our capitalist system. We are worried about unfair monopoly, not monopoly per se.

Under modern antitrust law, corporations are free to become monopolies so long as they abide by the rules of the road and avoid a few obvious no-no's like predatory pricing. As a result, monopolies have become an unavoidable feature of our corporate landscape. As corporations have realized the great returns of concentrated market power, they have sought ways to grow bigger and faster. One of the most important breakthroughs in "bigness" came in the early 1900s from a little-known automobile company in Detroit.

five

THE ASSEMBLY LINE

O N JANUARY 5, 1914, HENRY FORD INVITED A SELECT GROUP OF three Detroit journalists out to his factory for a surprise announcement. Any enterprising journalist of the day would have leapt at the invitation. Ford had launched his Ford Motor Company just ten years before, but it had already become one of America's leading corporations. Its reasonably priced Model T automobile was pouring out of Ford's Highland Park factory at seemingly impossible rates and almost single-handedly turning America into a country of drivers. Ford himself had emerged as an unlikely national celebrity. His penchant for delivering folksy aphorisms to interviewers, combined with his grand theories about the future of the workplace, made him a popular figure in American homes and corporate boardrooms alike. On that frigid day in January, the three lucky reporters—one from the *Free Press*, one from the *Journal*, and one from the *News*—dutifully made their way out Woodward Avenue to Ford's headquarters, nicknamed the Crystal Palace for its giant glass windows lining the walls and roof.

When the three arrived, they were led to the office of one of Ford's lieutenants. Ford awaited them there, standing silently by the window "with an air of restless detachment from the business in hand." The lieutenant handed the reporters a two-page typed statement and began to read from it.

The announcement was nothing less than staggering. From that time on, the lieutenant read, all employees at the Ford Motor Company would receive five dollars a day for their work, more than double what they had been making. In addition, Ford was reducing the length of the workday, from the standard nine or ten hours typical in the automotive industry to eight hours. Finally, Ford was hiring: his company planned to bring on several thousand new workers in the coming days. As Ford explained to the reporters after the lieutenant had finished reading, "We believe in making twenty thousand men prosperous and contented rather than follow the plan of making a few slave drivers in our establishment multi-millionaires."[1]

When the reporters pressed Ford to clarify precisely who would be entitled to this unprecedented pay raise, Ford calmly explained, "The commonest laborer who sweeps the floor shall receive his five dollars a day."

"But Mr. Ford," one of the reporters replied in astonishment, "to-morrow morning there will be five thousand men out there in the street with brooms!"

Ford, unshaken, answered him, "No, nothing like that."[2]

In fact, it was not five thousand men who showed up the next day. It was ten thousand. On the following Monday, when the new pay system went into effect, twelve thousand more appeared. The job seekers had started lining up at the Ford employment office at 10 p.m. the previous night and spent a freezing night there, with temperatures near zero, all in hopes of landing a coveted position in Ford's factory. When the crowds grew so large that they blocked the entryway to Ford workers, the police shot fire hoses to disperse them, leading to a brief riot in the streets. Letters from around the country, fourteen thousand a week, streamed into the Ford mailbox, asking for jobs. Every American, it seemed, wanted to work for Ford.

Ford's plan was met with skepticism in some parts. Some worried that it would bankrupt small mom-and-pop companies who could not afford to pay their workers the same wages. Others worried that it would lead the Ford Motor Company into ruin when its sales inevitably slowed down. Some thought it would lead to higher car prices and thus shift the burden of higher wages onto consumers. Still others worried that all that money in the pockets of workers and all that leisure time was a recipe for vice and debauchery. The *New York Times* wrote that Ford's plan was "tinged with the utopian quality" and warned that "serious disturbances in the automobile industry labor market will, of course, follow." "The Ford Company cannot hire all the men," the newspaper wrote, "yet there will be unrest and dissatisfaction in the shops of other companies. Strikes are likely enough, and conditions of peace cannot be looked for until the equilibrium is somehow restored."[3]

Nearly everyone, however, agreed that Ford's plan was radical. The decision seemed to buck every tenet of traditional economic theory. Wages were supposed to be set by competition in the labor market. This competition was thought to be based on firms' desire to pay *less* for workers, not more. And while successful firms might offer a marginally higher rate to attract better workers, they weren't supposed to double the going rate at a single stroke. Ford himself described his plan as "the greatest revolution in the matter of rewards for its workers ever known in the industrial world."[4]

Henry Ford's motivations for the decision were complex. Part of the rationale lay in conditions at Ford's Highland Park factory: the company's moving assembly lines had greatly increased the speed with which automobiles could be constructed, and more laborers were needed to keep up with the machines. Another part of the equation was the morale of Ford workers: attrition rates were shockingly high, and Ford sought a way to encourage loyalty to his company. The competitive landscape of the automobile industry also played a role: while there were many automobile companies in America, the Model T was vastly more popular than any other car on the market, and Ford believed that he could sell as many cars as he could produce. But perhaps the most important reason for the five-dollar day was Henry Ford's vision of the role of the corporation in society. "The trouble with a great many of us in the business world," Ford wrote, "is that we are thinking hardest of all about the dollars we want to make. Now that is the wrong idea right at the start. If people would go into business with the idea that they are going to serve the public and their employees as well as themselves, they would be assured of success from the start."[5]

Ford's strategy proved remarkably successful. In 1913, Ford had managed to manufacture a grand total of 170,211 Model Ts. In 1914, the number rose to 202,667. In 1915, it rose again, to 308,162. By 1916, the Ford factory was producing over 500,000 cars a year. In 1920, around half of all the cars on America's roads were Model Ts. Ford Motor Company had transformed itself into one of America's greatest success stories, with businessmen and leaders from across the world visiting Ford's factories to learn the secret of its success.[6]

But the story of Ford's five-dollar day had a darker side. The offer came with strings attached. In order to be eligible for the extra pay, employees had to show that they led virtuous lives, a standard that the company itself defined. As the release announced, to receive the new pay, a worker had to "show himself sober, saving, steady, industrious and must satisfy the superintendent and staff that his money will not be wasted in riotous living." To enforce these rules, the Ford Motor Company created a "Sociological Department" to monitor workers, even going so far as to send investigators to their homes to snoop around and ask questions of wives, children, and neighbors. Ford Motor Company also expected superhuman productivity from its workers, an expectation that led to deteriorating conditions in the factory and heavy physical tolls on the workers themselves. Mass production, it turned out, along with its more direct effect of transforming consumer culture, also led to a major shift in what jobs looked like.[7]

But whatever the criticisms, Ford and his corporation gave America something more important than jobs and automobiles that day. They gave the nation a dream. James Truslow Adams, who first coined the term *American Dream* in his 1931 book *The Epic of America*, described the uniquely American ideal as "not a dream of motor cars and high wages merely, but a dream of a social order in which each man and each woman shall be able to attain to the fullest stature of which they are innately capable, and be recognized by others for what they are, regardless of the fortuitous circumstances of birth or position." Ford's message on that cold January morning was clear. With hard work and industry, you could get ahead in life.[8]

※ ※ ※

EFFICIENCY IS A tricky thing. We generally want things to be efficient: our lives, our markets, our workout routines, our airport screening processes, our baristas. But when you start digging into what precisely efficiency means, you quickly start running into aesthetic and moral quandaries. Take the example of the barista above. You would probably like your barista to make your morning cappuccino quickly. But if your barista told you that he could make your cappuccino more quickly by not steaming the milk, you would probably reply that that would not be efficient. It would not even be a cappuccino. What if your barista told you that he could make your cappuccino more quickly by preparing a bunch of cappuccinos the night before and then just serving the lukewarm coffees as customers came in and ordered them? You would probably reply that that would not be efficient either. You want your cappuccino to be made fresh. What if your barista could make your cappuccino more quickly by hiring a few dexterous child workers to help out with the frothing and the serving? You might say that that isn't efficient. It can't be efficient if it's illegal. What if your barista could speed up his cappuccino serving by a few seconds, but only by refusing pleasant conversation with you or increasing his risk of burning himself or sustaining an overuse injury? Are those efficient cappuccino-serving strategies? You might think that all of those are more efficient ways of making a cappuccino, or you might think that none of them are. The point here is that what we think is efficient depends on our values. Efficiency is inseparable from morality and, in some cases, may even conflict with it.

The most common justification of corporate power today, including monopoly power, is the ability of corporations to deliver efficiency. In ancient Rome, corporations could collect taxes more reliably than anyone else could. In Renaissance Florence, the Medici Bank could issue loans and store capital with an acumen and discretion not available anywhere else. In Elizabethan England, joint stock companies had unparalleled capital and expertise to trade with unexplored parts of the globe. All of these corporations had a claim to make about efficiency. They could do things better, faster, and more reliably than anyone else could.

There are many reasons why corporations are considered efficient vessels for trade and commerce as compared with other types of business or even the government itself. Their limited liability allows them to raise more money from the public at less cost. Their immortality lets them think for the long term. Their professional managers give them access to the brightest minds in business. But all of these are rather abstract ideas. They're hard to grasp.

A better question is how corporations themselves think about efficiency. What do they care about? What do they ignore or dismiss? Efficiency always involves trade-offs, and so when we think about the efficiency gains of corporations, it is worthwhile to examine how corporations define efficiency and how they go about achieving it.

To understand these questions, there is no better place to start than the dawn of the Age of Mass Production, that era of unparalleled productivity gains. While the basic ideas behind mass production had a long history filled with small, incremental improvements aimed at speeding up industrial production, there was one moment in which everything changed, when small steps turned into a giant leap.

THE HISTORY OF THE FORD MOTOR COMPANY IS, MUCH MORE THAN for any other corporation we have spoken of so far, the history of a single man. Henry Ford formed the company. He guided it. He made its key decisions. He is to the corporation what Romulus and Remus were to Rome: a founding myth, an idol, a leader responsible for everything that came after. Ford himself cultivated this image. Late in life, when his son contradicted him in an argument, he told him, "Young man, I invented the modern age." It was an exaggeration, but only a slight one. Ford's undeniable success, combined with his penchant for folk philosophizing, made him into the wise man of industry and corporatism. The Soviet Union asked Ford to send consultants to help them construct truck factories. Adolf Hitler modeled Volkswagen after his methods. The term *Fordism* entered the English lexicon to mean a style of corporate strategy that emphasized mass production, standardization, and mass consumption. Aldous Huxley, after reading Ford's autobiography during a transatlantic boat voyage, was so struck by it that he wrote a book imagining what a world inspired by the ideals of Fordism might look like. Published in 1932, *Brave New World* described a civilization transformed by the worship of Ford as a godlike figure—dates are measured from the year of Our Ford, Ford's Day is a national holiday, and the *Christian Science Monitor* has changed its name to the *Fordian Science Monitor*. The result is decidedly dystopian, with citizens organized into castes, drugged into a false sense of happiness, and indoctrinated to hate books and nature. "A love of nature keeps no factories busy," an official explains.[9]

But before all this, Ford was simply a young boy in Dearborn, Michigan, living on his family's farm and not particularly besotted with the farming life. He was born on July 30, 1863, in the midst of the

Civil War. Earlier that month, the Union had won the Battle of Gettysburg. Michigan was a frontier state at the time—it had only entered the union twenty-six years before—and most of the population earned its living through farming. But farming was not for Ford. He was afraid of horses, having had several accidents while riding them as a youth. He also didn't care for the endless toil of agriculture. "I have followed many a weary mile behind a plough and I know all the drudgery of it," he complained in his autobiography, *My Life and Work*. Instead of agriculture and husbandry, he was drawn to mechanics and engineering. In his free time, he liked to repair watches, taking them apart to tinker with their insides. In 1882, a neighboring farmer bought a portable steam engine that could be used to thresh grain and saw timber, and Ford was taken by the power of the machine. He learned everything he could about it, and before long his neighbor hired him to help run it. He became such an expert that the steam engine's manufacturer hired him to offer demonstrations of it across the state.[10]

Around this time, Ford started experimenting with the idea of a "horseless carriage," a vehicle that could move people and things on its own power. He had seen an Otto engine, the internal combustion engine made by German engineer Nicolaus Otto, and he experimented with building his own at the farm. The results of his attempts, however, were shoddy and unpredictable and always ultimately failed. Feeling that his rudimentary knowledge of electricity was holding him back, in 1891 he decided to move to Detroit to take a job as an engineer at the Edison Illuminating Company.

The Edison Illuminating Company was the brainchild of Thomas Edison, America's most famous inventor. Edison was as close to a celebrity as America had at the time. The Wizard of Menlo Park had invented a dizzying array of world-altering technologies, from the automatic telegraph to the phonograph to the world's first commercially usable light bulb. Newspapers avidly reported on his every venture. Ford was naturally starstruck. To Ford, Edison's greatest accomplishment was showing how corporations and business could be a force for good in society. Ford said of Edison that "his work has not only created many millions of new jobs but also—and without qualification—it has made every job more remunerative. Edison has done more toward abolishing poverty than have all the reformers and statesmen since the beginning of the world." Ford worked hard for Edison's company and rose quickly through its ranks, making chief engineer in 1893 after just two years at the company.[11]

But throughout his time at Edison, Ford continued to work on his horseless carriage in the shed at the back of his house on Bagley Avenue, tinkering and improving and learning. After five restless years, on June 4, 1896, Ford finally had a working prototype. He finalized it after a forty-eight-hour binge of nearly nonstop work, with the last pieces coming together at 4 a.m. He proudly called it the "Quadricycle." It was not much to look at, at least to the modern observer. The carriage was simply a seat borrowed from a buggy. The wheels were taken from a bicycle. The gas-powered engine had a mere four horsepower and two speeds, slow and fast. Slow meant a speed of around ten miles per hour. Fast meant a speed of twenty. There was no steering wheel to speak of, just a bar that could be adjusted to the left or to the right. As he wheeled the Quadricycle out of the shed, he realized that it was too wide to fit through the door. Without hesitation, he took an axe and knocked out the offending brick wall. He then drove the vehicle out onto the street. His friend James Bishop, who had helped him with the project, biked ahead to warn off any pedestrians. The spin was a success. The Quadricycle made it down Grand River Avenue and back, only dying once. In the coming weeks, Ford would take more rides around the town, and soon the Quadricycle became a curiosity throughout Detroit. As Ford described his early automobile, "It was considered to be something of a nuisance, for it made a racket and it scared horses. Also it blocked traffic. For if I stopped my machine anywhere in town a crowd was around it before I could start up again. If I left it alone even for a minute some inquisitive person always tried to run it." Ford resorted to carrying a chain with him whenever he took the vehicle out, locking it to a lamppost when he had to leave it unattended.[12]

Ford's experiments with cars earned him a reputation in town and, in 1896, one of the defining moments of his early career. In the summer of that year, Ford, still working at the Edison Illuminating Company, received an invitation to the annual Edison Convention being held at the Oriental Hotel in Manhattan Beach, New York City. On the last night of the convention, Ford was seated at the same table as Thomas Edison. Conversation eventually turned to electric carriages, and Ford's boss, Alexander Dow, pointed to Ford and remarked, "There's a young fellow who's made a gas car." Edison, famously hard of hearing, asked Ford to move closer and tell him about it. He peppered Ford with questions about his invention, covering everything from ignition to piston action. Ford, finding it easier to illustrate the workings of his automobile than narrate them, grabbed a menu and started sketching everything out. By the time he was done, Edison was flabbergasted. Banging his fist down on the table, Edison shouted, "Young man, that's the thing; you have it. Keep at it! Electric cars must keep near to power stations. The storage battery is too heavy. Steam cars won't do it either, for they have to carry a boiler and fire. Your car is self-contained—it carries its own power-plant—no fire, no boiler, no smoke, no steam. You have the thing. Keep at it." Hearing these words from Edison, his idol, was deeply moving to Ford. "That bang on the table was worth worlds to me," Ford said later. "No man up to then had given me any encouragement. I had hoped that I was headed right, sometimes I knew that I was, sometimes I only wondered if I was, but here, all at once and out of a clear sky, the greatest inventive genius in the world had given me a complete approval." He rededicated himself to his machine.[13]

As Edison's words indicated, Ford was not the first to invent a self-powered vehicle in America. That honor went to Charles Duryea, whose gasoline-powered "motor wagon" was first test-driven in 1893. Other models included cars that looked like wheelbarrows, or bicycles, or covered wagons. Whatever the exterior looked like, each needed a source of power, of which there were three basic types. First, there were steam-powered cars, which had tremendous acceleration but took an eternity to get started, as they needed time to build up steam. Second, there were electric cars, which were easy to start but slow and of limited range. Finally, there were gas-powered cars, which were noisy and notoriously unreliable. In the beginning, the steam-powered car was most popular and for a while seemed like the inevitable winner. But over time, as better engines were manufactured, the gas-powered car, to Ford's relief, took over.[14]

By 1899, Ford had significantly improved his Quadricycle and felt ready to launch a company around it. To do so, he turned to William Murphy, a lumber and real estate baron in Detroit. Murphy had been interested in "horseless carriages" for some time and had followed Ford's progress with curiosity. He made Ford a promise: if Ford could drive him from his home at Putnam and Woodward, out Grand River Avenue to Farmington and Orchard Lake, and back home by Pontiac—a journey of around eighty miles—Murphy would back his company. And so, on a Saturday afternoon in July 1899, Ford showed up at Murphy's house. "I am ready to take you on the ride," he told Murphy. The journey went off without a hitch, and Murphy lived up to his word. After several other wealthy Detroiters agreed to invest, the Detroit Automobile Company was formed on August 5, 1899.[15]

The Detroit Automobile Company proved a complete disaster, in part because of tensions built into its structure. Ford, despite being the brains behind the operation, had been relegated to the lowly rank of "mechanical superintendent." The wealthy investors received all the corporation's most prominent positions: Clarence Black, Detroit's city controller, was named president, and the investors controlled the board of directors. This quickly led to conflict. The managers of the company wanted Ford to put out a car as quickly as possible. Ford wanted to release the best car he was capable of making, however long that might take. Ford's perfectionism kept delaying production. By the fall of 1900, over a year after its founding, the company still hadn't produced a single car. Every time the investors pushed Ford to start building, he demurred. He would take the car out, notice something wrong with it, remark, "Come on, boys, we'll have to pull this to pieces," and then start again from scratch. In November 1900, the exasperated board of directors held a meeting to ask Ford for an explanation. Ford skipped it. He told a friend to inform the board that he was out of town. This excuse was the straw that broke the camel's back, and the board promptly shut the company down, laying off its workers and dissolving the corporation in January 1901.[16]

Undeterred, Ford formed a new company, this one called the Henry Ford Company, on November 30, 1901. Again, though, Ford's obsessive fiddling doomed the endeavor. Once again, impatient stockholders grew concerned at Ford's failure to produce a working car. This time, though, Murphy, who had invested in Ford's company, hired a local engine machinist named Henry Leland to review Ford's work. Ford, furious at the slight, left the company. Leland proved so adept at manufacturing that Murphy decided to keep running the company despite Ford's departure. A few years later, the venture would become the Cadillac Automobile Company, and it would emerge as a long-term competitor of Ford.

All these early false starts generated a skepticism toward capitalists and stockholders that Ford would hold throughout his life. "I'm not going to have a lot of rich people tell me what to do," Ford would say. He became convinced that they did nothing but undermine and distract true visionaries. In his autobiography, he wrote of his stockholders as greedy, simpleminded men: "I could get no support at all toward making better cars to be sold to the public at large. The whole thought was to make to order and to get the largest price possible for each car. The main idea seemed to be to get the money. And being without authority other than my engineering position gave me, I found that the new company was not a vehicle for realizing my ideas but merely a money-making concern—that did not make much money."[17]

But Ford did get one good thing out of these early failures: time to experiment and learn. He came to believe that what consumers wanted from a car was simple: it had to be cheap, it had to reliable, and it had to be durable. By 1903, he and his team of engineers finalized a prototype of a new car designed around those requirements. They called it the Model A. It had room for two occupants, the driver and a passenger, and, with the addition of a detachable bucket seat, potentially two more. It had eight horsepower and two speeds. It weighed 1,240 pounds, relatively heavy for cars of the time, but it cost just $750. With a prototype now ready, Ford was finally ready to move to the next stage: production. On June 16, 1903, he incorporated the Ford Motor Company. This time around, he made sure that he had a large stake in the company and the ability to control its day-to-day decisions. He was the largest shareholder, with 255 of the 1,000 shares, giving himself just over a quarter of the company. The Dodge brothers, John and Horace, who had a machine shop that would build the engines in the Model A, each subscribed for 50 shares; James Couzens, who would become Ford Motor Company's chief business manager, subscribed for 25. While Ford was not the president of the company—John Gray, a prominent Detroit banker and heir to a candy fortune, was given the largely ceremonial title—as vice president he had effective control of the company.

Ford quickly set to work. The company built an assembly plant on Mack Avenue and brought on twelve employees to handle assembly, paying them each $1.50 a day. The Dodge brothers were hired to provide prebuilt engines and body parts. Needing a logo for the cars, one of the young toolmakers, Harold Wills, took a printing set that he had used as a teenager to make calling cards, put *Ford* in cursive, and then drew an oval around it—the famous Ford logo that is still in use today.

The Model A was designed to be simple, durable, and, most importantly of all, cheap: the $750 starting price was significantly less than that of cars such as the Packard Model F, which cost over $2,000.

On July 15, 1903, a little less than a month after being formed, the company sold its first Model A. Ford Motor Company was off to a start.

Over the coming months, sales increased quickly. The dozen workers in the Ford factory could make around fifteen cars a day, and they soon found that they could barely keep up with demand. By the spring of 1904, demand for the cars so outstripped his factory's capacity that Ford purchased a larger site. With sales came profits, and even from the very beginning, the company made a substantial margin on its cars. In the first three months of operation, Ford Motor Company made a profit of $37,000, around $72 million in today's value. It paid a dividend of 2 percent in October 1903, 10 percent on November 21, 1903, 20 percent in January 1904, and 68 percent on June 16, 1904—a total of $100,000 in the first year of its existence. Within fifteen months, it had paid dividends of more than 100 percent of total initial investments. In the fall of 1904, sales averaged $60,000 per month. In the spring of 1905, it produced around twenty-five cars a day, using three hundred workers. As Ford wrote, "The business went along almost as by magic." The company was growing, and fast.[18]

Ford's operating philosophy, which proved overwhelmingly successful, was to make as many cheap cars as he could, as quickly as possible. He was not concerned about demand. As he said,

> You need not fear about the market. People will buy them alright. When you get to making the cars in quantity, you can make them cheaper, and when you make them cheaper you can get more people with enough money to buy them. The market will take care of itself. . . . The way to make automobiles is to make one automobile like another automobile, to make them all alike, to make them come through the factory just alike; just as one pin is like another pin when it comes from a pin factory, or one match is like another match when it comes from the match factory.

In the coming years, Ford built on his success by creating new designs. In 1906, the company sold 8,423 of its new Model N car, a record. But Ford knew that he could do better.[19]

Ford's grand dream had always been to build a car for the masses, one that would be reliable yet cheap, simple yet durable, an automobile for all Americans. He called it the "universal car." In order to make the universal car, though, he still had work to do. The Model A, for all its simplicity, proved more unreliable than predicted, unable to withstand the rigors of a life on the bumpy roads of America. He needed to find better raw materials that would be strong, light, and long-lasting.

In 1905, Ford made an accidental discovery that helped solve the durability problem. Attending a car race in Palm Beach, Florida, he witnessed a terrible crash involving a French car. He wandered over to look at the wreckage and noticed an odd-looking piece of metal. On inspection, he discovered that it was a valve strip stem and that it was surprisingly light and strong. He did not recognize its material. When he asked others to take a look, they could not identify it either. Finally, he handed the piece to his assistant and told him, "Find out all about this. That is the kind of material we ought to have in our cars." After some research, the assistant discovered that the stem was made of a French steel containing vanadium, and, as Ford had observed, it proved remarkably light, strong, and durable. Convinced that vanadium steel could transform his cars, Ford set out to find a source of it domestically. After learning that no steelmaker in America could produce it, Ford Motor Company hired an English metallurgist to design methods for producing it commercially. Because vanadium steel required a hotter furnace than typical steel, Ford worked with a specialized steel company in Canton, Ohio, to test and produce the alloy. Vanadium steel would become, in the words of Ford, "our principal steel."[20]

In 1908, Ford finally had his universal car. The Model T was the culmination of all his years of tinkering and designing and testing.

It had a twenty-horsepower engine, weighed twelve hundred pounds, and could reach forty-five miles an hour. It had an entirely new design: the Model T was the first production car that had its steering wheel on the left (the better to see oncoming traffic) rather than the right (the better to see rural ditches). It sold for just $850 in the first years, and the price would drop later. The Model T met all of Ford's conditions, and he knew it. In connection with the release of the Model T, he announced, "I will build a motor car for the great multitude. It will be large enough for the family but small enough for the individual to run and care for. It will be constructed of the best materials, by the best men to be hired, after the simplest designs that modern engineering can devise. But it will be so low in price that no man making a good salary will be unable to own one—and enjoy with his family the blessing of hours of pleasure in God's great open spaces."[21]

The American public snapped up Model Ts, just as Ford had predicted. In the year from October 1908 to September 1909, the company made over ten thousand cars, most of them Model Ts, and all of them sold out. The car was in greater demand than the company could supply.

FORD'S SEARCH FOR A WAY TO CUT PRODUCTION COSTS WHILE INcreasing production speeds led to his greatest discovery—indeed, to one of the most important innovations of modern capitalism. This was the concept of mass production and its essential ingredient, the assembly line. While the desire to produce large quantities of goods quickly was not new, the traditional response had been to throw manpower at the problem: hire more miners to extract more gold, hire more weavers to produce more cloth, hire more graders to lay more track. To the extent that corporations tried to make production more efficient, they were generally tinkering around the edges, making small improvements based on gut instinct and passed-down wisdom. But in the late 1800s, business leaders and engineers had begun to study production methods scientifically, to measure and test production processes objectively using experimentation and data. This new "scientific management" movement found its greatest proponent in Frederick Winslow Taylor, a mechanical engineer who had devoted himself to applying engineering principles to industry. Taylor believed that modern industry was woefully inefficient because it failed to use rational, testable methods for improving its systems, instead relying on instinct and rules of thumb. Taylor undertook "time studies" to understand how small changes in factory operations could improve production rates. In these studies, he would time with a stopwatch how long it took workers to perform their tasks, testing out different tools and methods. He would then use these studies to identify faster, more efficient processes for workers. He argued that work was a science. It was essential to test procedures to find out which worked and which didn't, then to standardize the best procedures, all in the name of speeding up work.

Henry Ford was an early convert to scientific management principles, and in 1910, when Ford Motor Company moved into the legendary Highland Park factory, he purposely designed it with these principles in mind. Instead of housing different parts of the assembly process in different buildings, he placed them all in one enormous building. In order to ensure that lighting was optimal, he placed massive glass windows around the structure, along with skylights and glass roofs—a design that earned it the name the Crystal Palace. In order to rationalize production, he placed machines in the sequential order in which a car was assembled. Workers had bins placed near them with all the parts they needed, so that they could grab a part, install it, and then quickly turn to the next car and repeat.

The Highland Park factory laid the foundations for the rise of the assembly line. Ford wrote of the evolution of the concept, "The first step forward in assembly came when we began taking the work to the men instead of the men to the work. . . . The net result of the application of these principles is the reduction of the necessity for thought on the part of the worker and the reduction of his movements to a minimum. He does as nearly as possible only one thing with only one movement." Ford had put a rudimentary assembly line in place in 1906, when manager Walter Flanders had had the idea of giving each worker a specific task to perform in the assembly of the Model N and placed the chassis on a truck to be pushed from station to station. But the real breakthrough came in 1912, when William Klann, a foreman at the Ford Motor Company, visited the Swift & Co. meatpacking plant in Chicago and saw how quickly the packers could "disassemble" pigs placed on a moving trolley overhead. In 1913, Ford introduced the moving assembly line for one part of the Model T, the flywheel magneto that formed the ignition system for the vehicle. Previously, individual workers would assemble entire magnetos from a pile of materials located next to them. A skilled worker could, on average, complete a magneto in twenty minutes. But Klann broke down the assembly process into twenty-nine different tasks and had each worker perform just one of them, with twenty-nine men located along a moving belt in the order in which assembly typically took place. This small change produced a miraculous result. Suddenly, a magneto could be assembled in not twenty minutes but thirteen. When foremen discovered that the process was slowed down by workers having to bend over to reach the trolley, they raised it and reduced assembly times to seven minutes and then five. The simple change — of breaking down assembly into simple, standardized tasks — had quadrupled output. Soon the moving assembly line was introduced into all areas of the plant. By 1914, it had dramatically reduced the time needed to make a Model T. Whereas previously assembling the car's chassis had taken twelve hours and twenty-eight minutes, in the summer of 1914 it took one hour and thirty-three minutes.[22]

The Crystal Palace had transformed itself into the most efficient system of production the world had ever seen. In 1913, the year before the introduction of the assembly line, Ford produced 68,733 Model

Ts. In 1914, the number soared to 170,211. Production accelerated as the company refined its methods through constant experimentation. In 1915, the company produced two hundred thousand Model Ts, then three hundred thousand, then five hundred thousand. By 1918, it was producing over seven hundred thousand cars a year. Ford Motor Company was now producing half of all US automobiles.[23]

The Crystal Palace may have seemed like a glistening citadel of capitalism to the outside world, but to observers who witnessed its workings firsthand, it was a terrible thing to behold. Author Julian Street visited the Highland Park factory in 1914 and was deeply shaken by the experience. In his book *Abroad at Home*, he devoted a chapter, titled "The Maecenas of the Motor," to the factory: "The machine shop is one room, with a glass roof covering an area of something less than thirty acres. It is simply unbelievable in its size, its noise and its ghastly furious activity." He knew that there was a method to the factory's organization, but he could hardly believe it, surrounded as he was by "whirling shafts and wheels, its forest of roof-supporting posts and flapping, flying, leather belting, its endless rows of writhing machinery, its shrieking, hammering, and clatter, its smell of oil, its autumn haze of smoke, its savage-looking foreign population—to my mind it expressed but one thing, and that thing was delirium." It was busy and loud and chaotic.

> Fancy a jungle of wheels and belts and weird iron forms—of men, machinery and movement—add to it every kind of sound you can imagine; the sound of a million squirrels chirking, a million monkeys quarreling, a million lions roaring, a million pigs dying, a million elephants smashing through a forest of sheet iron, a million boys whistling on their fingers, a million others coughing with the whooping cough, a million sinners groaning as they are dragged to hell—imagine all of this happening at the very edge of Niagara Falls, with the everlasting roar of the cataract as a perpetual background, and you may acquire a vague conception of that place.[24]

In practice, the Ford factory was less about the triumph of machine over man and more about turning man into machine. This may have been good for production numbers, but it was decidedly unpleasant for the man. And it turned out that morale had a greater effect on efficiency than Ford had bargained for. Frederick Winslow Taylor had predicted that the assembly line would roughly double production, but in fact, the differential was much less. In 1909, the first full year that Ford manufactured the Model T and before the assembly line had been introduced, the 1,548 workers in the factory produced on average 1,059 cars a month, or 0.68 cars per worker. In 1913, after the introduction of the assembly line, the 13,667 workers in the factory manufactured on average 15,284 automobiles a month, or 1.12 cars per worker. In other words, worker productivity had increased 65 percent, a substantial sum, but far from what Ford had projected. The company conducted a productivity study at the plant to identify what accounted for the discrepancy, and two key factors stood out: absenteeism and high attrition. Both were directly connected with worker dissatisfaction. In 1913, the Highland Park factory reported a 10 percent rate of "daily absences," meaning that on any given day, of the 14,000 employees, 1,400 were out, most of them claiming to be sick. Attrition was bad as well: the rate of turnover was 370 percent, meaning that for every job at the plant, the company had to hire 3.7 workers a year due to departures. Attrition and absenteeism were expensive for the company, as they required new workers to be trained or other workers shifted into new areas of the plant. They also hurt efficiency. Ford concluded that, to fix his factory, he had to fix his labor problem.[25]

And so, on January 1, 1914, New Year's Day, Ford met with all of his head executives. Ford began the meeting by telling the story of a recent tour he had made of the factory with his son. Walking through the assembly room, they encountered two workers fighting. Ford was ashamed to have his son witness it. He remarked that men acted like "savages" when they had barbarous living conditions, and they had barbarous living conditions when they were paid subsistence wages. If executives shared in the profits of the company, and customers did as well, why shouldn't the laborers? He started writing down on the blackboard the year's budget, and when he got to wages, he remarked that they were too small relative to profits. He started with an average wage of $3. Then he recalculated for $3.50. When one executive protested, Ford ignored him, raising it next to $4 and then to $4.50. Couzens, his second in command, watching all this time in disgust, remarked, "Well, so it's up to $4.75. I dare you to make it $5." So Ford did. On January 5, the board met and authorized the raise. Later that day, Ford made his announcement to the world.[26]

FORD'S NEW SYSTEM OF MASS PRODUCTION OF LOW-PRICED CARS by highly paid workers proved remarkably profitable, but it also created a series of unintended consequences that would forever change the landscape of corporate life. These consequences affected every constituency within the Ford corporation: the shareholders, the workers, and the consumers. Ford Motor Company was always immensely profitable. In 1916, those profits had risen to $60 million, an enormous sum that would be worth approximately $1.5 billion today. One might have expected that shareholders of such an obviously thriving company would be happy. But some shareholders thought that they were getting a raw deal. In 1916, Ford decided not to issue any special dividends, which it had been regularly paying out for the last five years. Ford explained that he needed the cash to invest in a new and better factory, and he did not want to waste it on a dividend. For two shareholders in particular, John and Horace Dodge, though, this change of heart rankled. Together they held 10 percent of Ford Motor Company, a stake they had held since the company's founding in 1903. They had done well from the investment. Their initial investment of $10,000 had earned them a total of $5.5 million in dividends. But in 1914, they had formed a rival automobile company, the Dodge Brothers Motor

Company, and they needed cash to run it. So when, in 1916, Ford started planning a smelter at River Rouge and reduced dividend payouts, the Dodge brothers were livid.[27]

On September 28, 1916, John and Horace Dodge wrote Ford a letter, complaining about his new dividend policy. They demanded that Ford call a board meeting "to distribute a large part of the accumulated cash surplus as dividends to the stockholders to whom it belongs." Ford ignored the letter, and so, on November 2, 1916, the brothers filed suit in Michigan. They asked the court to prevent Ford from pursuing his expansion plans and to force the company to distribute 75 percent of its cash surplus as dividends to shareholders. Adding insult to injury, the Dodge brothers filed their suit the day after the wedding of Henry Ford's son, Edsel, a ceremony the Dodge brothers had attended. Ford was naturally furious. Neither side backed down, and so the case eventually went to trial. The high-profile suit made front-page news across the country, particularly when Ford took the witness stand. The Dodges' attorney, Elliot Stevenson, asked Ford to explain how he thought a corporation should be run. "Let me say right here," Ford remarked, "that I do not believe that we should make such an awful profit on our cars. A reasonable profit is right, but not too much. So it has been my policy to force the price of the car down as fast as production would permit, and give the benefits to users and labourers—with resulting surprisingly enormous benefits to ourselves." Stevenson pressed him:

STEVENSON: And . . . you were not satisfied to continue to make such awful profits?

FORD: We don't seem to be able to keep the profits down.

STEVENSON: You are not able to keep them down; are you trying to keep them down? What is the Ford Motor Company organized for except for profits, will you tell me, Mr. Ford?

FORD: Organized to do as much good as we can, everywhere, for everybody concerned.

STEVENSON: Do you know anything in the law that discusses anything about doing people good, in connection with the manufacture of automobiles, or any other manufacturing business?

FORD: I don't know very much about law.

Ford's commentary—that he was running the company to "do as much good as we can, everywhere, for everybody concerned"—proved devastating to his case. As the Dodges' lawyer argued, Ford "wanted glory at the expense of the stockholders." All the Dodges wanted was for Ford to run the company to "make as large profits as possible." "When a business is run only to extend that business and not to make profits it is being run unlawfully," the Dodges argued.[28]

The court, clearly troubled by Ford's contempt for his investors, ruled in favor of the Dodges. The Michigan Supreme Court later upheld the decision in an opinion that has since gained near-legendary status in corporate law. In it, the court set out a strikingly shareholder-oriented view that elevated the interests of capitalists above all others:

A business corporation is organized and carried on primarily for the profit of the stockholders. The powers of the directors are to be employed for that end. The discretion of directors is to be exercised in the choice of means to attain that end, and does not extend to a change in the end itself, to the reduction of profits, or to the nondistribution of profits among stockholders in order to devote them to other purposes. . . . It is not within the lawful powers of a board of directors to shape and conduct the affairs of a corporation for the merely incidental benefit of shareholders and for the primary purpose of benefiting others, and no one will contend that, if the avowed purpose of the defendant directors was to sacrifice the interests of shareholders, it would not be the duty of the courts to interfere.

There could be no starker illustration of the conflict between shareholders and society—and a court had just stepped in and said that, where they conflict, the shareholders will win.[29]

Ford, always suspicious of shareholders and capitalists, whom he now took to calling "parasites," had had enough. Just a month after the Michigan Supreme Court handed down its decision, on March 6, 1919, Ford announced that he planned to leave Ford Motor Company to start up a new car company. He did not want to deal with minority shareholders who were constantly demanding their dividends and who now felt emboldened to challenge his business judgment in court. It was a bold play, and it worked. The shareholders, spooked by the prospect of losing the company's visionary leader, started to unload their stock. Ford snapped it all up through an anonymous buyer. It cost him over $100 million, but in his mind, it was worth it. The shareholders were gone. The company was all his.

HENRY FORD ALSO HAD A TEMPESTUOUS RELATIONSHIP WITH HIS workers. His five-dollar day was something of a Faustian bargain. Employees were paid a good salary and worked fewer hours, but the benefits came at a cost. The shift to the assembly line brought with it an overweening emphasis on speed, and workers were expected to work hard and fast. As one worker at the Highland Park factory explained, "The one word every foreman had to learn in English, German, Polish and Italian was 'hurry up.'" Charles Madison, a line worker who joined the company soon after the plan came into effect, described the constant pressure. "The harried foreman told me that my operation had been timed by an efficiency expert to produce a certain number of finished parts per day," he wrote. "I timed myself to see what I could actually do, and realized that I might achieve the quota only if all went well and I worked without letup the entire eight hours." The production quotas made no allowance for breaks for lunch or to go to the bathroom, let alone for rest, so Madison "managed to keep the machine going while munching [his] sandwich." When he failed to meet his quota on the first day, the foreman scolded him. The next day, an "efficiency timekeeper" came to his station with a stopwatch and observed him work. The timekeeper watched him like a hawk for the next hour, taking notes occasionally, and then reported to the foreman that Madison was too slow and was making no effort to speed up. Madison resigned himself to the inhumane system in hopes of earning his five dollars a day. He was therefore shocked when he received his first paycheck, only to learn that he was being paid just twenty-five cents an hour. The foreman informed him that "the arrangement was to begin paying five dollars a day only after a worker had been with the firm six months and had proved his ability to maintain his quota requirement."[30]

Assembly line work could be physically and emotionally debilitating. Workers were stuck in often uncomfortable positions for hours at a time, performing repetitive actions at high speed. It was a recipe for injury. One worker, Anthony Harff, recalled the story of an artist friend he had managed to get hired at the factory. "First night I picked him up and took him home, he said he was awfully tired," Harff remembered. The friend had been assigned to a "squatty position" underneath the fenders of cars on the assembly line, and he could hardly stand up straight when his shift was over. "He'd come home at night, and he would sit in a chair and he didn't care whether he ate dinner or not. He just had to sit in an upright position for a while. He was just so tired, and his body ached so that he didn't care whether he moved or not." After three days, the friend refused to return to the factory. It was this kind of treatment that led John Steinbeck to write in *The Grapes of Wrath*, a book that revolves heavily around automobiles, "I don' want nothin' to do with nothin' of Henry Ford's. I don't like 'im. Never did. Got a brother worked in the plant. Oughta hear him tell."[31]

Ford Motor Company also coupled its industry-leading pay with an expectation that its employees demonstrate "good moral character." In connection with the five-dollar-day plan, Ford created a new

"Sociological Department" tasked with enforcing the requirement. Employing as many as two hundred investigators, the department snooped on employees, gathering intelligence about their personal habits, their families, their housing, and their neighborhoods. They would drive around Detroit, armed with long lists of employees and their addresses, and stop at their houses to ask questions of the inhabitants and neighbors. A reporter described a typical interaction:

> "Does Joe Polianski live here?" he asks.
>
> "Yes, he lives here all right."
>
> "What sort of a man is Joe—pretty good fellow?"
>
> "*Sure*, he's a *fine* man."
>
> "What does he do evenings?"
>
> "Always home evenings, goes to bed early."
>
> "Does he drink?"
>
> "No! *No!* He not drink."
>
> "What does he do with his money—does he save any?"
>
> "*Sure*, he save. Some of it he send to old country to help old folks, some of it in bank."
>
> "Well, now, if Joe should get more wages what do you think he would do with it?"
>
> "Save it and buy a house, I guess."

These investigations carried real consequences. If workers were found to have lied to the department, they would be let go. If the investigators concluded that they were insufficiently thrifty or sober, their wages could be docked.[32]

Ford's patriarchal, all-seeing, all-knowing approach to employment had its advantages, though, particularly for families. At a time when very few women worked, wives and children were heavily dependent on men to provide for them. As one employee said of Ford's Sociological Department, "I do know this, that if they weren't taking care of their children and they were divorced, and the husband wasn't paying his alimony and maybe the wife wouldn't bother him, all she had to do was go down to the Sociological Department and they just kept that out of his pay . . . They took care of a lot of children." The company was also ahead of its time in caring for its employees' long-term health and well-being. It developed several groundbreaking programs to support its workers. In 1913, it created an employee savings and loan association to help workers build up wealth. Its legal department provided free assistance for home purchases, citizenship applications, and debt relief. It had a medical department that by 1920 had twenty rooms, ten doctors, two dentists, two pharmacists, and an anesthetist. Because many of Ford's workers were immigrants, the company established a language school to teach English. Fordism even won over famous muckraker Ida Tarbell, who called his plan "a thoroughly worthwhile and deeply human method." She concluded, "The truth is the Sociological Department at Ford's seems to hate to give up a man as much as the Sales Department hates to give up an order."[33]

Ford's view of himself as the savior of the common man made it hard for him to sympathize when workers occasionally complained. He never seemed to grasp the dehumanizing nature of the mass-production system he had created. This was a man, after all, who said, "Work is our sanity, our self-respect, our salvation. So far from being a curse, work is the greatest blessing." When labor unions witnessed an upsurge of interest in the 1930s, he advised his workers to shun them at any cost. "A man loses his independence when he joins a labor group of any kind and he suffers as a result," he told an interviewer. "Competition in industry will guarantee workers a fair wage, but labor unions destroy this competition." To Ford, the labor union movement was more a conspiracy of wealthy capitalists than it was a symptom of true worker grievances. It also played into his anti-Semitic prejudices. "International financiers are behind the labor unions because they want to control industry and kill competition. They are the cause of all these strikes." Ford failed to see that there could ever be a conflict between managers and their employees. "This habit we have of talking of 'labor' as if it were a class apart from others; as if 'labor' and 'business' were two antagonistic opposites. Most of the business men of this country came out of labor. Where else can they come from? I belong to 'labor.' It is all I have done all my life." He always believed that the best way to promote the interests of workers was to give managers a free hand in setting wages and conditions. The invisible hand of the market would ensure workers a good job on fair terms. "You would be surprised to know to what extent responsible managers willingly burden themselves with these things because they believe that in so doing they are making perhaps a contribution to social progress greater than any commodity they can make. . . . If an employer pays his men less than they earn, he lays himself liable to anything that may happen to him. The first thing that happens is that he gets poor work and a poor product and loses his business." Over time, Ford's attitude toward the labor movement only solidified. "Labor unions are the worst things that ever struck the earth," Ford said in 1937.[34]

The stage was set for a reckoning. As early as 1915, Ford was hauled before the Congressional Commission on Industrial Relations to answer questions about his treatment of workers. They asked him why Ford Motor Company had assumed "so large a measure of responsibility, not only for the labor conditions in their plants, but also for the social and moral surroundings of their employees" and whether it was "desirable for a corporation to assume so large a measure of control of employees." Ford dodged the questions, explaining that his aim was "simply to better the financial and moral status of the men." But the Great Depression brought the conflict to a head. Conditions in the Ford factory had declined during the Depression—there were fewer jobs, and the ones that still existed were even more exhausting due to the notorious "speed-up" of the assembly line. Toilet breaks on the assembly line were prohibited unless a substitute was available. Lunch breaks were cut to fifteen minutes. One worker described his experience in harrowing terms: "At the first tick of the bell he reaches for his lunch with one hand, while the other is busy shutting off his machine.

His legs seem to instantly lose their starch and he crumples into a sitting posture, usually upon the floor. The lid of the lunch box opens as if by magic, and quicker almost than the eye can follow he has a sandwich in hand and is chewing on the first bite. . . . Consequently he has to cut mastication to the limit and bolt his food if he was going to get it all down." Fed up, some workers began talking about unionizing. In the 1930s, the United Auto Workers (UAW) had organized a series of strikes in factories across the United States. When Ford got wind of the rumors, he deployed his "Service Department," a team nominally devoted to security but in reality a group of thugs and mob figures, to intimidate workers. They would snoop around and listen to employee conversations during lunch hour. When a strike broke out at the General Motors factory, the foremen were ordered to form an emergency squad that would kick employees who dared strike out of the factory immediately and turn them over to service men, who "would take care of them." One Ford worker explained that the service men could be easily identified by their "cauliflower ears and broken noses."[35]

Workers and management would clash violently twice during the 1930s. On March 7, 1932, a crowd of twenty-five hundred people marched on the River Rouge plant in Dearborn, Michigan, demanding better working conditions and the rehiring of laid-off workers. When they arrived at the entrance to the factory, policemen met them along with Ford security forces. When the police fired tear gas canisters to disperse the crowd, the protesters responded by throwing rocks. The fire department then showed up and directed their hoses toward the protesters. When Ford's head of security was knocked unconscious with a rock, the police opened fire with shotguns and pistols, and the crowd charged back with cudgels and pipes in their fists. In the end, five workers died and dozens were injured in the "Dearborn Massacre." Five years later, violence struck again. On May 26, 1937, leaders of the UAW marched to the River Rouge factory, along with a group of reporters and photographers. The organizers planned to hand out leaflets with pro-union messages to Ford workers. When the Service

Department found out about the plan, it sent a security detachment to stop them at a pedestrian overpass leading to the factory. After ordering them off the property, the Ford security forces proceeded to beat the labor organizers mercilessly. "They would knock us down, stand us up, and knock us down again," one union member recounted. The president of the labor union was thrown down a flight of concrete stairs. Photographers trying to capture the violence had their cameras grabbed away and smashed. When one photographer got away in a car, the Service Department chased after him, and he was forced to hide out in a police station for safety. The attack would come to be known as the "Battle of the Overpass."[36]

The mounting conflict between workers and corporations led to intervention by the federal government. In 1933, Franklin D. Roosevelt signed into law the National Industrial Recovery Act (NIRA) to increase wages and employment. Among other things, it established the right of workers to form unions and ordered major industries to draft "codes of competition" to set wages, hours, and conditions. When the National Automobile Chamber of Commerce wrote a code for the automobile industry, Ford simply refused to sign it. The NIRA proved ineffective, though, so in 1935 Congress went further, passing the Wagner Act, which again guaranteed workers the right to bargain collectively and, this time, established a National Labor Relations Board (NLRB) to enforce the right. The NLRB would later investigate Ford and find the company guilty of violating the Wagner Act. Only in 1941 did workers finally have the chance to vote on unionization. The results were overwhelming: 97 percent of workers voted in favor of unionization; a mere 3 percent voted against.

PERHAPS THE FARTHEST-REACHING CONSEQUENCE OF FORD Motor Company and the ideology of Fordism was felt outside the company, in the rise of a culture devoted to consumption. Ford had always placed an emphasis on the wants and needs of the buyer. It was his insight into the mass audience for cars that led him to his Model T design. It was his insight into how much a consumer could afford to pay that led him to strive to push down the price of his car beneath $500, a feat he finally achieved in 1914. But the revolutionary system of mass production that Ford pioneered in the 1910s required an accompanying revolution in consumer culture. Mass production required mass consumption. Ford needed large numbers of buyers to snap up the hundreds of thousands of cars that were now pouring out of his factories every year. And so, somewhere along the line, Ford decided he needed to do more than just cater to existing needs. He needed to create new ones.

When Ford introduced the five-day workweek in 1926, he explained that the necessity of giving workers free time to cultivate their appetites had driven him to do so. He understood the powerful influence that leisure exercised on desire. "The country is ready for the 5-day week," he said. "Without it the country will not be able to absorb its production and stay prosperous." To Ford, there was an inexorable connection between free time and shopping. "Business is the exchange of goods. Goods are bought only as they meet needs. Needs are filled only as they are felt. They make themselves felt largely in leisure hours. The man who worked 15 and 16 hours a day desired only a corner to lie in and a hunk of food." But Ford went further than just understanding the link between consumption and lifestyle. He believed that consumption had value in itself, writing that "nothing could be more splendid than a world in which everybody has all that he wants."[37]

In order to generate demand for his cars, Ford developed nationwide advertising campaigns that played off Americans' desires and beliefs, illustrated with eye-catching graphics. One 1924 advertisement showed a woman gathering fiery-red autumn leaves in a pasture and boasted of "freedom for the woman who owns a Ford." "To own a Ford is to be free to venture into new and untried places," the ad read. Another ad showed a man helping a young woman from a car and remarked "a very pretty girl and a charming scene from California." "He tours in it, travels in it, hunts in it, climbs mountains and crosses deserts, and the more he demands of it, the more its performance surprises him," read another ad. When Ford realized that many potential buyers simply were not earning enough to afford his cars, the company launched a buy-on-credit scheme, the Ford Weekly Purchase Plan. "Buying begets buying, if the things are there to buy," Ford said. "There is no consumer's dollar. Thinking of consumers as having definite incomes is only going back to the old days when the saturation point for goods was supposed to be fixed."[38]

Ford understood what he was doing quite clearly. He told an interviewer, "Well, say, we're creating new wants in folks right along, aren't we? And we no sooner get those wants satisfied in one class of society than another class bobs up to present its needs and demands. The wants keep right on increasing, and the more wants the more business, isn't that so?" Perhaps no one understood Ford's strategy better than Norval Hawkins, who headed up the company's sales and marketing department for over a decade. Hawkins wrote a book on his theory of sales, titled *The Selling Process*. In it, he wrote that salesmen had to appeal to people's hearts, not their minds. "A man's emotions, not his thoughts, control his desires. . . . No one was ever reasoned into buying. . . . Desire means want, and a man wants things, longs for things with his heart. He realizes a lack, and has a heart hunger for something to fill his lack. . . . We all realize the truth of this. But have we all been applying the principle in our selling efforts to persuade and to create desire?" Hawkins applied these principles to great effect at Ford. His psychological-attack-through-advertising method spread throughout the industry, and his mottoes are repeated in advertising theory today.[39]

Fordism created a world oriented around the consumer, one in which individuals were constantly bombarded by the message that, if they could just get that one shiny new object, they would finally be happy. The age of consumerism was beginning to take shape. By 1936,

John Maynard Keynes, one of the foremost economic minds of the twentieth century, could write, entirely seriously, that "consumption—to repeat the obvious—is the sole end and object of all economic activity."[40]

FORD, UNLIKE THE OTHER COMPANIES WE HAVE STUDIED SO FAR, never went out of business. But it did change. From its inception in 1903 until 1945, Ford Motor Company had been dominated by the figure of Henry Ford. But somewhere along the line, Ford's competitors caught up. In the 1930s, General Motors and Chrysler surpassed Ford, earning greater profits and selling more cars (in 1933, General Motors sold 650,000 cars, Chrysler, 400,000, and Ford, 325,000). Part of this shift can be explained by General Motors' and Chrysler's own improvements: they had copied wholesale Ford's assembly line, and Ford's competitive advantage slowly disappeared. But part of the shift was caused by failures of leadership at Ford itself. In its cultlike devotion to its founder and CEO, Ford the corporation succumbed to Ford the individual's biases and omissions. Ford proved rigid at times, unwilling to build new models or tinker with his cars' designs, even after other companies began offering superior vehicles. New voices in management went unheard, including those of Ford's own son, Edsel, who made a vain attempt to modernize the company.[41]

In 1945, Ford finally stepped down from the company at the age of eighty-two. Control shifted from Ford to a network of executives, directors, and managers. The company started acting more like a modern corporation. As Harvard economist John Kenneth Galbraith described it, "Ford had become a bureaucracy. The notion of personality was draped all over the organization, but control had passed from owners to management."[42]

But the echoes of Ford's legend would reverberate through American culture for decades. Jack Kerouac drove a 1937 Ford in his beatnik novel *On the Road*. James Dean drove a souped-up 1949 Ford Mercury in *Rebel Without a Cause*. The "Greased Lightning" in

Grease is a 1948 Ford De Luxe. It was no exaggeration when John D. Rockefeller called the Ford Motor Company the "industrial marvel of the age."[43]

爾 爾 爾

THE ASSEMBLY LINE was a tangible illustration of corporate efficiency at work. By standardizing production methods and simplifying worker tasks, the assembly line led to an immediate and dramatic increase in the productive power of corporations. Just as remarkably, its fundamental insight—that groups of humans could do more work, faster, by breaking down production into separate steps and then performing those steps in a physical line—was not particularly intuitive. Was it better to break tasks up? Or was it better to put them together? One could imagine plausible arguments on both sides. Theory could only do so much here. Experience was needed. Corporations sought out this experience, tested it, and discovered the answer.

Today, mass production and its effects are everywhere. Consumer products—from cars to phones to computers to appliances—are more abundant and cheaper than they have ever been in history. Shiny new gadgets roll off assembly lines and onto store shelves (or into Amazon warehouses) at incredible, relentless rates. It is often more expensive to repair an item than to simply buy a new one precisely because of the efficiencies of mass production and the inefficiencies of lone workers. Unprecedented standards of living are available to billions of people around the world because of the advances in efficiency spearheaded by corporations and their forward-thinking managers. Mass production is truly a corporate miracle.

But sometimes, even miracles are impure. Making more things for less effort seems like a win-win. Ford certainly thought so. But mass production created new and different problems, both within and outside corporations. Within the corporation, it created a working environment that proved draining and exhausting and often simply dehumanizing and cruel. Outside the corporation, it created new appetites for consumption as an end in itself and, perhaps worse, incentives for corporations to generate those appetites on a societal scale. Mass production, it turned out, was a dangerous recipe for materialism, waste, and environmental destruction. It took time for society to come to grips with the full extent of the problem, and it is still dealing with the repercussions.

The rise of the assembly line made corporations more productive than ever and generated consumer demand to match. The next decades would witness a dramatic growth in trade and commerce. But a new evolution in the corporate form would expand the horizons of the corporation even further. The multinational corporation would knit the world together into a single globalized market.

six

THE MULTINATIONAL

O N October 17, 1973, just eleven days after the armies of Syria and Egypt launched a surprise attack on Israel, a group of Middle Eastern oil ministers met in Kuwait City to consider a new and dangerous military tactic. Arab nations had long considered using their vast stores of oil to pursue geopolitical aims, but now the time had finally come to deploy the oil weapon. After eight hours of debate, the group of countries, including Saudi Arabia, Iraq, Iran, Kuwait, Qatar, and Abu Dhabi, announced that they would cut their production of oil and place an embargo on oil shipments to the United States, Israel's closest ally. They promised even more draconian cuts in the future if their demands—that Israel withdraw its troops from the territories it had occupied during 1967's Six Day War and that the United States cease military support for Israel—were not met. Mohammad Reza Pahlavi, the shah of Iran, proclaimed that the United States "will have to realize that the era of their terrific progress and even more terrific income and wealth based on cheap oil is finished. . . . Eventually they will have to tighten their belts; eventually all those children of well-to-do families who have plenty to eat at every meal, who have their cars, and who almost act as terrorists and throw bombs here and there, they will have to rethink all these aspects of the advanced industrial world."[1]

The oil embargo presented an enormous challenge to the United States. In the previous few decades, the demand for oil, both domestically and worldwide, had skyrocketed. For nearly a century, coal had been the primary source of energy for developed economies, but after World War II, petroleum surpassed it. Petroleum possessed a number of advantages over coal. It was liquid, which meant that it could be transported more easily. It was energy dense, providing more fuel for any given amount of it. It was easily refined into other forms and uses. And it was relatively clean burning, not creating the kinds of "death fog" that had turned the air of major cities like London into pea soup for much of the previous century. The ensuing oil boom fueled economic growth and higher living standards across the world, transforming cities and homes and transportation. American production of oil had not kept up with rising demand. Instead, more and more of the oil that Americans consumed came from abroad—of the 17 million barrels of crude oil that they used each day in 1972, 6.4 million, or roughly 38 percent, were imported. Western Europe imported almost 90 percent of its oil from Arab countries. So the announcement that the major oil-producing nations of the Middle East were cutting production and banning shipments to the United States was a big problem. Without oil, the economy couldn't run.[2]

President Richard Nixon had had ample warning about the threat. The Arabian-American Oil Company (known as Aramco) had been sending increasingly urgent messages for months, alerting the administration to the combustible situation in the Middle East. Aramco was a consortium of four of the largest American oil companies—Exxon, Mobil, Texaco, and Standard Oil of California—formed to produce oil in Saudi Arabia. Its executives had been in the habit of advising presidents on Middle Eastern affairs. Exxon even assigned a representative to the State Department to keep it up to date on new developments in the region. On October 12, 1973, the chairmen of Aramco sent Nixon a letter warning that if the United States increased military support for Israel, a "snowballing effect" of retaliation from Middle Eastern countries could "produce a major petroleum supply crisis." "Much more than our commercial interests in the area is now at hazard," they wrote. "The whole position of the United States in the Middle East is on the way to being seriously impaired, with Japanese, European, and perhaps Russian interests largely supplanting United States presence in the area, to the detriment of both our economy and our security."[3]

The warning came too late for action, though, and the oil embargo began in earnest after the Kuwait conference. In the coming months, the price of oil would quadruple, from three dollars a barrel to twelve dollars. On November 7, 1973, Nixon delivered a nationally televised speech warning the American people that the nation faced "the most acute shortage of energy since World War II." He called on citizens to make sacrifices for the greater good of the country. They should turn down thermostats, carpool to work, and drive under fifty miles an hour. Two months later, in January 1974, he repeated the plea, announcing in a radio address to the nation that, despite the real and substantial efforts by Americans to reduce their energy use, the country was facing a large shortfall in oil supply. To those who questioned the severity of the problem, he recounted a story about Winston Churchill.

> The burden of energy conservation, of cutbacks and inconvenience, of occasional discomfort, continued concern is not, I can assure you, an artificial one. It is real. During the Second World War, Winston Churchill was once asked why England was fighting Hitler. He answered, "If we stop, you will find out." If we should choose to believe that our efforts in fighting the energy crisis are unnecessary, if we permit ourselves to slacken our efforts and slide back into the

wasteful consumption of energy, then the full force of the energy crisis will be brought home to America in a most devastating fashion, and there will be no longer any question in anyone's mind about the reality of the crisis.[4]

Oil companies came in for major criticism at the time, both from Nixon and from the public. In the same speech in which he warned of the severity of the oil crisis, Nixon pledged to "do everything in [his] power to prevent the big oil companies and other major energy producers from making an unconscionable profit out of this crisis. . . . Private profiteering at the expense of public sacrifice must never be tolerated in a free country." Aramco found itself in a difficult position. The Saudis had tasked it with implementing the embargo. On October 21, 1973, Sheikh Ahmed Zaki Yamani, the Saudi minister of petroleum and mineral resources, had met with Frank Jungers, Aramco's president, to go over the new export rules. As Jungers reported, "A discussion of the complexities evolved with the Saudis entirely aware that the program would be very difficult to administer, but they are looking to Aramco to police it." It did not help that Exxon and other oil companies reported a banner year in 1973. Exxon's earnings had risen 59 percent over the previous year, not a good headline during a time of energy crisis.[5]

But Nixon failed to mention the important role that the big oil companies were playing, not in creating the oil crisis, but in lessening it. Nixon's own efforts to solve the oil crisis had proved largely ineffectual. His lead negotiator with the Middle Eastern countries, Secretary of State Henry Kissinger, knew next to nothing about oil markets. As Kissinger told his aides, "Don't talk to me about barrels of oil. They might as well be bottles of Coca-Cola. I don't understand." The government's efforts to get the oil the country did have into the hands of consumers also failed. Before the embargo began, the United States had introduced an allocation system aimed at distributing supplies of gasoline evenly around the country. But the rigid regime made it harder to shift oil from one region to another based on demand. Drivers, worried that local gas stations would run out of fuel, started to top up their tanks as much as possible. Long lines at gas stations sometimes reached around entire city blocks and could require waits of an hour or longer. Some states enacted gas-rationing plans that allowed motorists with even- and odd-numbered license plates to fill up on alternate days. Citizens grew confused and frustrated by the conflicting messages they were receiving from their politicians.[6]

While government stood paralyzed, Exxon, America's largest oil company, sprang into action. In 1970, Exxon produced around 15 percent of the world's daily demand of forty million barrels of crude oil and natural gas. It had interests across the globe, including many projects in the Middle East. It had a subsidiary in Libya, a 30 percent interest in Aramco in Saudi Arabia, a 7 percent interest in Iran's consortium, and a 12 percent interest in the Iraq Petroleum Company, as well as subsidiaries in Qatar, Abu Dhabi, and Lebanon. In all, the Middle East accounted for nearly half of Exxon's global production of 6.2 million barrels a day. So Exxon was at the epicenter of the oil crisis. From the very beginning, it used this position to blunt the effects of the embargo on world markets. On October 8, 1973, two days after the commencement of the Yom Kippur War and before the announcement of the production cuts, Exxon had sent its director for the Middle East to Vienna to negotiate lower oil prices with delegates from the Organization of Petroleum Exporting Countries. When the negotiations failed, Exxon realized that, if Western economies were to survive the oil embargo, a supreme effort of coordination by private oil corporations would be required. Over the next several weeks, it negotiated intensively with the other "Seven Sisters," the world's largest oil companies, to coordinate oil shipments. In the end, the group settled on a complex system of "equal suffering"—or "equal misery," as Royal Dutch Shell termed it—to help smooth the embargo's effects out across countries. In effect, the system of equal suffering required the oil companies to prorate oil supplies based on how much countries had been consuming before the crisis began, so that each would receive a similar percentage decrease, rather than having one country face a huge shortfall while others faced none. Once the Seven Sisters had settled on their goals, the companies began shifting around supplies based on geography, timing, and the oil embargo's rules. Oil from Arab countries went to nonembargoed states. Oil from non-Arab countries went to the embargoed ones. Exxon increased its exports of flexible, unembargoed oils from Iran, Nigeria, Venezuela, and Indonesia to the United States, while it sent its embargoed crude oil to Europe. Japan, on the other hand, received more from Indonesia and Arab nations and less from Iran.[7]

Exxon was only able to pull off this complicated international arrangement because of its multinational reach. It had a long history of navigating the global economy and had developed an intricate and interlinked system for producing, refining, shipping, and distributing oil to all its markets. The epicenter of this system lay on the twenty-fifth floor of Exxon's Manhattan headquarters, located on Sixth Avenue and Forty-Ninth Street. There, Exxon managers manned rows of TV screens, recording the movements of the five hundred Exxon tankers moving between sixty-five countries. The innovative computer system, called "Logics," connected Exxon's offices in New York to its worldwide branches from Houston to Tokyo. The system worked remarkably well. During the embargo, the distribution of oil to the United States from major oil companies dropped 17 percent, Europe's dropped 18.6 percent, and Japan's dropped 16 percent. It was estimated that, absent the oil companies' redirecting of sources, the US supply of oil would have been reduced 29 percent. The Federal Energy Administration, in a report on the embargo, concluded that "U.S. companies helped to blunt the edge of the Arab oil weapon by redistributing global supplies so that the construction of supplies was fairly evenly allocated. . . . It is difficult to imagine that any allocation plan would have achieved a more equitable allocation of reduced supplies."[8]

But the oil embargo also put on display just how integral oil corporations had become to national power. This put them in the difficult spot of balancing political pressures with corporate ones. Throughout the embargo, Exxon confronted aggressive demands from governments to favor their own countries or, somewhat less often, their allies. John Sawhill, director of the US Federal Energy Office, told oil companies "to bring as much as possible" to the United States, while Henry Kissinger later told them "to take care of Holland" when it was hit by the embargo. Japan's minister of international trade and industry, learning that the oil companies were planning to redirect unembargoed oil from Indonesia to the United States, summoned the major oil companies to his office and warned them not to divert any oil away from Japan. In the United Kingdom, Prime Minister Edward Heath invited the chairmen of British Petroleum and Shell to Chequers, the country house reserved for the head of government's use, and ordered them to maintain oil deliveries to his country at 100 percent of their pre-embargo level. "It became clear to us that it wasn't a business operation, but a political one," an Exxon executive said of the experience. When journalist Anthony Sampson asked an Exxon manager if Exxon felt like it was ruling the world, the manager replied, "No, the world was ruling us."[9]

Recognizing that this dependence on Middle Eastern oil had become a major vulnerability, both for itself and for American consumers, Exxon set out to do something about it. This meant finding oil somewhere, anywhere, outside the Middle East. Over the next decade, Exxon stepped up efforts to find and develop oil fields in places previously believed impossible to work in, because of their remoteness, their inaccessibility, or their weather. In the coming years, Exxon developed major fields in Alaska, Australia, Malaysia, and the North Sea. These discoveries would pay large dividends in the years to come and greatly increase the world's supply of oil.

But until new fields came online, for five months in 1973, Exxon kept the world turning.

器 器 器

AN UNCLE OF mine once found a baby alligator in a pond in Mississippi. He took the alligator back home to Austin, Texas, and raised it in his backyard pool as a pet. In the beginning, the alligator was small and cute, but, as one might expect, and as he should have known, the alligator soon grew into a larger and decidedly less cute beast. Eventually, my uncle grew scared of the alligator and took to keeping his distance from it. One day, he came home to discover that the alligator had escaped. We never saw it again, although I did happen upon a small alligator in Town Lake in downtown Austin a few years ago, and I like to think that it was a distant relative of that old alligator.

Wild animals have a way of outgrowing their owners. So do corporations. The corporation was a product of the nation-state—nations created them and imbued them with their rights and privileges. But beginning in the twentieth century and accelerating after World War II, the corporation started to outgrow the nation-state. Corporations had always sought to break down barriers to trade, from the warring kingdoms of the late Middle Ages to the treacherous seas of the Age of Exploration. Traditionally, though, international business was a fraught affair, one with major costs and risks. It was only in the post–World War II years, when countries were tearing down trade barriers and embarking on grand international economic treaties, that conditions became favorable enough for the widespread emergence of the multinational corporation. Freer trade, cheaper shipping, and improvements in communication and information technology all made it possible for corporations to become truly global creatures, turning into sprawling corporate empires that controlled webs of subsidiaries and divisions around the world. They could own raw materials in one country, manufacture products in another, and sell them in yet another, all while maintaining control within the same corporate entity. These multinational enterprises tapped into the basic economic truth of comparative advantage: whenever two individuals, or countries, have different capacities, they can gain from interacting with one another. The multinational corporation used comparative advantage on a global scale, drawing from whatever a country's economy had to offer.

Multinational corporations proved to be the driving force behind the new phenomenon of globalization. In the afterwar years, national economies became increasingly interdependent as supply chains went global and people and ideas crossed borders as never before. International corporations encouraged these developments, not just by taking advantage of the economic prospects of cross-border trade but also by attracting the world's best and brightest and training them to succeed in the new world. A new kind of cosmopolitan capitalism began to take shape.

But what kind of actors would multinationals be on the world stage? Freed from the clutches of the nation-state, would they become dangerous predators preying on local communities? Or would they blend seamlessly into their local surroundings, enriching the international economic system? More prosaically, how would governments regulate them, if they could always move their operations abroad to evade restrictions they deemed too onerous? Would the rise of the multinational lead to a race to the bottom among nation-states as countries competed to attract businesses to their jurisdictions by watering down corporate responsibilities and obligations? The multinational corporation was a new breed of corporation, and it raised fundamental questions about the relationship between capitalism and democracy.

Exxon, one of the first and most powerful multinational corporations, is an object lesson in the promise and peril of global enterprise.

IN 2006, JOURNALIST THOMAS FRIEDMAN WROTE AN ARTICLE IN the magazine *Foreign Policy* titled "The First Law of Petropolitics." In it, he made a stark claim: "Oil wealth impedes democracy." In his view, there was an inescapable connection between oil and oppression. As oil prices increased, he argued, political and economic freedoms decreased. The mechanism behind this perverse relationship was simple. The ruling class of oil-producing countries used the windfall wealth from oil sales not to develop their economies or open up educational opportunities but rather to bribe or repress social groups pressing for change. No wonder, then, that the list of countries with the largest proven oil reserves coincided closely with the list of the world's most repressive governments. "The price of oil and the pace of freedom always move in opposite directions," he wrote. Friedman's article was deeply influential in policy circles and led to renewed criticism of an already-unpopular group: the oil companies.[10]

It is hard to think of a class of companies so deeply reviled as Big Oil. In the minds of many, the very term "oil company" is synonymous with avarice, corruption, and environmental destruction. Oil companies are eternally connected with such disasters as the *Exxon Valdez* oil spill off the coast of Alaska, the *Deepwater Horizon* spill in the Gulf of Mexico, and global warming. They are accused of bolstering up kleptocrats and dictators around the world in return for priority access to their oil reserves. And somehow, despite all these problems, they remain some of the most profitable companies on earth. It isn't hard to come up with good reasons for censuring them.

But, perhaps precisely because of the appeal of these criticisms— oil companies do bad things and profit from them—it is easy to lose sight of why oil companies have risen to their positions of power and wealth. In short, they rose to power because they filled a need. Society needed energy, and they provided it. Oil was abundant, transportable, and energy rich. It allowed us to keep our lights on, our cars running, and our economies humming. Without oil, economies would fail, and people would suffer; with it, they could thrive. Oil companies understood this opportunity very early on, and they created vast corporate structures to cater to it. They studied geology to find oil underneath the ground in hidden deposits around the globe. They invented new methods of drilling and transporting and refining. They set up corporate operations in dozens of countries to handle distribution and marketing.

All of this to ensure that the world's most precious resource kept flowing to satisfy humanity's seemingly insatiable demand for it.

To understand the wide-ranging effects that oil, energy, and multinational corporations have had in shaping our world, there are few better places to start than Exxon. Exxon has long ranked as one of the most profitable companies in the world. Its revenues regularly exceed those of entire countries. It has billions of barrels of oil in reserve and hundreds of affiliates dotting the globe. Following the history of Exxon Mobil Corporation, though, is not a simple feat. Its story meanders like the Nile, flowing along tributaries and forks and streams, at times branching away and at others reuniting. At various times, it has been known as Standard Oil of New Jersey, Socony, Vacuum, Humble, Esso, Exxon Corporation, and ExxonMobil. For simplicity's sake, we will refer to the company primarily as Exxon, with exceptions made where necessary to distinguish major changes in its form.

Exxon began life as Standard Oil. In 1870, John D. Rockefeller, a thirty-year old businessman in Cleveland, Ohio, formed the Standard Oil Company to take advantage of the city's growing business in oil refining. In the 1860s, kerosene had emerged as a cheap and reliable form of lighting, replacing the expensive and notoriously sputtery whale oil that had been used in lamps previously. Kerosene came from petroleum, a kind of "rock oil" discovered just sixty-nine feet below the earth's surface at Titusville, Pennsylvania, in 1859 and soon found in many other locations in the United States. Rockefeller recognized that kerosene would prove tremendously popular. In a very real sense, it would bring light to the country. Most Americans could not afford whale oil to light their lamps and so normally went to sleep soon after sunset. Cheap kerosene lamps meant that, suddenly, Americans could stay up to eat, drink, read, and entertain themselves.[11]

From the very beginning, Rockefeller's ambitions for his company were grand. "The Standard Oil company will some day refine all the oil and make all the barrels," he once said. His prediction proved more or less correct, although his methods proved somewhat less than admirable. In the coming years, he would threaten, cajole, and pressure his competitors into selling out or shuttering their companies, using every tactic imaginable to eliminate what he called "ruinous competition." He more or less wrote the book on how to become a monopolist. He negotiated with railroad companies to give him better rates for transporting his oil to market and even managed to convince the railroads to pay *him* any time a competitor shipped its own oil on the railroads. He sold oil at below-market rates to put his smaller competitors out of business and then raised prices immediately after they went under. He hid his interests in other businesses by using shell companies. He employed spies to steal information about what other companies were doing and charging. Soon Standard Oil would earn the nickname the "Octopus" for the way in which its tentacled grip grasped for everything. In 1879, Standard Oil controlled 90 percent of America's refining capacity. In 1891, it produced a quarter of America's total crude oil output. "The day of combination is here to stay," Rockefeller proudly announced. "Individualism has gone, never to return."[12]

But like the railroad companies of that era, Standard Oil overplayed its hand, and its deceptive and bullying tactics soon earned it the ire of the nation. For years, lawmakers and citizens had been complaining about Standard Oil's unfair business practices but had been stonewalled by the company. As one Standard Oil executive explained it to Rockefeller in 1888, "I think this anti-trust fever is a craze, which we should meet in a very dignified way and parry every question with answers which while perfectly truthful are evasive of bottom facts." But in 1902, Standard Oil met its match, in the form of a "muckraking" investigative journalist working for *McClure's Magazine* named Ida Minerva Tarbell. Tarbell had grown up in Titusville, the site of the first big oil boom in America. Standard Oil had ruined her father's oil company, and so she had a particular bone to pick with Rockefeller. In 1902, after several months of research into how the company worked behind the scenes, she began publishing a series of articles in *McClure's*. These articles eventually turned into a book, and they uncovered all of Standard Oil's dirty secrets—its deceptive business practices, its anticompetitive agreements, its legislative maneuvers. In one telling sequence, she asked a senior company executive whether Standard Oil ever sought to manipulate legislation. The executive replied, "Oh, of course, we look after it! They come in here and ask us to contribute to their campaign funds. And we do it, that is, as individuals. . . . We put our hands in our pockets and give them some good sums for campaign purposes and then when a bill comes up that is against our interests we go to the manager and say: 'There's such and such a bill up. We don't like it and we want you to take care of our interests.' That's the way everybody does." It was hard to dispute Tarbell's damaging conclusion: "Mr. Rockefeller has systematically played with loaded dice, and it is doubtful if there has ever been a time since 1872 when he has run a race with a competitor and started fair."[13]

President Theodore Roosevelt, who had been elected in 1901 on a trust-busting platform, was determined to make use of the country's landmark antitrust law, the Sherman Antitrust Act. He reserved some of his worst feelings for Standard Oil. In a major address in 1908, he cited the company by name and said that "every measure for honesty in business that has been passed during the last six years has been opposed by these men on its passage and in its administration with every resource that bitter and unscrupulous craft could suggest and the command of almost unlimited money secure." He ordered an investigation of the company, and in 1906 the federal government filed suit, alleging that it had systematically violated the antitrust laws. After Tarbell's investigations, Standard Oil had little chance of succeeding, and in 1911 the US Supreme Court ordered it broken up.[14]

But the breaking up of Standard Oil was also a moment of genesis. By 1911, Standard Oil was an enormous company; even broken up, its pieces would be giants by any normal standards. The Supreme Court ordered that it be broken up into thirty-four separate, independent companies but paid little attention to evening up the actual size of the new entities. Standard Oil of New Jersey, the largest of the pieces, retained almost half of Standard Oil's total value—it would become Exxon. But the other pieces were large too. Standard Oil of New York, the next largest, had 9 percent of Standard Oil's value and would become Mobil. Standard Oil of California became Chevron. Standard Oil of Ohio became the American branch of British Petroleum. Continental Oil became Conoco. They would all become major players in the new world of Big Oil.

IT WAS A GOOD TIME TO BE AN OIL COMPANY. BY THE EARLY 1900S, it had become clear that petroleum had many more uses than illumination. Other industries had begun to embrace oil as their primary energy source, including steamships, railroads, and cars. It was in 1903, after all, that Henry Ford had founded his motor company and in 1908 that his Model T came out. The next decade would witness an exponential increase in car ownership. Between 1914 and 1920, the number of registered motor vehicles in the United States rose from 1.8 million to 9.2 million. By 1930, it reached 23.1 million. The car boom sparked an oil boom. In 1910, gasoline surpassed kerosene in sales for the first time in history, and the trend only accelerated afterward. Exxon, as the country's largest oil company, was in the pole position to capture this dramatic shift in the way that America powered itself.[15]

But first Exxon had to survive a world war. In the years leading up to World War I, both the US and the British navies had begun to transition from coal- to oil-powered ships. Oil-powered battleships had several advantages over coal-powered ones. They had greater top speeds and faster acceleration. They didn't shower the sailors with smoke and ash. And they didn't have to devote increasingly large numbers of men to shovel coal from bunkers to furnaces—oil, after all, was liquid. In 1912, Winston Churchill, then the first lord of the Admiralty, announced that from thence forward, the Royal Navy would only build oil-powered vessels.[16]

This presented something of a problem, though, once war broke out in 1914. England had switched over to oil, but it produced no oil domestically. Instead, it depended on imports from its allies, particularly the United States and, above all else, from Exxon. In 1914, the United States was producing 266 million barrels of oil a year, or around 65 percent of global output. Most of its exports went to Europe—the United States provided around 80 percent of the Allies' wartime petroleum. Exxon alone accounted for a full quarter of all the Allies' oil. But still, it was almost not enough. In the later stages of the war, recognizing that American oil was keeping the Allies afloat, German submarine fleets began targeting Exxon tankers as they made their way across the Atlantic. Between May and September 1917 alone, German submarines sank six of them. The British navy began running short of fuel. Desperate telegrams to the US government were dispatched warning that unless more oil was shipped, the Royal Navy's fleet would be useless. The American ambassador to London wrote in July 1917, "The Germans are succeeding. They have lately sunk so many fuel oil ships, that this country may very soon be in a perilous condition—even the Grand Fleet may not have enough fuel. . . . It is a very grave danger." Walter Long, Britain's secretary of state for the colonies, repeated the warning, saying in October 1917, "Oil is probably more important at this moment than anything else. You may have men, munitions, and money, but if you do not have oil, which is today the greatest motive power that you use, all your other advantages would be of comparatively little value."[17]

But the US government was simply not equipped to respond to the urgent messages from its allies. It did not have reliable information about oil production within the United States and knew little about its transportation systems. Instead, it turned to the oil companies to spearhead the effort to save the Allies' fuel source. Exxon's president, Alfred Bedford, helmed a new National Petroleum War Service Committee, which orchestrated the flow of oil to where it was most needed. In February 1918, the Allies went further, creating an Inter-Allied

Petroleum Conference to coordinate international oil supplies and shipments among the Allies. Exxon, again, led the way: it largely ran the conference in partnership with its major international competitor, Royal Dutch Shell. The combination of better organization and more protection for oil tankers helped solve the oil problem and power the Allies to victory.

AFTER THE TREATY OF VERSAILLES ENDED WORLD WAR I, EXXON began looking for the next big thing—and found it, increasingly, abroad. The interwar period was a time of dizzying growth in the demand for oil, but Exxon constantly fretted about not being able to produce enough of it. The US government shared this fear, worrying that there simply was not enough oil to be found beneath American soil to satisfy domestic demand. Between 1911 and 1918, American consumption of oil had risen 90 percent. Domestic production, meanwhile, had only increased 50 percent. Exxon simply couldn't keep up. The prospects looked dire. In 1919, the director of the US Bureau of Mines predicted, "Within the next two to five years the oil fields of this country will reach their maximum production, and from that time on we will face an ever-increasing decline." And so, increasingly, Exxon began looking for oil outside its home country.[18]

Exxon's new president, the larger-than-life Walter Teagle, led the charge. Teagle had risen to the helm of Exxon in 1917 when he was just thirty-nine years old, but he quickly came to dominate the company in a way that few had done since the age of Rockefeller. Standing six feet, three inches tall and weighing in at almost three hundred pounds, he had a way of filling a room. He spoke directly and bluntly and never shied from conflict—his underlings called him simply "the Boss." He was known as a tough negotiator. "He haggled over everything," said a colleague. "He'd trade and trade and trade. If it was company money, he'd think he was paying too much for a five cent cigar and try to get it for four." But Teagle also had deep technical knowledge of the industry. He had been such a brilliant student at Cornell University's mechanical engineering school—he wrote his senior thesis on the desulfurization of crude oil—that the department asked him to join the faculty there. He declined the offer and instead entered the oil business.[19]

When Teagle rose to the presidency of Exxon, he had a clear agenda. Teagle had long believed that Exxon's Achilles' heel was the lack of proven crude oil reserves. He believed that Exxon needed to search actively for oil around the world and not just in the United States. This was not an obvious decision at the time, and other directors resisted his search for oil as too risky. As one said, "We're not going to drill dry holes all over the world. We're a marketing company." In fact, crude oil production was just 16 percent of Exxon's refinery output. But, hardheaded as he was, Teagle won the day, cajoling the directors into supporting his decision to ramp up efforts to acquire foreign reserves. In 1920, at a celebration for the fiftieth anniversary of Standard Oil, he announced Exxon's new direction: "The present policy of the Standard Oil Company is to be interested in every producing area no matter in what country it is situated."[20]

The US government actively supported Exxon in its hunt for oil abroad. After their experience in World War I, Congress and the White House had learned the vital strategic importance of oil to America's national security. George Otis Smith, director of the US Geological Survey, argued that the government should "give moral support to every effort of American business to expand its circle of activity in oil production throughout the world." The State Department began instructing its consulates on the "vital importance of securing adequate supplies of mineral oil both for present and future needs of the United States." When foreign governments sought to shut out American oil companies from their concessions, the American government pressured them to allow American companies access or risk losing access to the American market. In 1920, this policy was enshrined in law as the Minerals Leasing Act, which provided that companies of foreign countries that discriminated against American companies could not acquire any interests in US minerals.[21]

Teagle's adventures in international trade greatly expanded Exxon's reach. First came Venezuela. In 1919, Exxon sent geologists to the South American country, and they came back unimpressed. As one of the geologists, who visited the Maracaibo basin and recommended against investing, reported, "Anyone who stays there a few weeks is almost certain to become infected with malaria or liver and intestinal disorders which are likely to become chronic." But the fact that one of Exxon's main competitors, Royal Dutch, was investing millions in the country convinced Teagle to overrule his geologist and invest anyway. At first, this looked like a bad decision. Other companies struck oil in Venezuela, but Exxon only managed to negotiate concessions for areas that were small and in undesirable locations.[22]

The company's largest concession happened to be forty-two hundred acres located underneath Lake Maracaibo. An officer joked that if it didn't have oil, they could at least go into the fishing business. Conditions there proved just as dangerous as Teagle's geologist had warned. Engineers sent down to the country to develop the concession found few passable roads, most of them traversable only by oxcart, almost none by car. Maps tended to be unreliable, with drillers constantly finding rivers where maps told them to expect jungles and jungles where they expected rivers. Disease was rampant, and hostile indigenous tribes regularly attacked their compounds. After a driller was killed by an arrow as he sat on the porch of the company's cafeteria, Exxon ordered that all jungle be cut back around the camp for at least the range of an arrow. But in 1928, Exxon struck oil. The company had improved its technology for underwater drilling and found enormous deposits in the Maracaibo. Teagle's bet paid off handsomely. Other subsidiaries were soon opened in Mexico and Bolivia.[23]

Next was the Middle East. In 1925, Exxon had sent geologists to Iraq on a joint expedition with representatives from Anglo-Persian Oil Company and Royal Dutch Shell, and they had come back convinced of the region's potential. One particularly valuable site was Baba Gurgur, a field near Kirkuk in a Kurdish region of the country. There, burning natural gas spewed from the ground in giant flames and had done so for as long as anyone knew. Plutarch had written in his *Parallel Lives* that the locals had set a street on fire with oil to honor the arrival of Alexander the Great. In 1927, when drilling started, a giant gusher spewed fifty feet high—containing it took the companies eight days. In 1928, Exxon signed a concession agreement with other major oil companies granting them rights over a sprawling region comprising modern-day Turkey, Syria, Iraq, Qatar, Saudi Arabia, Yemen, and Oman. The agreement would come to be called the "Red Line Agreement" for its reliance on a hand-drawn map outlining the prewar boundaries of the Ottoman Empire, and it would prove perennially contentious but also profitable.[24]

Teagle also launched ventures in the Soviet Union and Germany. In 1920, Exxon had bought out the Russian oil concerns of the wealthy Nobel family, which had fled the country during the Russian Revolution. The investment proved ill-conceived. In 1921, when Vladimir Lenin announced his New Economic Policy, he had made conciliatory statements toward Western enterprise. "We cannot by our own strength restore our shattered economy without equipment and technical assistance from abroad," he wrote. The Soviet Union would welcome doing business with "the most powerful imperialist syndicates." But soon it became clear that Lenin's comments would be honored more in the breach than in the observance. The Soviet Union had no intention of honoring concessions to foreign companies and simply took the oil and sold it for themselves. Furious at the snub, Teagle refused to have anything more to do with the Soviets. "I know I am old fashioned in feeling this way, but somehow or other the idea of trying to be on friendly terms with the man who burglarizes your house or steals your property has never appealed to me as the soundest course that could be pursued toward him." Lenin's successor, Joseph Stalin, was, if anything, even more hostile toward Western oil companies. He commented that his early work had been devoted to instilling "unlimited distrust of the oil industrialists."[25]

Things went more to Teagle's satisfaction in Germany. Teagle had visited the factories of I. G. Farben, a large chemical conglomerate, in 1926 and come away deeply impressed. "I had not known what research meant until I saw it," he said. "We were babies compared to the work I saw." Convinced of the wisdom of allying himself with Farben, Teagle had Exxon sign an agreement with the conglomerate to exploit its patented process for creating synthetic oil out of coal. In return, Exxon gave Farben a 2 percent interest in Exxon's stock. Over the next two decades, the two companies would share research and exchange patents. Later, Teagle would be accused of turning a blind eye to the role of I. G. Farben in promoting the Nazi war effort. Farben's directors would eventually be convicted of war crimes at the Nuremberg trials for, among other things, using slave labor from the Auschwitz concentration camp, next to which it had built a factory.[26]

By the time of World War II, Teagle had transformed Exxon. It was no longer a "marketing" company with a chaotic administration and a smattering of foreign interests. It was now a truly multinational corporation with a highly effective central administration, a sophisticated research department, and a network of over one hundred affiliates around the globe. Part of this was due to Teagle's own determination to transform the company according to his vision. But part of it was due to the undeniable rise in the importance of oil. As Secretary of the Interior Harold Ickes wrote in 1935, "There is no doubt about our absolute and complete dependence upon oil. We have passed from the stone age, to bronze, to iron, to the industrial age, and now to an age of oil. Without oil, American civilization as we know it could not exist."[27]

WITH THE OUTBREAK OF WORLD WAR II, EXXON WOULD ONCE again find itself at the center of an American war effort. The Axis powers, desperate for oil supplies to power their armies, were driven to some of their most fateful decisions by the need to secure oil fields. Japan's attack on Pearl Harbor in 1941 was part of a broader plan to acquire oil sites in the East Indies, which the American fleet in Pearl Harbor might have threatened. As one Japanese admiral said, "If there were no supply of oil, battleships and any other warships would be nothing more than scarecrows." Germany's invasion of Russia was motivated at least in part by a desire to acquire oil fields in the Caucasus, with Albert Speer, Germany's minister for armaments and war production, saying that "the need for oil certainly was a prime motive" in the decision. German U-boat wolf packs prowled the Atlantic Ocean near the American coast to target oil tankers sailing to England. As German general Erwin Rommel explained, "The bravest men can do nothing without guns, the guns nothing without plenty of ammunition, and neither guns nor ammunition are of much use in mobile warfare unless there are vehicles with sufficient petrol to haul them around."[28]

Back at home in the United States, Exxon was busy trying to produce and transport as much oil as possible to support the war effort. Just as in the last war, American oil would be essential to the Allied cause. In 1941, President Franklin D. Roosevelt announced a lend-lease program that committed the United States to supplying the Allies with massive amounts of oil, and he appointed Harold Ickes as the petroleum coordinator for national defense to oversee the effort. Ickes found that the Allies were in a desperate situation. In July 1941, his deputy told him that England's oil supply was "nothing less than shocking . . . grave in the extreme." Britain had just two months of fuel left for the navy and five weeks of motor gasoline. So Ickes turned to Exxon and the other major American oil companies and asked for their help. He requested that they reduce their deliveries to American gas stations so that there would be more left for the Allies. He spearheaded an antitrust exemption from the Justice Department to allow the oil companies to speak with each other about operations and to allow them to pool supplies. In order to encourage more exploration for oil and spur greater production, he helped ensure that companies could receive favorable tax deductions for their drilling expenses.[29]

These efforts paid off. During the war years, America's oil production ramped up enormously. In 1940, American oil companies produced 3.7 million barrels a day; by 1945, they produced 4.7 million a day. More than half of all tonnage shipped from the United States in World War II was oil. And nearly all the oil used by the Allies came from US oil companies. Between December 1941 and August 1945, the Allies used 7 billion barrels of oil. Six billion of those barrels came from the United States. For its part, Exxon invested in building the capacity to make one-hundred-octane gasoline for high-performance aircraft, and in the Battle of Britain in 1940, its fuel helped British Spitfire fighter planes outperform the Luftwaffe's eighty-seven-octane Messerschmitts. Oil helped the Allies win the war. In a toast to Winston Churchill at a wartime banquet, Stalin remarked, "This is a war of engines and octanes. I drink to the American auto industry and the American oil industry."[30]

THE UNITED STATES AND EXXON EMERGED FROM THE WAR TRIUM-phant. Over the next two decades, the American economy would be the wonder of the world, with gross domestic product (GDP) and living standards soaring at historic rates. Between 1945 and 1970, the nation's GDP increased from $228 billion to $1.1 trillion, a postwar boom that brought unheard-of affluence to middle-class workers across America. They, in turn, spent their wealth on bigger houses, more cars, and new appliances. All of this led to even greater demand for oil. Between 1945 and 1950 alone, gasoline sales increased 42 percent. Exxon's profits reflected this dizzying rise. In 1950, the company had income of $408 million. By 1957, the number had risen to $805 million. It had more than 250 subsidiaries and affiliates operating in 140 countries and dependencies. It had operations in every major producing and consuming nation in the world.[31]

To manage this sprawling corporate empire, Exxon devised a process for developing talent from within its ranks. The "Exxon System" focused on hiring only the best and the brightest, typically students straight out of college or graduate school, almost always with degrees in technical fields like chemical engineering, petroleum engineering, or civil engineering. Once new hires arrived at the company, they were subjected to a battery of assessments that would evaluate and rank them, on a twice-yearly basis, on their perceived performance. To ensure that employees understood the entire Exxon universe, executives would move offices frequently—one senior vice president told an interviewer that he had been relocated sixteen times in his career. Top performers would often be sent to Exxon's Baton Rouge refinery, which became known as "the Academy" for its grooming of future senior executives. Above all else, the Exxon System stressed loyalty. Exxon rewarded employees with high salaries and long careers if only they demonstrated their devotion to the company. As one of Exxon's public affairs experts put it, "When I came here, I was told that Mobil shouts and Exxon whispers."[32]

Precisely this kind of talent and global reach allowed Exxon to rise to the challenge presented by the oil embargo of 1973. Only a multinational could be equipped to explore the globe and distribute its oil in an increasingly interconnected world economy. But even for Exxon, the challenge was not easy. As the company wrote in its annual report for 1975, "Exxon is directing its efforts to other parts of the world which offer good prospects for new energy sources." But, the report acknowledged, "many of these potential reserves are located in technically challenging areas such as the deep waters beyond the continental shelf or in the far reaches of the Arctic." One executive would later recount that Exxon's push in the 1970s to develop sites like Alaska, the North Sea, Malaysia, and the Bass Strait in Australia required superhuman efforts from its teams. "We made it happen by sleeping on desks, fighting the big war."[33]

Consider, for example, Exxon's development in Prudhoe Bay. The North Slope of Alaska is a land of tundra and sunless winters, home to the eerie green lights of the aurora borealis and roaming herds of caribou. Prudhoe Bay is located off the northern shore around 250 miles above the Arctic Circle. It has fiercely cold weather and strong winds. It also happens to be home to North America's largest oil field, which Exxon discovered on December 26, 1967. On the day that Exxon struck oil there, the temperature was thirty degrees below zero. But the discovery was monumental: the Prudhoe Bay field was estimated to contain ten billion barrels of oil, which represented around 30 percent of total US oil reserves in 1977. Initially, the logistical challenges of drilling and transporting oil from the frozen reaches of Alaska seemed insurmountable. But after the oil embargo of 1973 gave new urgency to the project of finding oil outside the Middle East, Exxon moved forward. Its research team developed new technology to deal with the icy conditions, including ice islands and gravel causeways to support drilling and production. In 1977, Exxon and its partners completed an eight-hundred-mile pipeline across the state to connect Prudhoe Bay to the southern shore of Alaska. By 1986, the Prudhoe Bay field was Exxon's largest producer of oil.

Meanwhile, in the North Sea, Exxon had to deal with entirely different problems. As one skipper reported, "There's nothing quite as vile as the North Sea when she's in a temper." Storms formed and dispersed in a matter of minutes. Waves a hundred feet tall battered ships. Gale-force winds howled across the surface. Life on the North Sea was treacherous and fickle. But by the early 1970s, oil companies had begun to find oil there in copious amounts. Estimates of the Brent oil field alone came to billions of barrels. The question, again, was how to extract the oil from such harsh environments. The weather was so unpredictable that workers could not be evacuated ahead of storms, and so they had to ride them out on the platforms. The waves and wind stressed these platforms, and weldings kept splitting apart. In 1965, a British oil rig had fallen apart, killing thirteen people. Exxon had to invent new technologies and processes to protect its workers.[34]

One of the key problems in deepwater drilling was how to deal with the tendency of the waves and wind to cause platforms to resonate, or sway. If the drilling structure swayed at the same rate as the waves, the effect would be amplified, causing potentially catastrophic stress to steel structures. Exxon's research team worked on new kinds of drilling structures, such as "compliant" towers that would be attached directly to the ocean floor through long steel cables radiating outward to the seabed. They tested these structures in the Gulf of Mexico. An Exxon official described the sheer scope of the operation:

> It was a remarkable day in that the Gulf of Mexico was flat . . . just like a tabletop. There were all manners of pieces of equipment out there—tugboats and launch barges and headquarters barges and helicopters. At the appointed hour at a signal to be given, they were going to press the button, blow those explosive bolts, and [the tower] would slide off and float that way and then they would upend it and tow it to the site. If it came off in any way sort of cockeyed, because it was so long and so slender, it could flex and it could have been trashed.

The installation went off without a hitch. These sorts of innovations made the North Sea accessible to oil companies and helped pave the way for a great expansion of worldwide oil production.[35]

THE POSTWAR PERIOD WAS A TIME OF TRULY UNPRECEDENTED prosperity for Exxon. In the first fifty years of *Fortune*'s list of America's largest corporations, Exxon ranked in the top four every year. It often came first. But Exxon's prosperity also highlighted a new and dangerous shift in the way that corporations saw themselves. Exxon was the first of a new breed of multinational enterprise that did business throughout the world, wherever a profit was to be found. Exxon's offices were filled with globes and world maps, denoting the new international reach of the corporation. Its revenues often dwarfed those of the countries in which it was operating. But as the corporation outgrew the nation-state, it increasingly saw itself as unbeholden to it. Exxon was no longer an American business. It was a global one. And if it was a global business, where did its loyalties lie?

It just so happened that Exxon's product, oil, was found in places without strong traditions of democratic governance. Beginning in the postwar period, Exxon found itself consistently accused of doing business with tyrants and autocrats, from the Soviet Union to the Middle East. Its experience in Saudi Arabia was emblematic. In 1946, an Exxon official had visited that country and reported back "with his eyes popping." "His advice . . . always was 'Go after the elephants,' and leave the little things alone," the official said. "And man, this was a real elephant." Convinced that Exxon needed to acquire an interest in Saudi Arabia, the board sent John Suman, an Exxon director, to meet personally with Saudi king Ibn Saud. The meeting went off famously: one official reported back that Suman and Ibn Saud "took to each other like a couple of old Indians and within fifteen minutes were joking and slapping each other's legs, and he [Suman] authorized us to send a cable that afternoon which would let us go ahead and exercise our purchase option on the Aramco shares." In 1947, Exxon joined the Arabian-American Oil Company, or Aramco, to export Saudi oil. But the enormous profits from the venture, much of which flowed to the House of Saud, helped the Saudi monarchy maintain a social and religious system that was at odds with Western values and would, in the decades to come, be blamed for spreading extremism around the Muslim world. Ironically, the Aramco agreement was finally signed on March 12, 1947, the same day that Harry S. Truman announced the Truman Doctrine, committing the United States to "support free peoples who are resisting attempted subjugation by armed minorities or by outside pressures."[36]

Some commentators asserted not just that Exxon did business with bad regimes but that it actually helped create them. The broader phenomenon came to be known as the resource curse: countries rich in oil tended to be poor in other ways, such as economic development, civil rights, and equality. The oil business, as Thomas Friedman argued, undermined democracy. In Iran, for example, a populist prime minister, Mohammad Mosaddegh, came to power in 1951 and nationalized the Anglo-Iranian Oil Company, a British venture. Alarmed by Mosaddegh's Communist rhetoric, the Central Intelligence Agency and Britain's MI6 orchestrated a coup d'état that unseated Mosaddegh and reinstated the repressive Shah Mohammad Reza Pahlavi. Afterward, the question arose of who would continue the oil business in Iran. The State Department feared that if oil production didn't start again, Iran's economy would fail, leading the country into the Soviet sphere of influence. But given the deep unpopularity of Anglo-Iranian within the country, it was decided that American companies should head the effort. Secretary of State John Foster Dulles appointed Herbert Hoover Jr. as a special representative to negotiate with American companies, and he eventually convinced Exxon to lead the venture. Orville Harden, Exxon's vice president, wrote to Dulles to explain the decision: "From the strictly commercial viewpoint, our company has no particular interest in entering such a group but we are very conscious of the large national security interests involved. We, therefore, are prepared to make all reasonable efforts." Exxon entered into a venture, known as the Iranian Oil Participants, with six other major oil companies, including British Petroleum, Royal Dutch Shell, and Chevron. The Iranian Oil Participants would be a lightning rod for Iranian outrage for the next two decades until, after the Iranian Revolution of 1979, the company was nationalized.[37]

Exxon was no longer a power that was subordinate to nations. It stood above them. It lived longer. It was richer. It was faster and more decisive. Even countries as powerful as the United States had to go to Exxon to ask for its assistance. "We see governments come and go," Lee Raymond, Exxon's famously combative CEO, told an interviewer. "We operate in a lot of countries around the world and have for a long time that wouldn't necessarily meet the definition of democracy the way you define it. That's the nature of this business." But to more and more observers, the nature of Exxon's business undermined US interests around the world. It had grown so large and international that it did not see itself as owing allegiance to any country. Raymond stated this explicitly at times. At an energy conference in Washington, DC, for example, a participant asked Raymond if Exxon would build more refineries within the United States, rather than abroad, in order to prevent gas shortages in the country. "Why would I want to do that?" Raymond asked in return. "Because the United States needs it for security," the participant replied. "I'm not a U.S. company and I don't make decisions based on what's good for the U.S.," Raymond shot back.[38]

Like Frankenstein's creature, the multinational had broken free of the clutches of its creator. It now roamed the world unbound, seeking profit wherever it could be made. In future years, a growing clamor of policymakers, academics, and regulators voiced worry that the multinational presented a set of intractable problems for societies, which depended on them but couldn't control them. As Harvard scholar Detlev Vagts described the critique, the multinational "essentially free of moral or legal constraints . . . grinds remorselessly toward its financial and technological objectives, 'el pulpo' (the octopus) spreading its tentacles over the world and holding other countries, in particular the less developed, to ransom."[39]

BUT THERE WAS ANOTHER PROBLEM THAT HAD LESS TO DO WITH structure and more to do with substance—to be precise, the black, gooey substance that was petroleum. Exxon was an oil company. It was in the business of selling petroleum, and it was very good at it. No one had ever sold so much oil to so many people for so long. And yet no one really knew what the consequences of extracting and burning all of that oil would be for the world and the environment, at least not in the beginning. In fact, for much of the twentieth century, oil was thought of as a *solution* to environmental problems. After all, it replaced, for the most part, coal, and coal was a notoriously dirty fuel, generating everything from acid rain to lethal fog. A move away from coal seemed initially like a win for the environment. But eventually, the harmful environmental effects of oil started to make themselves felt.

The first issue to surface was the problem of oil spills. It had always been known that drilling for oil involved a certain amount of leakage. When drills penetrated high-pressure reservoirs of oil beneath the surface, the oil would often come "gushing" out of the hole and spew upward, sometimes hundreds of feet into the air. The so-called Lucas Gusher at Spindletop in Texas, for example, shot out one hundred thousand barrels of oil a day and was only capped after nine days of effort. Exxon's own strike at Baba Gurgur in Iraq in 1927 flowed at the rate of ninety-five thousand barrels a day. But it was one thing when oil leaked on the ground, where it would more or less stay where it fell. It was another when it happened at sea. In 1989, the oil tanker *Exxon Valdez*, carrying a load of oil that had been piped from Prudhoe Bay to the port at Valdez, Alaska, struck a reef in Prince William Sound. The resulting spill, estimated at around 10.8 million gallons of crude oil, spread quickly, lapping ashore on rocky beaches for hundreds of miles surrounding the area. Images of oil-coated seabirds and otters broadcast by television networks testified to the enormity of the harm and brought worldwide attention to the dangers of oil. And there were much bigger, deadlier spills to come. In 2010, BP's *Deepwater Horizon* spilled 200 million gallons of oil into the Gulf of Mexico before it was capped. The 2004 Taylor Energy spill, in the same body of water, was never contained and, by one estimate, could continue releasing crude oil into the surrounding waters for one hundred years.[40]

Global warming proved an even more pernicious problem. Beginning in the 1960s, as oil consumption was skyrocketing, scientists observed increases in carbon dioxide in the atmosphere, raising questions about what was causing the change and what it might mean for the world. As late as 1962, Humble Oil—an Exxon subsidiary—was running ads with giant pictures of glaciers, accompanied with the headline "Each Day Humble Supplies Enough Energy to Melt Seven Million Tons of Glacier!" But as evidence accumulated, it became clear that the burning of fossil fuels led to carbon dioxide accumulation, and the change in atmospheric carbon dioxide was causing the global climate to shift. In 1979, the National Academy of Sciences published a landmark study on the subject, concluding that if emissions of carbon dioxide continued to increase, significant climate change would likely result. But it also issued a warning that it could take time before the full effects of climate change would be felt: "The great and ponderous flywheel of the global climate system, may be expected to slow the course of observable climatic change . . . [and] a wait-and-see policy may mean waiting until it is too late." In 1981, James Hansen, a scientist working at NASA, published an article in *Science* magazine connecting climate change to oil consumption. He found that world temperatures had increased over the last century, that this rise was attributable to greater carbon dioxide in the atmosphere, and that the atmospheric changes were caused primarily by "anthropogenic" burning of fossil fuels, not natural climate variability. If fossil fuel consumption continued to increase, Hansen warned, it would cause major environmental changes around the globe, from droughts to melting of icebergs to rising sea levels. By the late 1980s, global warming had become a major worldwide concern, and in 1988 an Intergovernmental Panel on Climate Change was established to study the phenomenon and propose solutions.[41]

Exxon watched this science develop with great interest—its business model, after all, depended on convincing people to buy and burn oil. The prospect of greater regulation of the use of fossil fuels was a serious threat, as the passage of the Clean Air Act in 1963 and the Energy Policy and Conservation Act in 1975 had made clear. And so Exxon started to take action, funding its own scientific studies and lobbying against climate change regulation. In 1980, just a year after the National Academy of Sciences report, Exxon hired an astrophysicist from Harvard, Brian Flannery, to study climate change and publish research on the topic. Flannery's conclusions, it so happened, often cast doubt on the science of climate change and on efforts to reduce it. A common talking point was that the science was "uncertain." In a 1996 speech to Esso Italiana, Flannery stated, "Scientific, technical and economic understanding [of climate change] remain limited by enormous uncertainty. Not the type of uncertainty where findings are known within some limited precision, plus or minus some factor. Rather we are simply ignorant. We don't know how to describe what may happen. Descriptions of impacts of climate change are based either on unverified models full of untestable assumptions, or often on sheer speculation." He also cast doubt on the promise of proposed alternatives to oil: "Even with well funded, long term research and development there is no guarantee that alternative energy technologies will be environmentally, socially, and economically acceptable."[42]

Flannery's conclusions were echoed at the very highest levels of Exxon. In 1997, for example, while the landmark environmental treaty, the Kyoto Protocol, was being negotiated, CEO Lee Raymond gave a speech at the Fifteenth World Petroleum Congress in Beijing that included the following: "Let me briefly address three key questions: Is the Earth really warming? Does burning fossil fuels cause global warming? And do we now have a reasonable scientific basis for predicting future temperature?" While Raymond did not answer any of these questions explicitly in the rest of his talk, the direction in which he leaned was clear. On the question of whether Earth was really warming, he talked about how "natural fluctuations in the Earth's temperature have occurred throughout history." On the question of whether fossil fuels caused global warming, he talked about how "most of the greenhouse effect comes from natural sources, especially water vapor." On the question of predicting future temperatures, he quoted an anonymous climate modeler who said, "The more you learn, the more you understand that you don't understand very much."[43]

Much of Exxon's effort against climate change regulation took place under the umbrella of anonymizing industry groups. The American Petroleum Institute (API), a trade group representing petroleum companies including Exxon, strongly opposed climate change regulation. After the Kyoto Protocol was signed in 1997, for example, the API sent a memo to its members outlining a multimillion-dollar effort to fight "precipitous action" on climate change. An Exxon representative participated in developing the draft plan, which stated that "victory will be achieved when average citizens 'understand' (recognize) uncertainties in climate science; recognition of uncertainties becomes part of the 'conventional wisdom.'" In order to achieve this goal, the API planned to "identify, recruit and train a team of five independent scientists." It was important that the recruited scientists be "individuals who [did] not have a long history of visibility and/or participation in the climate change debate." They would then develop a "global climate science information kit for media including peer-reviewed papers that undercut the 'conventional wisdom' on climate science."[44]

Climate change presented the world with a new kind of problem. Unlike most corporate evils from the past, which tended to have local causes and local harms—if a Union Pacific train ran into a cow, the cow's owner knew whom to sue and where to lobby if he wanted recompense—climate change was a truly international phenomenon. Emissions from factories in China affected the climate in Texas, and vice versa. Reductions in emissions in one country might be offset by increases in another. Governments were ill-equipped to deal with this sort of problem, which seemed to require a coordinated international agreement of the sort that was hard to come by in the modern era. Exxon's own attempts to defeat climate change regulation only made the problem even more insoluble. Even today, a comprehensive solution remains out of reach.

The history of Exxon is, in a way, the history of the twentieth century. Exxon rose from the ashes of Standard Oil and assembled the world's first truly multinational corporation. By the middle of the twentieth century, its crack team of geologists, engineers, and physicists had fanned out across the globe to find and extract the oil that the world desperately demanded to fuel its economic growth. Plentiful oil helped fuel economic expansion in America and abroad and brought enormous riches to corporate shareholders. During this time, the company stood at the forefront of energy innovation, creating new technologies to work in the world's most extreme environments, from the North Sea to Alaska. But Exxon also created new problems for society that seemed more intractable than ever—it did business with dictators and autocrats, its multinational structure undermined its connection to single nation-states, and its very product was soon found to be destroying the environment. Big Oil was a big headache.

※ ※ ※

THE MULTINATIONAL CORPORATION represented an important shift in the nature of capitalism. Corporations, long the creatures of local governments, were freed from the clutches of their creators. Enterprises no longer did business primarily in a single country and with a single domestic market. Now, they wheeled and dealed wherever and whenever it made sense—regardless of jurisdictions or borders, currencies or languages. Today, we see the result of this dramatic shift in the corporate form everywhere. All of America's largest corporations today would rightly qualify as multinationals. Walmart, Amazon, Apple, Exxon, and Facebook are all truly global entities.

From a corporate structure perspective, the rise of the multinational enterprise meant that, increasingly, corporations were made up of complex webs of foreign affiliates and subsidiaries, each with its own function and role within a single overarching business. Corporations could shift employees around the world as demand arose. Capital, intellectual property, equipment, and products all flowed between these various entities in order to maximize profits. These far-reaching structural changes worked a subtle shift in the mind-set of corporate executives. Increasingly, they thought in global, not national, terms. Sometimes this was because they were of a different nationality than the corporation that employed them. Sometimes it was because they had spent time in a foreign office. Sometimes it was simply because they had had to learn to negotiate cultural differences to succeed in a corporation that sprawled across the globe.

The multinational corporation provided a lesson in the benefits of free trade and globalization. Multinationals provided jobs, goods, expertise, and revenue to countries that had long been shut out of the international economic system. Multinationals produced goods more cheaply than ever, giving consumers plentiful access to products that otherwise might have been prohibitively expensive. In the case of the oil companies, multinationals also had the benefit of providing energy for the international economy to keep humming. In many ways, then, the multinational showcased all that corporations had to offer the globe. When humanity came together in a spirit of cooperation and enterprise, extraordinary things happened.

But once again, this new version of the corporation proved dangerous when in the hands of the unscrupulous, the reckless, or simply the shortsighted. It should come as no surprise that the rise of the multinational in the post–World War II world coincided with the rise of the world's most pressing multinational problem: climate change. Multinational corporations had a way of seeking out the most advantageous jurisdictions to do business in, the ones that promised greater profits for shareholders. While this sometimes meant finding new resources or markets, it often meant seeking out countries with more favorable regulations—ones that imposed lower taxes, or fewer restrictions on employment conditions, or laxer environmental rules.

With corporations lobbying for rule changes, countries suddenly found their hands tied. They could either increase environmental protections and risk losing corporations to countries with looser rules, or they could relax their own environmental standards and keep corporations and their desperately needed jobs. Too often, governments chose abject surrender. The result, not just in environmental regulation but also in other areas, like tax and employment law, was what scholars of international relations call a "race to the bottom." Regulatory competition between countries caused governments to water down their laws in ways that ultimately harmed the public.

With corporations now rivaling and sometimes surpassing the power of countries, a question arose in the minds of close watchers of capitalism. Was this the end of history for the corporation? Had it reached its final, most muscular form? Or did it have a few more shape-shifts in store?

seven

THE RAIDER

IN 1976, TWO ECONOMISTS WROTE AN ARTICLE THAT CALLED into question everything we thought we knew about the corporation. In "Theory of the Firm," University of Rochester professors Michael Jensen and William Meckling argued that the structure of the corporation was rotten. Economists had long assumed that the corporation was a profit-maximizing entity: that it pursued its self-interest in a rational and considered way. But Jensen and Meckling argued that this was all wrong. In order to understand how a corporation worked, we needed to look inside of it, to open up the "black box" and peer in at the incentives of the people who worked there. And, as Jensen and Meckling pointed out, these incentives were a jumble of conflicting and problematic signals, which they referred to as "agency costs." Stockholders owned corporations, but they delegated decisions to a group of professional executives. The executives had interests of their own that did not perfectly align with those of the stockholders who had chosen them, let alone with those of the workers beneath them.

Instead of raising worker wages to improve productivity, they could use that cash to pay themselves bigger bonuses. Instead of issuing dividends to shareholders, they could buy corporate jets or golf club memberships. While stockholders could always vote directors out of office, most investors did not have the time or inclination to go over the line-item expenses of managers with a fine-toothed comb, and even if they did, they would never be able to spot the myriad ways in which waste crept in. For Jensen and Meckling, the root of the problem lay in the separation of ownership and control at the foundation of the corporation since the times of ancient Rome.

Jensen and Meckling were not the first to point out the paradox at the heart of corporations. Adam Smith himself reached a very similar conclusion in *The Wealth of Nations*. Smith believed that the shareholders of his day knew little to nothing about the business of the joint stock companies they owned. Instead, they were simply content to receive dividends at the end of the year. Directors similarly did not care much about how the business of their corporation went, as they were "the managers rather of other people's money than of their own." They considered it beneath their station to pay attention to small matters of profit and loss. With no one at the helm, joint stock companies were disasters waiting to happen. "Negligence and profusion, therefore, must always prevail, more or less, in the management of the affairs of such a company," Smith wrote.[1]

Jensen and Meckling provided a vocabulary for understanding Smith's original intuition about the flaws of corporations. Their article would mark a turning point in the history of corporate law, and future scholars would refer to their work early and often. But it also reached an unusually broad audience outside the halls of academia. At a time when CEO pay had started a long and vertiginous rise, "Theory of the Firm" struck a chord. To much of the public, it seemed that corporations had become an enemy of the state, not an ally. Newspapers were filled with stories of executives and their giant mansions, exotic vacations, and million-dollar bonuses. Capitalism had lost its way. The modern corporation was no longer an exemplar of industry and efficiency; it was a symbol of greed and excess. Jensen and Meckling's article explained why.

Near the end of the article, though, Jensen and Meckling offered a ray of hope. In what seemed like a passing comment, they speculated about a different type of company, one that would prove stronger, more resilient, and better designed than the hopelessly flawed modern corporation. "Why don't we observe large corporations, individually owned, with a tiny fraction of the capital supplied by the entrepreneur, and the rest simply borrowed?" they asked. Jensen and Meckling admitted that most people found the very question silly. Didn't everyone know that businesses had to raise money and that the best way to do this was to sell stocks to the public? Wasn't this the lesson we had learned from the East India Company over three hundred years ago? No, Jensen and Meckling defiantly replied. "The fact is that no well articulated answer to this question currently exists in the literature of either finance or economics." Moreover, there were strong reasons to believe that if a firm's owner managed the company himself, the company would prove more rational, if for no other reason than that the owner presumably knows what he wants. "If a wholly owned firm is managed by the owner, he will make operating decisions which maximize his utility," Jensen and Meckling concluded.[2]

In a coincidence of fate worthy of a Dickens novel, in the same year that Jensen and Meckling wrote their article, a group of brash former investment bankers founded a new firm that adopted, more or less wholesale, the professors' speculative reforms. Their firm, Kohlberg Kravis Roberts & Co. (KKR), would launch broadsides against many of the country's biggest companies, accusing them of mismanagement and waste. Their raids proved spectacularly successful, and soon an entire industry of copycats sprang up to mirror their tactics. The age of the corporate raider had begun.

※ ※ ※

I LIKE TO tell my students that private equity is a tale of two Gordons.

The first Gordon is Gordon Gekko. In this lens, private equity firms and their managers are real-life versions of Oliver Stone's immoral banker from the movie *Wall Street*. They believe that "greed is good," that all is fair in love and business, and that, in the free market, avarice is a competitive advantage. The Gordon Gekko view of private equity is a morality tale about those who create nothing and yet take everything.

The second Gordon is Flash Gordon. Seen in this light, the realm of private equity is not the immoral world of *Wall Street*. It is the noble, self-sacrificing one of the Flash Gordon comic books. It is populated by all-American polo players who graduated from Yale and then transform into superheroes devoted to saving the world from destruction and waste. Private equity managers, in this tale, are real-life heroes, bringing new energy and vigor to our economies.

These two schools of thought tell very different stories about what private equity is and how it works. The Gordon Gekko school understands it as being primarily about wealth extraction—charging high fees to pension funds, driving hard bargains with struggling companies, firing and mistreating workers, exploiting tax loopholes, and then selling companies to the gullible public at inflated prices. This is a bleak vision. The Flash Gordon school understands private equity quite differently. Private equity firms leave everyone they touch better off. Pension funds get better returns. Struggling companies get access to world-class expertise and financial guidance. Jobs are created. Government revenues are increased. Communities are enriched. This is an optimistic vision.

You might think that we could solve these debates by just looking at the numbers. Have private equity buyouts led to more new jobs or more layoffs? Have pension funds earned better returns from their private equity investments? Have tax revenues increased or decreased? What happened to stock prices after private equity firms took their companies public? These sound like simple, straightforward questions that could be easily measured. They are not. For one, it is hard to actually get comprehensive data about private equity. The industry is notoriously secretive, and getting proprietary data about it is difficult. For another, people disagree about what the points of reference should be. At what point should you measure job numbers? Against what benchmark should you measure private equity returns? Scholars have debated these matters for years, and no consensus picture has emerged.

Today, though, there is no debate about the fact that private equity firms have dramatically altered the landscape of corporate America. They own many of America's largest companies, in areas as diverse as hospitals, real estate, and toy stores. Their managers have become some of the wealthiest people in the world, earning mind-bogglingly high salaries year after year. Private equity's influence in politics has been similarly outsized. A better understanding of the modern corporation, then, begins in 1976, with the dawn of the Age of the Raider.

JEROME KOHLBERG HAD IT ALL. IN THE EARLY 1970S, THEN IN HIS mid-forties, he had risen to the heights of investment banking as the head of Bear Stearns's prestigious corporate finance group. He had already had an illustrious career marked by an uncommon degree of prudence and principle. He had studied at Swarthmore as an undergraduate and been so taken by the Quaker ethos that he liked to call himself a "Jewish Quaker." He later earned an MBA from Harvard and a law degree from Columbia. After a short stint as a law clerk, he joined Bear Stearns, where he remained for twenty years. Nearly everyone who met him was struck by one thing: his remarkable sense of ethical duty, of a commitment to doing things the right way, to putting the interest of his clients first. In meetings with executives who were considering doing business with his firm, he would often say, "We're all on the same side of the table." "Jerry was a hands-off, elder statesman figure," one officer who worked with him remarked. "He was constantly talking about integrity." He had joined Bear Stearns's corporate finance group because he thought it gave him a chance to help companies grow, to work alongside them as a trusted advisor and not just a piggybank: "I liked the long-term thinking," Kohlberg explained. "I liked working with management and bringing more than just financial legerdemain." Outside work, his favorite things were his children, his trumpet, his books, and his tennis game (his son, James, became a professional tennis player).[3]

Bear Stearns was an odd place for a man of Kohlberg's ilk to work. Even in the high-octane world of Wall Street, Bear Stearns stood out for its aggressive culture. Its longtime managing partner, Salim "Cy" Lewis, was a former professional football player and shoe salesman known for a ferocious temper and a cutthroat mind-set. He often ridiculed subordinates, on everything from their trading decisions to their choice of clothing. He had a reputation for holding grudges forever if someone said the wrong thing around him. Candidates for positions at the firm would often be greeted in their interviews with a single question: "How do you feel about money?" Nonetheless, nearly everyone agreed that Kohlberg floated above Bear Stearns's no-holds-barred culture.[4]

He did so, in part, by carving out a niche for himself that he believed to be both profitable *and* ethical. That niche was an innovative financial transaction that he invented called a "bootstrap" deal. In the early 1960s, many of the founders of companies from the World War II boom economy were beginning to retire. They wanted to cash in on the success of their firms, and yet they also wanted their businesses to live on after them, to leave a legacy. Often, their children did not want to take over the companies, and these proprietors certainly did not want to sell out to the competitors they had been fighting off for years. It was a hard nut to crack. Kohlberg cracked it. His idea was to allow aging owners of family companies to cash out but remain in control of their companies for just a bit longer. Kohlberg would find a group of investors willing to put up cash to buy the company from the founder, and then he would negotiate an agreement with the founder to keep some stock in the company and stay on as CEO for a period of years to guide it through the transition. These were friendly deals that left all parties satisfied: the founder pocketed a hefty profit from the company before eventually turning over the keys to the trustworthy hands of Kohlberg, who would sell the streamlined company at a multiple over its purchase price.

Kohlberg's deal with Stern Metals in 1965 illustrated his playbook. In that year, Kohlberg learned that H. J. Stern, the seventy-two-year-old founder of the dental products company, was looking to raise cash to provide his children with an inheritance. Stern did not trust his children to run the company, and so he did not want to relinquish control just yet. "A company isn't like an oil well, where all you have to do is hold a pan out and collect oil," he told Bear Stearns. "It's like a violin. And I'm not sure my sons have what it takes to play the violin." After long negotiations with Stern, Kohlberg put together a plan. Kohlberg formed a company, owned by a group of investors he had located, and used it to buy Stern Metals for $9.5 million, using $1.5 million of investor funds and $8 million in funds borrowed from banks and insurance companies. H. J. Stern kept some stock in his company and continued to run it. Eight months later, Kohlberg sold a portion of his stock, which he had originally bought for $1.25 a share, to the public for $8 a share. He used the cash to acquire new companies and expand Stern Metals' market. When the company went public two years later, investors received back a whopping eight times their initial investment. Stern was so happy that, in a dinner thrown to celebrate the deal, he toasted to Kohlberg and Bear Stearns. "We mutually pledge to each other our lives, our fortunes, and our sacred honor," Stern solemnly declared.[5]

Kohlberg's leveraged buyouts were complicated transactions, though, and he needed help structuring them. To do so, he brought in two associates, George Roberts and Henry Kravis. Roberts arrived first. The son of a Houston oilman who had spent time in jail for tax evasion, Roberts gave off an air of detached reserve, as if he were constantly analyzing the odds. Perhaps he had acquired the icy demeanor during his high school years at Culver Military Academy in Indiana, where he remembered waking up at 4 a.m. to shovel the snow. In college at Claremont, he spent his free time typing out letters to Fortune 500 CEOs on his Hermes typewriter and suggesting potential takeovers in return for a small finder's fee for his trouble. None took him up on the offer. After college, he attended the University of California, Hastings College of the Law and then went to work for Bear Stearns, where he met Kohlberg. Soon, the two were working closely together. When he eventually transferred to Bear Stearns's San Francisco office, he convinced Kohlberg to choose his cousin Henry Kravis as his replacement in New York.

On paper, Kravis looked very similar to Roberts. Like Roberts, he was the son of an oilman. Like Roberts, he spent time at a boarding school and attended college at Claremont. Like Roberts, he had been interested in finance from an early age, and he wrote his senior thesis on convertible debentures. After college, he went to Columbia Business School before landing at Bear Stearns. But the similarities ended there. Whereas Roberts was reserved and analytical, Kravis was flashy and brash. He was a constant presence on the New York social scene, attending galas and throwing parties. He liked to wear Italian pants and Gucci loafers. On his thirtieth birthday, he drove a Honda motorcycle he had received as a gift inside the interior of his Park Avenue apartment.

There may have been personality differences between the trio of Kohlberg, Kravis, and Roberts, but all three shared a sharp-edged focus on financial success. In 1971, the founder of Cobblers Industries, a shoe company that Kohlberg had bought, walked up to the roof of the company's factory during a lunch break and committed suicide. When Kohlberg found out, he was furious. "Jerry called me and screamed, 'The fucker jumped off the roof!'" an investor in the deal remembered. Cobblers eventually went bankrupt, and the investment was a total loss. George Roberts could be hard-nosed too. "Never fall in love with anything except your wife and kids," he said.[6]

By the mid-1970s, relations between the trio and the rest of Bear Stearns had deteriorated. The returns from Kohlberg's bootstrap buyouts had declined significantly, and Cy Lewis thought that they should abandon the losing tactic and refocus on Bear Stearns's core corporate finance business. Kohlberg disagreed. He still believed in his bootstrap deals and thought the declining profits were just the result of a few bad apples—the strategy itself was a good one. So in 1976 he approached his two young protégés about the prospect of leaving the bank and starting up their own shop. Kravis and Roberts, eager to make a name for themselves, both leapt at the idea. When Roberts went to inform Cy Lewis about his decision to leave Bear Stearns, Lewis tried to dissuade him. "You know, young man, you're making a terrible mistake," Lewis said. "No one has ever left this firm and been successful." But Kohlberg, Kravis, and Roberts all believed that their new shop would prove the exception.[7]

ON MAY 1, 1976, KOHLBERG KRAVIS ROBERTS & CO. OPENED ITS doors to the world. In the beginning, it must be admitted, those doors were a bit shabby. They were operating on a thin budget and had to cut costs wherever possible. Kohlberg put in $100,000 of his own money, while Kravis and Roberts invested $10,000 each. They set up office on Fifth Avenue in Midtown Manhattan in the Mutual of New York Building, which looked like a Holiday Inn. They did, however, manage to convince the previous tenant to let them keep the drab furniture that was already there, primarily metal desks, gray carpets, and generic art. This was no longer the high-flying world of Bear Stearns.

The trio crisscrossed the country trying to drum up business wherever they could, but there was no denying that it was a hard-scrabble affair. When their first associate, Bob MacDonnell, visited a grain-handling equipment company in South Dakota in the winter to discuss buying it for around $3 million, the owner took him outside in the minus-fifteen-degree weather and asked, "Do you want to plink?" MacDonnell had no idea what he was talking about, but before he knew it, the owner had pulled out his .32 revolver and started shooting at Campbell's soup cans. "Let's see how many of these you can hit!" the owner shouted. No one kept a record of how many cans MacDonnell hit that day, but presumably it wasn't many. The owner declined to sell.[8]

Raising money from investors was equally rocky. Their initial goal had been to raise $25 million from institutional investors, and they networked tirelessly with banks and insurance companies. Nevertheless, after two months, none had bitten. KKR's track record was simply too short and too risky. Then, one day, they received a call from Henry Hillman, a wealthy venture capitalist based out of Pittsburgh. Kravis had met with Hillman a week before and been told that Hillman would give him an answer within two weeks. But six days later, Hillman's associate called. "Did you not like us?" he asked Kravis. Kravis, flustered, asked what he was talking about. "The minute you walked out of the door we made our decision," the associate replied. "Our decision is, we'd like half the fund." Hillman had just committed to a $12.5 million investment. The experience with Hillman convinced the trio that individual investors, not institutions, might be a better source of funds. So in the summer of 1976, KKR turned to the time-tested fountain of wealth for every well-connected businessman: family and friends. This effort proved more fruitful. A few months later, they had managed to find seven investors, including Kravis's father, who were willing to invest $50,000 a year to pay for the firm's expenses. In return, the investors received the option to participate in and profit from any buyout transaction that KKR made. It was a win, but it was not everything they had hoped for. Individual investors, even wealthy ones, had their limits. The next year, after one of the investors had received four requests for additional capital in a period of less than twelve months, he called

Kravis up to complain. "Henry, you're going to bankrupt me," he told the chastened Kravis.[9]

KKR now had enough money, however, to finally start buying companies. Its first investments were few and far between, and relatively small, but turned out to be quite profitable. In 1977, KKR bought three companies. It paid $26 million for AJ Industries, a Los Angeles jet-refueling company; on its sale eight years later, investors received forty-four times their investment before fees. KKR bought L.B. Foster, a Pittsburgh drilling-equipment company, for $106 million; twelve years later, investors received back six times their money. US Natural Resources, an Oregon-based coal-machinery company, sold to KKR for $22 million; seven years later, investors would receive back twenty times their money.

With a few deals under their belts, Kohlberg, Kravis, and Roberts could tell that they were onto something. And if their financial engineering worked for these small companies, wouldn't it work for bigger ones too? The trio thought it would. But in order to target bigger fish, they needed more investments—and bigger ones. So, in 1978 they went out and raised a buyout fund. Now that they had a slightly longer track record, they could target the institutional investors who had passed on their offers the first time around. This time, it worked. By the end of the year, they had raised a buyout fund of $30 million. Their investors included such major players as the insurance company Allstate, the bank Citicorp, and the pension fund Teachers Insurance. Now they were playing in the big leagues.

Flush with cash, KKR started scouring the market for a major corporation that it deemed ripe for a takeover. Its big break came when Kohlberg, flipping through the *New York Times* in the summer of 1978, came across a short article, hidden deep in the business section, about a company called Houdaille Industries. Houdaille was a classic example of the conglomerate corporation that ruled the markets of 1970s corporate America. It was a sprawling company: it had begun life as a manufacturer of hydraulic shock absorbers in Buffalo, New York, but over the years had diversified into construction, gravel quarries, machine tooling, industrial pumps, and much more. The company was conservatively run, with a large cash balance and minimal debt. The article also pointed out that its CEO, Gerald Saltarelli, was sixty-seven years old, well past "normal retirement age." All this led the columnist to ask, "Is Houdaille Industries . . . a takeover candidate?" When Kohlberg read the story, he knew that Houdaille was a perfect target for his bootstrap deal. There was just one problem: no one thought that a conglomerate company of Houdaille's size could ever be bought in a leveraged buyout, not even Houdaille's own investment bankers at Goldman Sachs. There was no way to raise that amount of debt from lenders. But the trio of financial whizzes at KKR thought otherwise.[10]

In August 1978, Kohlberg and Kravis flew down to Fort Lauderdale, Houdaille's new headquarters, to meet Saltarelli and pitch their plan to him. They laid the charm on thick. "It was a very soft sell," Saltarelli recounted afterward. Kohlberg walked Saltarelli through his firm's history and how they approached business. Kravis described what the company's balance sheet would look like after the buyout (hint: it would be heavily indebted). "I'm sure, knowing how you've run your company in the past, that this is going to scare you," Kravis explained as he handed over a packet containing the projected financials. "You're telling me initially that it's not going to work. I'm telling you: I think it will work." Saltarelli remarked that he hoped to retire soon and wanted to hand over the reins to his two subordinates, executive vice president Phil O'Reilly and treasurer Don Boyce. Kohlberg and Kravis reassured him that they would respect that decision.

The next step was getting O'Reilly and Boyce, the heirs apparent, on board. To that purpose, Kohlberg invited the two to visit him at his vacation home in the Virgin Islands. When they arrived, Kohlberg presented them with an offer they couldn't refuse: new employment contracts that raised their salaries to $200,000 a year for O'Reilly and $100,000 for Boyce, increases of more than 50 percent over what they had been making. Saltarelli, for his part, would make $5.2 million on the sale of his stock. The numbers were too good to pass up, and after some initial reluctance, Houdaille and KKR reached a deal.[11]

Building the deal structure was just as important as building the relationship. Tax considerations were paramount. An analysis of Houdaille's financial situation had convinced Kravis that, by layering on debt, KKR could cut Houdaille's tax burden roughly by half. But Kravis wondered if they could reduce it even further, perhaps even to zero. In order to do so, they would need to engage in a maneuver known as step-up depreciation. The basic idea was to increase the value of the company's assets so that the company could take bigger depreciation deductions on those assets in future years. It turned out that Houdaille had lots of old assets, like factories and equipment, that it had historically held on its books at very low values. KKR's accountant at Deloitte analyzed these assets and concluded that the company could increase its value by around $100 million, allowing additional tax-deductible depreciation for Houdaille of $15 million.[12]

Doing so would require complicated corporate structuring, though, and KKR hired Skadden, one of Wall Street's most powerful law firms, to handle the documentation. Skadden, in turn, devised a transaction of Dickensian complexity. For example, on March 5, 1978, HH Holdings Inc. held a "meeting" at KKR's office, which was attended by a single person, Kravis, who was its sole director. At this "meeting," Kravis proposed eighteen resolutions to himself and approved them by a 1–0 vote. Several days later, he did the same with HH Acquisition Corporation, another piece of the transactional puzzle. Later, when an error was discovered in an agreement between Houdaille Associates and HH Holdings, Kravis, in his capacity as the general partner of Houdaille Associates, wrote a letter to himself, in his capacity as the president of HH Holdings, requesting his own consent to amend the agreement. Fortunately, Kravis was in an agreeable mood and wrote back to himself that his offer was "accepted and agreed to." The Securities and Exchange Commission (SEC), perplexed by the transaction structure, asked the group to create an organizational chart showing the various entities and where they stood in relation to each other. The resulting chart looked like a spiderweb. The KKR associate working on the deal printed out a three-foot-wide copy of it and hung it on his office wall. He proudly told visitors that it was "the control room of the Three Mile Island nuclear plant."[13]

When KKR announced its $355 million leveraged buyout of Houdaille, a tremor ran through corporate America. No one had ever thought that a company of Houdaille's size could be bought by a small firm like KKR. It had been conventional wisdom in boardrooms around the country that only corporate blue chips, like General Motors or Exxon or Ford, could afford to spend that kind of money on mergers and acquisitions (M&A). "When Houdaille came along, it got everybody's attention," said Richard Beattie, a lawyer at Simpson Thacher & Bartlett who represented KKR on its early deals. "Up to that point, people walked around and said, 'What's an LBO?' All of a sudden this small outfit, three guys—Kohlberg and Kravis and Roberts—is making an offer for a public company. What's *that* all about?"[14]

The Houdaille investment would prove to be a landmark deal for the industry, not just because it alerted everyone to what KKR was up to but also because it inspired others to get into the game as well. One of the firm's early admirers was Stephen Schwarzman, then a thirty-one-year-old investment banker at Lehman Brothers. When he heard about the deal, he grabbed a copy of the bond prospectus outlining the terms to understand how it could be done. "I read that prospectus, looked at the capital structure, and realized the returns that could be achieved," Schwarzman said. "I said to myself, 'This is a gold mine.' It was like a Rosetta stone for how to do leveraged buyouts." Six years later, Schwarzman founded his own private equity firm, Blackstone, which would grow into one of the world's largest.[15]

The Houdaille deal introduced the world to private equity, a type of business that would soon become a major, if controversial, feature of the corporate landscape. It was a strange model. Rather than buying and selling goods, private equity bought and sold corporations. This hyper-financialized strategy turned corporations into yet another a commodity, a thing to be traded and exchanged as the bankers saw fit. But some observers doubted that private equity managers really could improve on the corporation and wondered what effects they would have on the health of the broader economy.

KKR's PRIVATE EQUITY MODEL PROVED SPECTACULARLY SUCCESS-ful. Throughout the twentieth century, stocks in the S&P 500 index returned around 10 percent a year. KKR, meanwhile, targeted returns of 40 percent a year for its investors, and it generally outperformed this metric. In 1983, the firm claimed to have earned average annualized returns of 62.7 percent. These were unheard-of numbers, so high that they could hardly be believed even by the investors who were receiving them. Where was all the money coming from?[16]

KKR's basic strategy relied on the "leveraged buyout," sometimes referred to as a management buyout. The playbook was simple. First, KKR raised a fund from wealthy investors, typically large institutions. Second, it bought companies, using the cash from the fund as well as a hefty portion of borrowed money to pay the purchase price. Third, it ran the company for a few years and then sold it, hopefully at a profit, to the public or another buyer. There was nothing particularly magical about these components. "Buy low, sell high" had been a corporate mantra at least since the days of the East India Company. But in the hands of financial wizards like Kohlberg, Kravis, and Roberts, they transformed into something elemental and powerful.

To begin with, the trio displayed a remarkable talent for finding people willing to give them oodles of money. Their inaugural fund in 1976 had aimed to raise $25 million and didn't even come close to reaching that number. In 1978, though, they raised a fund of $30 million. Then, in 1980, they raised a $357 million fund. By 1987, they had raised five funds amounting in total to $2.4 billion. Where did all this money come from? Investors in the first fund had included an insurance company and a bank, but the real driver in future years would be pension funds. In the 1970s, the retirement savings of millions of teachers, firefighters, and civil servants around the country had been parked in giant pools of capital that had steadily grown into some of the largest investors in corporate America. These funds were watched over by state bodies such as the California Public Employees Retirement System and the Teachers Retirement System of Texas, which sought to ensure that the pension funds enjoyed sizeable returns on their investments in order to pay out the benefits they had promised to retirees. For the most part, though, these pension funds were run by government workers on government salaries. KKR realized that they were ideal investors: they controlled enormous amounts of capital, they weren't interested in managing it directly, and they were captivated by the possibility of doing business with some of the most powerful and connected people on Wall Street. Roberts did much of the marketing because, as Kohlberg said, he was good at "recognizing that power is money, and . . . getting close to it and staying close to it."[17]

One early investor was the Oregon Investment Council, a body that controlled the state's retirement funds. Roger Meier, the council's chairman, was heavily courted by George Roberts and eventually invested $178 million in KKR's buyout of Fred Meyer Inc., an Oregon-based retailer. After board meetings, Roberts would invite Meier to play doubles tennis at the Beverly Hills Hotel with himself and the hotel pro, who happened to be Alex Olmedo, a former Wimbledon champion. "It was delightful," Meier would say of the experience. "Here was a little yokel from Portland, Oregon, operating with really some pretty fantastic high fliers. I was pretty impressed." Oregon's investment in the Fred Meyer deal was the largest single investment the Oregon Investment Council had ever made, amounting to around 8 percent of all of the pension fund's assets. It was a risky bet, but it paid off handsomely. By the time the company was sold, the pension fund had earned an annual return of 53 percent. In future years, Oregon would be a reliable and sizeable source of capital for KKR, and

Meier would become a close friend of Roberts's. Other states, seeing the outsized returns that Oregon was earning, followed its lead. In 1982, Washington's and Michigan's pension funds invested in KKR's private equity fund, as did Harvard University's powerful endowment. Iowa at one point had $347 million, or around 10 percent, of its total $4 billion invested in two KKR funds. The chairmen of state pension funds turned into vocal promoters of KKR and its stable of financial wizards. The head of Washington State's pension fund said in a 1989 interview, "If you had to name, on the fingers of one hand, the people who have had the greatest influence on U.S. capitalism in the second half of the twentieth century, those three guys are there."[18]

KKR structured its relationship with the pension funds to ensure that it would receive ample compensation for taking their money. The partnership agreements governing the investments contained a veritable thicket of fees payable to KKR. The most important of these were the management and carried-interest fees. These might best be analogized to a salary and a bonus. The management fee, like a salary, was paid to KKR annually regardless of performance, while the carried-interest fee, like a bonus, was contingent on results, fluctuating based on how well its acquisitions went. A typical management fee in KKR's deals would pay the firm, every year, between 1.5 and 2 percent of all the money it had raised. To give a sense of the magnitude, the fund's 1982 management fee was $4.5 million a year; the fund's 1986 management fee was $27 million. These fees were stackable: KKR could earn management fees on each of its funds, so the firm was making tens of millions of dollars a year simply for taking investors' money. The carried interest, on the other hand, gave KKR a percentage of any profits it made from buying and selling companies. A typical carried-interest fee gave KKR 20 percent of any profit above a certain threshold (or "hurdle")—in effect, it had to beat the market in order to earn the fee. But other fees abounded as well: there were investment banking fees, transaction fees, and fees for the use of KKR associates whom KKR placed on the boards of its portfolio companies. In the late

1980s, transaction fees alone came to around $100 million for KKR. Together, these fees composed ample profits, year in and year out, for the firm. "It's very Machiavellian," one investment banker remarked of the fee structure. "It's as if KKR set up its limited partnerships according to the guiding principle of: 'How do we make tons of money with almost no risk to ourselves?'" Not all investors were happy about this, but as long as returns were good, they felt they had no option but to pay up.[19]

The second part of the KKR strategy, the bread and butter of the private equity industry, was the leveraged buyout itself. The idea behind the leveraged buyout was to use debt to leverage a small amount of cash into a larger one. Just like mortgages allow homebuyers to buy a bigger or more expensive house than they would be able to afford with their savings alone, leveraged buyouts allowed KKR to buy bigger, more expensive companies than their cash on hand would have allowed them to do. Leverage also supercharged returns. Consider, for example, a hypothetical purchase of a company for $100 million. Let us assume that, after a year of careful management, the company could be sold for $110 million. If KKR bought the company entirely with its own cash, it would receive a return of exactly 10 percent: it bought the company for $100, sold it for $110, and pocketed $10. A 10 percent return would be perfectly respectable and would roughly match the average return of stocks. But what if KKR borrowed a portion of the purchase price? KKR typically borrowed anywhere from 70 to 95 percent of the total purchase price of the companies they bought, so let us assume that KKR used $10 million of its own capital and borrowed the rest, or $90 million. At the end of the year, KKR could still sell the company for $110 million. It could then pay off the $90 million of debt and have $20 million left. Now, its initial $10 million of cash had turned into $20 million—a return of 100 percent, all through the magic of debt. Of course, debt is not free. KKR had to pay interest on the money it borrowed, and the higher the interest rate, the harder it was to make money. KKR, recognizing this, turned to a newfangled debt market being developed by an investment banker named Michael Milken.[20]

In the 1980s, Michael Milken had transformed the sleepy world of bonds into a churning profit machine for his investment bank, Drexel Burnham Lambert. Operating out of his Beverly Hills office, Milken developed a market for so-called junk bonds, risky debt issued by debt-laden or struggling companies. Junk bonds had long been considered off-limits to most mainstream investors. They were considered too risky and too unlikely to pay off. But Milken became convinced—and, more importantly, convinced buyers—that if he could package these junk bonds together into a portfolio, they would outperform the bonds of more conservative, stable companies. Milken's junk bond business was soon helping companies issue billions of dollars in debt every year—in 1983 alone, Drexel sold $4.7 billion in junk bonds. But the real supercharger behind junk bonds was the rise of leveraged buyouts. KKR realized that junk bonds could finance their acquisitions, allowing them to raise more debt, for less, and faster. In 1984, KKR accepted a bid from Milken to finance its $330 million acquisition of Cole National, an eyewear and toy company, and Kravis was shocked by how easily Milken found buyers for the risky debt. It was "the damnedest thing I'd ever seen," Kravis said. For the rest of the decade, KKR and Drexel would form an inseparable duo. Between 1984 and 1989, KKR used Drexel for thirteen transactions, and KKR, in turn, was Drexel's largest borrower. One Drexel banker said of the relationship between KKR and Drexel, "It was one of the most symbiotic relationships of all time. They blessed us and we blessed them." Drexel and Milken profited handsomely from the relationship. In his best year, in 1987, Drexel paid Milken $550 million.[21]

The final part of the private equity playbook was running the businesses KKR bought. You might assume that, if the business of private equity was making companies more valuable so they could be sold for a profit, the firm's partners would be expert business managers, with a keen eye for honing and fine-tuning how businesses operated. But in fact, KKR took a remarkably hands-off approach to the companies it bought. The founders actively discouraged their portfolio companies from coming to them for advice on how to run their businesses. After KKR bought Motel 6 in 1985, the CEO of the company asked Kravis and Roberts for advice on what kinds of billboards the company should post near highways to promote its motels. After the meeting, Kravis pulled Roberts aside and told him, "We've got problems. Because if we, laymen as we are, have got to decide what the signs are going to look like, that's dangerous." Six months later, KKR replaced the CEO with another, presumably more self-reliant executive.[22]

Instead of making operational decisions for companies, KKR delegated decision-making to trusted executives at the companies themselves and loaded the executives up with performance incentives. KKR believed that, with enough financial interest in the company's profits, executives would find ways to make their companies more efficient. In most buyouts, KKR would give managers a substantial equity stake in the company, typically 10 to 15 percent. "When a manager has his own money invested and it's his company, he's going to come in a little earlier in the morning," Kravis explained. "He's going to think harder about that capital expenditure. Does he need the limousine and the corporate jet?" Roberts agreed: "A good local or regional supermarket chain with management ownership will be better run than the XYZ national chain that is publicly owned. If you start two chains up with similar resources, one owned by management who cares, and one owned by a large public company, the former will beat the pants off the latter every time." The incentives KKR offered to executives at their companies meant that, if the companies performed well, the executives would become fabulously rich. Don Kelly, who was brought in as CEO at Beatrice, one of KKR's companies, acquired shares for $5 million that would later be worth $166 million.[23]

Rule number one at KKR's companies was to cut costs, sometimes ruthlessly. Kravis believed that too many companies in corporate America had become weighed down by bloat and bureaucracy. "Companies build up layers and layers of fat," Kravis said. Private equity allowed them to shed that fat, to free themselves from "the paralyzing clutches of hidebound corporate bureaucracies." Two examples demonstrate how this process worked in practice. In February 1987, KKR announced that it was buying a glass bottle company called Owens-Illinois. A month later, in March, the company fired five hundred employees at its Toledo headquarters. It would also sell its two Gulfstream G-1 executive jets. Overall, corporate department spending dropped from $32.4 million in 1986 to $13 million in 1990. "We don't have assistants to assistants anymore," the chairman of Owens-Illinois said a year later. "In fact, we don't have assistants."[24]

KKR took a similar approach with Safeway, a grocery store chain that the firm bought in 1986. Again, steep cuts followed shortly after the acquisition. Within four years, Safeway had shed sixty-three thousand workers, through either direct layoffs or sales of underperforming stores. Before the buyout, the company's motto had been "Safeway Offers Security." After it, the company's new corporate statement, displayed prominently on a plaque in the lobby, touted "Targeted Returns on Current Investment." The cultural shift may have been jarring, but, to KKR, it was simply a needed corrective. "There was a complete layer of staff to get rid of," Kravis said of Safeway. "We gave them the courage and the discipline to do what needed to be done," Roberts reiterated. "When you clear away the brush, you release the growth potential of the remaining trees." Sure enough, profits increased. In all, KKR made back more than fifty times its initial investment when it sold off its remaining stake in Safeway thirteen years later.[25]

With all these ingredients in place, KKR unleashed a force never before seen in the history of capitalism. The returns on private equity were impossible to deny. The lowest average annual return on KKR's first five funds was 25 percent. The highest was 40 percent. Investors clamored to get in, and KKR kept growing. In 1987, it raised its biggest fund yet—a gargantuan $5.6 billion. Soon, other private equity firms were opening up too. An early rival, Forstmann Little & Co., opened in 1978 and raised a $2.7 billion fund. In 1985, Stephen Schwarzman, the young investment banker who had been so impressed by KKR's Houdaille deal, founded Blackstone. Even traditional investment banks like Morgan Stanley and Merrill Lynch had started doing leveraged buyouts. Leveraged buyout activity swept across corporate America, rising exponentially throughout the 1980s—from a total value of $3.1 billion in 1980 to $35.6 billion in 1987. Once, KKR had been a big fish in a small pond. Now, it found itself in an ocean.[26]

It was a remarkable story. Three friends opened a company in 1976 with $120,000 of personal savings. By the end of the 1980s, they had completed nearly $60 billion in deals, buying companies like Safeway, Duracell, Motel 6, Avis, and Tropicana. All three became enormously wealthy as a result. In 1986, *Forbes*, in its listing of the richest people in America, estimated that Kohlberg, Kravis, and Roberts each had a net worth of $180 million. Two years later, in 1988, their net wealth had nearly doubled to $330 million each. Success affected Kohlberg, Kravis, and Roberts differently, though. Kohlberg and Roberts maintained a relatively low profile in their public lives, rarely flaunting their wealth. One friend said of Kohlberg, "Getting Jerry to go out to a cocktail party is a major event." Kravis took the opposite approach. He bought an apartment on Park Avenue for $5.5 million and decorated it with Renoirs and French antiques. In the dining room, he placed a ten-foot-tall John Singer Sargent portrait of the Sixth Marquess of Londonderry at the coronation of Edward VII. In 1985, he married former model and fashion designer Carolyne Roehm, and the two became fixtures in New York's social circles. They hosted a private party at the Metropolitan Museum, with a recital by famous violinist Midori, a dinner of rabbit pie, and an exclusive tour of the new Degas exhibit. They held Christmas parties that were, in Roehm's words, "inspired by Dickensian themes." In an interview with *Esquire*, Roehm described their social lives: "Here we all were, and I looked around, and all the women were very attractive, and they all had successful husbands, and I was listening to the wonderful band music and looking at this incredible environment that [the host] and her decorator had created, and I thought, 'We are truly lucky.'"[27]

THE EXTRAORDINARY SUCCESS OF THE KKR MODEL OF CAPITALISM swept through the corporate world like a tsunami, with more and more companies succumbing to the deluge of corporate raiders. But as private equity worked its way through boardrooms across the nation, a mounting chorus of critics emerged. These critics raised concerns about the private equity revolution and its effects on corporations, workers, and society. Some of the harshest criticism came from within the ranks of private equity itself.

Workers complained first. Employees of companies KKR bought often found themselves out of work soon afterward or, if lucky enough to keep their jobs, suddenly found them crushing, if not unbearable. The end was often abrupt and devastating. In a Pulitzer Prize–winning *Wall Street Journal* investigation, reporter Susan Faludi explored the terrible human costs of KKR's takeover of Safeway. She told the story of James White, a Safeway trucker who had worked at the company for thirty years and lost his job after the takeover. He killed himself on the anniversary of his firing. She told the story of Robert Markell, who had worked in Safeway's Oakland office for twenty-eight years and also lost his job after the buyout. When he walked into the office one Monday morning, his boss informed him, with no advance notice, that "because of the takeover by KKR, [he was] no longer employed at Safeway" but that the company would pay him through the end of the week. Of those who kept their jobs, many complained that those jobs had changed, that they were treated no longer like human beings but rather as interchangeable and disposable parts. After KKR bought Owens-Illinois, one worker told the local *Toledo Blade* newspaper that morale at the company was at an all-time low. "I don't like O-I anymore," he said. "I don't feel proud of this place anymore." Observers worried that this kind of treatment of workers, grinding down their wages and employment numbers, might not be a viable way to run a company. It might work for a few years, but capitalism in that form was not sustainable.[28]

The government complained next. One concern was tax. To many observers, private equity firms appeared to be making an awful lot of profit simply from sending less money to Uncle Sam. Reducing tax payments had always been an essential part of KKR's playbook, and leveraged buyouts benefited from one enormous tax incentive at the very center of the US tax code: interest payments on debt were tax deductible, while dividend payments to shareholders were not. The differential treatment of equity and debt had long been a bête noire for tax scholars, who disliked its tendency to give companies strong reasons to load on debt rather than issue new shares. But KKR took full advantage of the quirk, along with other arcane provisions of the tax code. In the Houdaille deal, Kravis believed that he could halve Houdaille's tax burden simply by adding debt to the company; in fact, if they took advantage of a depreciation step-up maneuver that the accounting firm Deloitte had suggested, he might be able to pay no taxes at all. Safeway paid $122 million in taxes the year before its buyout; after the buyout, it *received* $11 million in tax refunds. RJR Nabisco, another acquisition, paid $893 million in tax the year before KKR bought it. In the year after, it paid only $60 million. Lower tax burdens were great for KKR and its investors, but government officials viewed them as a raw deal as tax revenue dried up.[29]

Another critique was that all this new debt that KKR was loading onto companies created a volatile economy in which companies were constantly teetering on the edge of bankruptcy as they raced to pay that debt off. When companies failed, the consequences reverberated throughout society, from workers to shareholders to local governments. Eaton Leonard, a fast-growing machine tool company that KKR bought in 1980, went bankrupt in 1986. EFB Trucking, another KKR company, was liquidated in 1985. Seaman Furniture, which KKR bought for $290 million in 1987, filed for bankruptcy in 1992. Other companies, such as Boren Clay and American Forest Products, had to have their debts restructured after struggling to meet them. Walter Industries, a home-building company that KKR had bought in 1987, filed for bankruptcy two years later, after victims of asbestos poisoning sued the company. Roberts explained the logic of his decision to his KKR colleagues in colorful terms. "Did you ever see the movie *Platoon?*" he said. "Well, there's this scene at the end where the captain's troops are being overrun in Laos. There's no way he can get them out. So he ends up calling an air strike on his own position, knowing that it will stop the enemy. Then at least he can get some of his men out. That's what we're doing. Tough times call for tough things." The government viewed the calculus differently. In 1984, SEC chairman John Shad put it as bluntly as he could: "The more leveraged takeovers and buyouts now, the more bankruptcies tomorrow."[30]

But it wasn't just government and workers who complained about private equity. Increasingly, private equity titans themselves spoke out about the abuses the industry had spawned. They worried that the outsized returns from this new type of financial engineering distorted capitalism. Too many of the country's brightest minds were devoting themselves to an industry that didn't create or invent or build—it simply rearranged. In 1988, Ted Forstmann, head of private equity firm Forstmann Little, wrote a bombshell article for the *Wall Street Journal* denouncing his own industry. In the article, titled "Corporate Finance: Leveraged to the Hilt," he wrote,

> Today's financial age has become a period of unbridled excess with accepted risk soaring out of proportion to possible reward. Every week, with ever-increasing levels of irresponsibility, many billions of dollars in American assets are being saddled with debt that has virtually no chance of being repaid. Most of this is happening for the short-term benefit of Wall Street's investment bankers, lawyers, leveraged buy-out firms and junk-bond dealers at the long-term expense of Main Street's employees, communities, companies and investors.

He compared the private equity industry's buyout kings to a herd of drunk drivers stumbling out of bars and into their vehicles on New Year's Eve. "You cannot tell who will hit whom, but you know it is dangerous." Kravis, for his part, responded that all the criticism aimed at KKR was misguided. "People say that R&D investment is cut back after an LBO to help pay interest, and that plants are closed, causing mass layoffs, and when subsidiaries are sold they disappear," he told *Fortune* magazine in an interview in 1989. "None of this is true. . . . We're not going to take the heart out of a corporation. People who produce things will stay. . . . Sure there are bad LBOs. But they are only hiccups in the business, the exceptions. Knock on wood, KKR hasn't had any like that."[31]

This wave of criticism hit KKR at a time when cracks had already begun to show within the firm itself. Kohlberg had first invented his "bootstrap" deal as a "friendly," or cooperative, transaction. He envisioned it as a win-win, a mechanism for helping founders of successful companies receive cash for retirement and allowing his investment bank a reasonable return for providing it. But by the mid-1980s, things had started to change within KKR. Kravis and Roberts wanted to chase bigger and bigger deals—in 1984, they completed the first leveraged buyout worth more than $1 billion. The firm grew as well, from three dealmakers in 1976, to eight in 1983, to fifteen in 1988. It was still a small shop, but it was no longer a business just between friends. And many of the younger, more ambitious dealmakers at the firm thought that Kohlberg's insistence on keeping buyouts "friendly" simply didn't make sense in the fast-paced buyout world of the mid-1980s. In their minds, Kohlberg didn't understand that the private equity world had changed. If KKR wanted to stay ahead, it needed to go hostile.

In a hostile takeover, a buyer seeks to acquire a target company *against* the wishes of the company's managers, such as its CEO and directors. Rather than negotiating an agreement with the leaders of the company, the buyer does an end around and takes its case directly to the shareholders. The tactic is controversial because it often devolves into aggressive attacks on the reputations and characters of the participants. The buyer criticizes the company's leaders as lazy and incompetent, and the leaders defend their records while simultaneously besmirching the buyer's. To win, the buyer must make its arguments with sufficient vigor and ferocity to convince the shareholders to accept the buyer's proposal over the objections of the incumbent management, which is often summarily dismissed after the acquisition is completed. Hostile takeovers were long considered a scandalous affair beneath the dignity of a reputable company, but by the 1980s, private equity firms were embracing the tactic.

Kravis and Roberts agreed with their younger colleagues that Kohlberg's misgivings about hostile takeovers were holding the firm back. It didn't help that, in 1984, Kohlberg suffered a blood clot in his lungs that nearly killed him; from that point forward, he suffered from problems associated with it, from headaches to fatigue. "Jerry was older and he never wanted to work as hard," Roberts later told an interviewer. "The reason Jerry was so negative was that he wasn't reading and understanding what was going on." Increasingly, Kravis and Roberts shunted Kohlberg aside on major decisions. When they told Kohlberg that they planned to launch a hostile tender offer for Beatrice, the twenty-sixth-largest company in the Fortune 500, Kohlberg objected, insisting that KKR stick with friendly deals. Kravis and Roberts ignored him, moving forward with the deal anyway.[32]

Professional tension inevitably led to personal tension. Kohlberg had always been reserved, preferring to spend his free time at home, playing tennis and reading novels and biographies. Kravis, on the other hand, lived in high society, attending galas and parties. Kohlberg thought this was too ostentatious. "It came between them to the point where Jerry couldn't stand to go to Henry's apartment on Park Avenue, there was so much wealth," a friend of Kohlberg's said in an interview. Things devolved quickly from there. One younger KKR partner described the messy conflict: "There were scenes when Jerry said, 'I founded this firm. You guys wouldn't be here without me.' None of us liked the way it worked out in the end." The final straw came in 1986, when Kohlberg learned that the firm had decided to award his son, Jim, who was an associate, a year-end bonus of just $500,000 rather than the $1 million handed out to other associates. Kohlberg was furious and quietly began to negotiate an exit. In 1987, he announced that he would leave the firm.[33]

KOHLBERG'S DEPARTURE MARKED THE END OF AN ERA FOR KKR. The elder statesman was gone. The firm was now firmly in the hands of Kravis and Roberts, who were younger, more ambitious, and more willing to take risks. Within two years, they had launched KKR's boldest, most expensive buyout ever, one that would make or break the firm.

In many ways, KKR's takeover of RJR Nabisco should have been a showcase for all that private equity had to offer the world of corporations. RJR Nabisco was a giant conglomerate that combined two businesses that seemed directly in conflict with one another. On one side of the business was Reynolds, a tobacco company that made Camel cigarettes and other popular tobacco products. On the other side of the business stood Nabisco, a wholesome biscuit company that had invented the Fig Newton, the saltine, and Ritz crackers. One observer characterized the combination as "mom and apple pie meet the skull and crossbones." Nabisco's corporate culture also seemed rife with excess and waste. Nabisco's CEO, Ross Johnson, reveled in spending the company's money on lavish projects: he had ten corporate jets, two personal maids paid for by the company, and $30,000 worth of eighteenth-century Chinese porcelain lining his office. He gave out $1,500 Gucci watches to executives and sponsored over-the-top events filled with celebrities at the Dinah Shore LPGA golf tournament. Executives enjoyed free country club memberships and company cars. Twice a day, a candy cart was wheeled around the headquarters delivering bonbons to the managers. As Johnson said,

"A few million dollars are lost in the sands of time." Nabisco seemed like the perfect example of KKR's theory that corporate America had become lazy and inefficient.[34]

But, somehow, somewhere, it all went wrong. Over the several months of hard-nosed and high-stakes negotiations between KKR and Nabisco's board, ultimately ending with KKR agreeing to buy Nabisco for $25 billion, the story became not so much about the disciplining effects of incentives as about overpowering and insatiable greed on the part of nearly everyone involved in the private equity business. As the details of the transaction leaked out, newspapers gleefully reported the eye-popping numbers. Massive amounts of severance pay were handed out to the top executives at Nabisco simply for leaving the company. After the deal closed in February 1989, Johnson resigned with a $53 million golden parachute. Edward Horrigan, head of the tobacco division of RJR Nabisco, received $45.7 million. Enormous fees were paid to the advisors and participants in the deal as well: the investment banks working for KKR made at least $400 million in fees, which by one estimate amounted to roughly $48,000 an hour for the work each banker put in. KKR itself received a $75 million transaction fee, in addition to its usual management fee and future carried interest. To celebrate the acquisition, KKR threw a closing dinner in the Pierre Hotel's grand ballroom with four hundred investment bankers, lawyers, and colleagues, where they dined on lobster, veal, and a three-foot-high cake decorated with Nabisco products, accompanied by Dom Perignon.[35]

The most damaging moment, among many, came when Johnson gave a long interview to *TIME*. The transcript read like a long list of things that CEOs should never say. When the *TIME* reporter asked Johnson for his opinion of the golden parachutes given to executives like himself, he replied, "My job is to negotiate the best deal that I can for my people," before admitting that in seven or eight years, he stood to make $100 million. Asked if anyone deserved that much money, Johnson said, "If he is an owner, he does. It's hard to answer.

Actually, it's kind of Monopoly money. . . . Making $100 million was
not my motive by any stretch of the imagination." Asked whether the
deal would be hard on employees, he replied, "While you are going
through the transition period it is. If you take 120,000 RJR Nabisco
people, yes, there will be some dislocation. But the people that I have,
particularly the Atlanta people, have very portable types of professions:
accountants, lawyers, secretaries. It isn't that I would be putting them
on the breadline. We have excellent severance arrangements." Sure
enough, after the deal closed, the job losses started. The number of
employees at RJR Nabisco headquarters was slashed from 400 to 150.
The tobacco division fired an additional 1,525 workers.[36]

Nearly everyone who looked at the deal was astounded by its bra-
zenness. *Business Week* ran a cover story on the transaction with the
title "The Debt Binge: Have Takeovers Gone Too Far?" The local
Atlanta Constitution newspaper ran a series of articles on the deal, as
well as a cartoon that showed a group of scared people standing in a ce-
real bowl on a Shredded Wheat box renamed "RJR Nabisco Shredded
Workers." "List price: 25 billion dollars," the cartoon's caption read.
Jim Hightower, the head of Texas's agriculture department, wrote a
New York Times op-ed pointing out that KKR paid $25 billion for a
tobacco and baking company, despite knowing next to nothing about
tobacco or baking. Kravis and Roberts, Hightower wrote, "couldn't
make a biscuit if someone kneaded the dough." There was more than
a little truth in this: Kravis himself admitted that he couldn't keep
track of all the products that Nabisco made.[37]

The Nabisco takeover turned KKR into a household name. It was
KKR's only deal in 1989, and yet it accounted for two-fifths of the
combined value of the nation's 371 leveraged buyouts that year. With
the addition of RJR to its portfolio, KKR now controlled $59 billion
in corporate assets, spread out across thirty-five companies—at a time
when the firm had just six general partners, eleven associates, and a
total staff of forty-seven. The only corporations that were larger were
General Motors, Ford, Exxon, and IBM, each of which had thousands

of employees. But the deal also crystallized all the criticisms of private equity that had been swirling around the industry for years—the excessive pay, the harm to workers and communities, the dangers of excessive debt. In the wake of the deal, scholars and policymakers began calling for new regulations to combat the scourge of leveraged buyouts. Robert Reich, a professor at the John F. Kennedy School of Government at Harvard, wrote an article arguing that America was paying a steep price for leveraged buyouts. "Investment bankers no longer think of themselves as working for the corporations with which they do business," he wrote. "These days, corporations seem to exist for the investment bankers." A quarter century before, the titans of American industry had been chief executive officers of large industrial companies. Today, they were investment bankers and private equity partners. Reich pointed out that the fees paid to bankers and lawyers on the Nabisco deal exceeded the total amount the United States had spent researching a cure for AIDS. He concluded, "Rarely have so few earned so much for doing so little. Never have so few exercised such power over how the slices of the American pie are rearranged."[38]

The wave of criticism led to a burst of interest in reforming private equity. In the following years, Congress held a series of hearings with buyout executives to interrogate them about their practices. Various reform proposals were bandied about, from abolishing tax deductions on interest from junk bonds to creating tax deductions for dividend payments. But all were shot down. The only effective brake on private equity's acceleration were two unrelated developments at the turn of the decade. The first was a rise in interest rates in the wider economy. Higher interest rates made debt more expensive, thereby making it harder for private equity firms like KKR to load their portfolio companies with bonds. The second development came when Michael Milken, the undisputed champion of junk bonds, was indicted for conspiracy and fraud in connection with his securities work. His investment bank, Drexel Burnham Lambert, pleaded guilty to mail and securities fraud and would eventually go bankrupt. Milken ultimately spent just twenty-two months in jail. President Donald Trump pardoned him in 2020. But Drexel Burnham's disappearance from the scene led to a hiccup in the junk bond markets that, at least for a while, slowed private equity's buyout spree.

Today, however, private equity has returned with a vengeance. Other private equity shops, like Blackstone, emerged and grew even bigger than KKR; one, Bain Capital, gained a measure of fame when a former executive, Mitt Romney, was named the Republican candidate for the presidency in 2012. The biggest change to KKR came in 2010, when the firm, for thirty years the raider of the lost public company, listed its stock on the New York Stock Exchange. It certainly seemed ironic: a company formed on the idea that the joint stock corporation had become too fat and lazy had become a joint stock corporation itself. But to Kravis, Roberts, and the other dealmakers at KKR, it made perfect sense. They had always been astute readers of the financial tea leaves, and the tea leaves told them to sell. By that point, KKR's portfolio had grown to $55 billion, a far cry from the $120,000 the founding trio had invested way back in 1976. Kravis and Roberts' stake in the company was estimated to be worth $1.65 billion. Disclosures that KKR made in connection with the listing put on stark display just how dependent the private equity model had become on fees rather than profits. In 2009, the firm paid Kravis and Roberts each $22 million. Only $500,000 of that came from carried interest, which is to say the profits from actually running the portfolio companies. Two of KKR's biggest holdings at the time were Toys "R" Us, the beloved toy store, and TXU Energy, a utility company providing electricity to the state of Texas. By 2017, both had gone bankrupt. Today, Forbes estimates Kravis's net worth to be $6.7 billion; George Roberts's is $6.9 billion.[39]

IN MAY 1987, THE MONTH OF KOHLBERG'S RETIREMENT, KKR held its annual conference with investors. The event resembled a gala more than it did a business meeting, with lavish surroundings and wealthy guests flying in from across the country. Over one hundred of KKR's largest investors attended, showing up at the glitzy Helmsley Palace Hotel on Madison Avenue in New York. They ascended the grand stairway of polished marble into the hotel's famous Versailles Ballroom, where they admired the gold and silver detailing, the giant mirrors, and the crystal chandeliers overhead.

Later on in the evening, Kohlberg, ever statesmanlike, strode to the podium to address his associates. It was a bittersweet moment for him. He was retiring from the company that he had founded a decade before. He took the moment to reminisce about what the firm meant, to himself and to the world.

Twenty years ago, I had a small dream that companies could be bought, and investments made, in undervalued businesses where we, as financiers, would put our money, time, and effort right alongside management. We would do everything in our power to ensure that our investment *and theirs* turned out well. We would *both* risk a great deal—capital and reputation.

I chose to mention this today because all around us there is a breakdown of these values—in business and government. It is not merely the difference between insider trading and legitimate arbitrage. . . . It is not just refusing a suitcase of cash, it is not just the overweening, overpowering greed that pervades our business life. It is the fact that we are not willing to sacrifice for the ethics and values we profess. For an ethic is not an ethic, and a value not a value, without some sacrifice to it. *Something given up, something not taken, something not gained*. We do it in exchange for a greater good, for something worth more than just money and power and position. The great paradox of this philosophy is that in the end it brings one greater gain than any other philosophy.

"We all must insist on a resurgence of these values," Kohlberg concluded. "Because if we do not, the great luck, hard work, intelligence, and decency that we have all brought to these successful investments will wither and decay. We must all insist on ethical behavior or we will kill the golden goose."[40]

And with that, Kohlberg left the stage.

It was a shocking speech, and one that took Kravis and Roberts, who had not known what Kohlberg planned to say, by surprise. The thinly veiled attack on Kravis and Roberts—on KKR itself—was hard to miss. It seemed like a breach of civility. Kravis and Roberts had done their best to hide the deep fracture in their relationship, but Kohlberg put it on display for all to see. It was clear that the speech stung.

Missing from Kohlberg's speech, however, were his own parting machinations. Before stepping down, he had negotiated hard with Kravis and Roberts on the terms of his retirement. Two months earlier, they had reached a settlement. The severance agreement gave Kohlberg the right to keep his shares in current KKR portfolio companies and to invest in future deals for the next nine years, as well as a few additional "perks," all paid for by KKR. These included reimbursement for a personal secretary and a driver. KKR also agreed to buy him a new Lincoln Town Car every year.[41]

※ ※ ※

THE RISE OF private equity marked a new era in the history of the corporation. By the 1970s, many believed that corporations had reached their final form: massive multinational companies with shares listed on national stock exchanges, a class of professional managers running them, and mass-produced goods and services flowing out their doors. The joint stock company seemed like an unstoppable force. But Kohlberg, Kravis, and Roberts saw something else. They saw an industry filled with bloated companies run by overpaid or incompetent CEOs. And they invented what they believed to be an antidote: the hostile takeover. They believed that money could be made by acquiring poorly run companies, making them more efficient, and then reselling them a few years later.

KKR and its private equity brethren bought dozens of companies over the next two decades. The sharp-elbowed tactics of corporate raiders made them the scourge of Wall Street, but they also forced big companies to adapt to a new world of shareholder empowerment—particularly after KKR successfully took over RJR Nabisco, a mainstay of corporate America. Leveraged buyouts proved to be unimaginably profitable. The new era of hypercapitalism, fueled by ever more sophisticated financial engineering, transformed the very nature of stock markets and spawned the modern M&A industry.

But the Age of the Raider also generated fear. The slash-and-burn strategies of private equity sometimes created short-term profits at the cost of long-term destruction. The parade of bankruptcies, layoffs, and employee complaints that followed many buyouts only strengthened these misgivings, including among some private equity managers themselves. For years, private equity raiders had been banging on the gates of corporate America. Now they had the keys to the kingdom, and they weren't entirely sure what to do with them.

The Age of the Raider centered on Wall Street and the world of finance. But the next great evolution in the corporation came from Silicon Valley, a place where computers and code mattered more than capital and carry.

eight

THE START-UP

T HERE ARE 7.8 BILLION PEOPLE ON EARTH; 3.3 BILLION OF
them are on Facebook.

No corporation in the history of the world has ever come anywhere
close to the sheer size and scope of Facebook (or Meta, as it has now
rebranded itself). Not Standard Oil. Not the East India Company. Not
the Medici Bank. Simply put, Facebook is unprecedented. In the evolution of the idea of the corporation, Facebook represents the apex
predator. It simply has no rivals. Users spend an average of fifty minutes a day using its services. Compare that with the time they spend
doing other things in their lives. Average Americans spend nineteen
minutes a day exercising and playing sports. They spend sixteen minutes reading. They spend nineteen minutes "relaxing and thinking."
And they spend *fifty minutes* on Facebook. The only leisure activity
that outranks Facebook scrolling is watching television (the average
American spends two hours and forty-nine minutes a day in front of
the tube).[1]

For a corporation that represents the culmination of hundreds of years of creative destruction, Facebook has a surprisingly friendly face. For many of its employees, the day begins with a free pickup by one of the company's luxury vans that shuttle back and forth between San Francisco and Facebook's Menlo Park headquarters or perhaps with a trip on one of the company's ferries sailing across San Francisco Bay. When employees arrive at Facebook's offices, they enter a realm that can only be described as a Disneyland for adults—which is no coincidence, given that the company brought in Disney consultants to help design the area. The "campus," as it is called, in a nod to its collegiate atmosphere, sprawls over fifty-seven meticulously manicured acres overlooking San Francisco Bay. Everywhere one looks, one finds trimmed lawns, lush trees, and meandering walkways. Free-to-use bikes are parked at racks peppered around the campus. Touches of whimsy abound: a yellow brick road à la *The Wizard of Oz* crosses one walkway, and alongside it stands Dorothy's house, with the Wicked Witch of the East and her ruby slippers squashed underneath it. Arriving in the central plaza, employees can sit at outdoor tables shaded by umbrellas and eat at gourmet restaurants, all of them free (with the exception of a few local options). If in the mood for Asian food, they can go to the noodle bar. If BBQ fits the bill, there is a BBQ shack. Those with a sweet tooth can visit the patisserie, piled high with muffins, cakes, cookies, and ice cream. Overhead, employees can marvel at the enormous jumbotron screen and a sign announcing that Facebook is "The Hacker Company." If employees want exercise, they can go to the gym, attend fitness classes, play basketball, or take lessons at the climbing wall. They can visit the video game arcade, or the music room, or the company barber shop. For a more mindful option, they can take in a mini forest of redwood trees planted in the middle of a plaza or stroll through the nine-acre rooftop park. Inside, the luxury continues. Bright colors and fun themes abound, with a bevy of Instagrammable walls, like the antigravity room, whose office chairs and computers are glued to the side walls. In the open-space work areas, expensive Aeron office chairs line the desks, and employees sit behind enormous screens wearing company-provided noise-canceling headphones.

Facebook's headquarters are a visceral reminder of the enormous societal transformation that the technology industry in general and Silicon Valley in particular have wrought over the last two decades. A website started by a computer whiz operating out of a Harvard College dorm room turned, almost overnight, into an $800 billion company, creating instant millionaires out of its early contributors. Mark Zuckerberg himself is worth an estimated $76 billion. The golden age of start-up culture dawned with Facebook.

And somehow, the most dominant corporation of the millennium gives away its most valuable product for free.

It's an unlikely story, but it's also an emblematic one. Facebook is no longer unique in the universe of corporations. Scores of companies today seek to model themselves on its basic template. We are witnessing a seismic shift in the structure of the corporation, and no one knows how the plates will settle.

※ ※ ※

THE START-UP IS a peculiar kind of corporation. It has a friendly face. A funny name. A quirky culture. Maybe a foosball table in its headquarters. In short, it's the cute and cuddly version of capitalism, the one that seems fun and relatable and, most importantly, cool.

Of course, start-ups have existed for as long as corporations have existed. Every corporation has to start somewhere. Otherwise, it wouldn't exist at all. In a way, then, the first start-up was the Roman company that offered to supply Scipio's army in Spain during the Second Punic War. It was an auspicious beginning for team incipient.

But when most people use the term *start-up*, they don't mean just any recently created corporation. Instead, they are describing a particular kind of corporation. Not every corporation fits the bill. Start-ups, unlike "regular" companies, are about technology. They are about growth. They are about the internet, and mobile phones, and platforms, and "sharing." They are overwhelmingly based in Silicon Valley.

Consider some of the most influential start-ups founded since the bursting of the dot-com bubble in 2000. Facebook. Airbnb. Instagram. Snapchat. Twitter. Uber. They all share a similar model. They take the internet, add some proprietary technology, and then let users take control: to rent their houses, to share their photos, to start conversations, to give rides. They are platforms. They aim to grow fast and dominate their markets, typically by acquiring users through low prices and gaining a reputation as the next "it" app, the one that is cool and pretty *and* useful. The typical employee is young and computer savvy and perhaps not so socially adept. The whole affair is likely being subsidized by a venture capital firm or two.

I am painting with broad strokes, but you get the picture. Start-ups are to corporations what meerkats are to African wildlife: a little smaller, a little more fun, and definitely not threatening or predatory like a lion.[2]

The only problem is that every meerkat, deep in his heart, wishes he were a lion.

The great promise of start-ups has always been that technology has an enormous capacity to improve human life, and the only thing holding us back is finding someone with the courage, the creativity, and, let's say it, the hubris to try it out. Hotels cost too much? Let's create a home-rental site. Taxis are too inconvenient? Let's create a ride-sharing site. Humans get lonely? Let's create a social network. Start-ups are here to give the gift of technology to the rest of us.

But of course, start-ups are not entirely altruistic. They seek to profit from the revolutions they bequeath to the world. As venture capital firms have found out, successful start-ups can be very, very profitable. It is easy to understand why. Most aim to become the dominant platform for whatever industry they happen to be operating in, be it real estate or transportation or media. The value of start-ups lies in their ability to create networks—of friends, coworkers, homeowners, drivers—and networks tend to be self-reinforcing. If all of your friends are using one social media site, you will likely use it too. If all the drivers are on one ride-hailing site, you will likely use it too. Growth begets growth. And growth eventually leads to profits, at least in theory.

The Age of the Start-Up began in earnest in the early 2000s, in the wake of the bursting dot-com bubble. The start-up was new and exciting and promised a better, more socially responsible corporation. But the question was always "At what cost?" At what cost did start-ups achieve their exponential growth? At what cost did start-ups craft dominant platforms? At what cost did start-ups, for the first time, allow billions of users around the world to connect seamlessly with each other? At what cost did venture capitalists provide capital to speculative new companies? Given the choice, would a meerkat stay a meerkat, or would it transform into a lion?

THE IDEA THAT A NINETEEN-YEAR-OLD COLLEGE STUDENT COULD found a billion-dollar company may not sound strange to readers today. We are used to seeing Silicon Valley start-ups turn into billion-dollar unicorns. The start-up ethos favors the young and the geeky. To many of us, it seems completely natural that anyone with a great idea and a talent with computers can create something world-changing. But this is certainly a novelty in the sweep of corporate history. Giovanni di Bicci de' Medici was thirty-seven when he founded the Medici Bank. Henry Ford was forty when he founded his Ford Motor Company. Jerome Kohlberg was fifty when he started KKR, and his comparatively baby-faced partners, Henry Kravis and George Roberts, were both a fully grown thirty-two. All of them had extensive experience in their industries before deciding to launch their ventures. Mark Zuckerberg, on the other hand, was a college sophomore at Harvard, taking classes in psychology and Roman art, shuffling around campus in his Adidas slides, and attending fraternity parties on the weekends. But by the time Zuckerberg turned twenty, his company, Facebook, had a million users. Depending on your perspective about the merits of youth, this may sound either refreshing or terrifying.

But the technology industry, particularly in the early 2000s, was a land of low barriers to entry. Anyone with a computer and an internet connection could start a website, and most users never looked to see whether the founder was of a respectable age. In fact, it still wasn't entirely clear what people would use the internet for. Most were still calling it the "World Wide Web." Would it be a repository of information? Would it be a means for communicating with one another? Would it be about commerce? Was it just a way to pirate free music? At the end of the 1990s, a slew of companies had soared to great heights on bets about what the future of the internet would look like, but most of them came crashing down when the dot-com bubble burst in 2000. So the internet question was still very much up in the air.

For Mark Zuckerberg, a sophomore living in Kirkland House at Harvard College, it was clear what the internet's killer application was: fun. Zuckerberg had grown up loving computers. He received his first one in sixth grade, and he quickly became obsessed with video games, particularly the world-domination game *Civilization*, which he played well into adulthood. But he wasn't content to simply play the games—he also wanted to create them, to customize them, to shape them in his own image. "I just liked making things," he told an interviewer. "Then I figured out I could make more things if I learned to program." In high school, he bought himself an introductory text on programming and took to writing computer code regularly when he was home from school. In the ninth grade, he wrote a program based on the world-domination board game Risk—his version centered on the Roman Empire. The player's opponent was Julius Caesar. "He was good, and I was never able to win," Zuckerberg said of his computer opponent in the game. It was a lesson, perhaps, in the fallibility of the human mind and the power of the artificial one—Zuckerberg had built something he himself couldn't understand, that he couldn't conquer, that, at heart, was a mystery to him.[3]

By the end of high school, Zuckerberg had emerged as a talented programmer. Like all ambitious teenagers in the age of the college admissions essay, he had a smattering of other interests. At Phillips Exeter, the elite private school he had attended since junior year, he fenced and studied the classics, learning Latin and Greek. But he spent most of his free time in front of his laptop. For his senior year project, he and a friend created a program called Synapse that kept track of the songs users played on their computers and then created playlists based on their preferences. Released in September 2002, the program made something of a splash in the online music world, even earning a mention from *Slashdot*, an early online tech publication with a cultlike following in the industry. After the *Slashdot* article came out, Zuckerberg received calls from some of the major corporations operating in the music space, from WinAmp to Microsoft. One of them purportedly offered $2 million for the program. But Zuckerberg turned them all down. "We wanted to go to college, so we said no," Zuckerberg told the Harvard student newspaper, the *Harvard Crimson*. Another thing irked him about the idea of selling his program to a large corporation. A corporation would seek to exploit his creation for profit. But that had never been his intention in creating it. "It's important to us that people are able to use the software for free," he said. "Software belongs to everyone."[4]

In the fall of 2002, after graduating from Phillips Exeter, Zuckerberg enrolled at Harvard. Studying at the Ivy League college was a momentous but short-lived event in Zuckerberg's life. He stayed there for a mere two years, and, by all accounts, his time was marked by social awkwardness and loads of skipped classes. Reading through early interviews and articles about Zuckerberg, a single feature appears with almost comical frequency. At some point, after being asked a question, Zuckerberg would simply stare back at the interviewer, not answering, for minutes at a time. One author, Steven Levy, referred to these episodes as "trancelike silences." Another described the look as an "intense stare that bordered on the psychopathic." Another named it "the eye of Sauron." "He will sit back and stare at people," one early coworker said. Despite the awkwardness, though, by his sophomore year, Zuckerberg had become something of a celebrity on campus due to a series of popular but controversial programs he launched at the university. All these programs had one thing in common: they took advantage of what was, for many of the eighteen-year-olds finding themselves away from home for the first time, a new experience: speedy internet and the leisure time to explore it. And it turned out that what they really liked to do with that time was look at what their friends (and, more importantly, their crushes) were doing.[5]

Zuckerberg's first program was called CourseMatch. Curious to find out what classes his friends were taking, Zuckerberg built a website that allowed students to log the courses they had registered for. Everyone who created an account could also see the courses that other students were enrolled in. The website proved a hit. "The thing that just struck me from the beginning," Zuckerberg said of his program, "is people would just spend hours clicking through. 'Here are the courses that people are taking, and, wow, isn't it interesting that this person is interested in these things?' It was just text, right? There was nothing that was super interesting there, but that just struck me as people have this deep thirst to understand what's going on with those around them." The program was so popular that it ended up breaking his laptop, which he had used to host the website.[6]

Zuckerberg's next effort would prove even more popular but also cause him significantly more trouble than just a busted laptop. Face-Mash was an unabashed copy of an already existing website called "Hot or Not," where users could look at pictures of people (primarily women) and vote on how attractive they were. Zuckerberg took this idea and transplanted it onto the Harvard campus, with predictably combustible results. He also, somewhat unfortunately for himself, blogged about it as he was writing the program, giving us a real-time view into his mind-set.

On the evening of October 28, 2003, in the middle of the fall semester of his sophomore year, Zuckerberg began blogging: " — is a bitch. I need to think of something to make to take my mind off her. I need to think of something to occupy my mind. Easy enough, now I just need an idea." At 8:13 p.m., he had found his idea: "I'm a little intoxicated, not gonna lie. So what if it's not even 10 p.m. and it's a Tuesday night? What? The Kirkland facebook is open on my desktop and some of these people have pretty horrendous facebook pics," he wrote, referring to the hardcopy directory that Harvard provided students and that contained pictures of his classmates. "I almost want to put some of these faces next to pictures of farm animals and have people vote on which is more attractive. It's not such a great idea and probably not even funny, but Billy comes up with the idea of comparing two people from the facebook, and only sometimes putting a farm animal in there. Good call Mr. Olson! I think he's onto something." An hour and a half later, he started working out the mechanics of how to create the site. Step by step, he proceeded to hack into the websites of each of Harvard's "houses," or dorms, and download students' pictures from them. He then put them on FaceMash, where people could see two photos and vote on who was more attractive. Zuckerberg understood that what he was doing was problematic, both legally and morally, but he proceeded anyway. "Perhaps Harvard will squelch it for legal reasons without realizing its value as a venture that could possibly be expanded to other schools (maybe even ones with good-looking people . . .). But one thing is certain, and it's that I'm a jerk for making this site. Oh well. Someone had to do it eventually." In the early hours of the morning, Facemash.com went live. Visitors to the site were met with the message "Were we let in for our looks? No. Will we be judged on them? Yes." Zuckerberg sent the link to a few friends and went to bed.

By the time Zuckerberg woke up, FaceMash had taken on a life of its own. It was an even greater sensation than CourseMatch: in just a day, 450 people had visited the site and voted a total of twenty-two thousand times. The average visitor, in other words, voted on fifty separate matchups comparing the attractiveness of their classmates. The sudden surge of internet use coming from Zuckerberg's dorm, Kirkland House, was so extreme that Harvard's information technology team scrambled to find the cause. Eventually, they simply shut down the internet for the entire dorm. Meanwhile, an uproar had started among several Harvard student groups about the demeaning nature of the site. The female president of Fuerza Latina, a Latin American student group, sent out an email to the group LISTSERV letting her members know about it: "I heard from a friend and I was kind of outraged. I thought people should be aware." The Association of Black Harvard Women complained as well.[7]

Zuckerberg, apparently chastised, shut the site down within a day of opening it up. The Harvard administration, though, decided to launch an investigation anyway and eventually accused him of breaching security by hacking into house websites, violating copyrights as well as individual privacy. Zuckerberg, facing potential expulsion from Harvard, appeared before the school's administrative board to defend himself and was placed on disciplinary probation. Afterward, Zuckerberg explained his actions to the student newspaper, the *Crimson*: "I understood that some parts were still a little sketchy and I wanted some more time to think about whether or not this was really appropriate to release to the Harvard community." After further reflection, he concluded that it was not. "Issues about violating people's privacy don't seem to be surmountable," he said. "I'm not willing to risk insulting anyone." And yet, Zuckerberg did learn one thing from his experience with FaceMash. People were more voyeuristic than he had thought.[8]

Zuckerberg would put that lesson to the test in his next project: Facebook.

WHEN FACEBOOK WAS LAUNCHED IN EARLY 2004, THE IDEA OF A "social network," where people could meet, connect, and share with friends online, was already in the air, culturally speaking. Other social media sites existed and were in widespread use. Friendster had launched nearly a year before, in March 2003, and counted more than three million users, who could create free profiles, describe their interests, list their relationship status, and add friends—all things that Facebook would go on to do. MySpace also attracted a wide variety of users, particularly artists and musicians, who used the site's customization features to attract fans. A week after launching Facebook, Zuckerberg told the *Crimson* that he had modeled Facebook on Friendster.

Another source of inspiration came from Harvard itself. As mentioned earlier, the university had long had a printed "face book," containing pictures of all Harvard's students, that was given to students every year. Many of these pictures were also available online, but, as Zuckerberg discovered when he tried to access them for his FaceMash site, they tended to be hidden behind password-protected house sites. The *Harvard Crimson* wrote an editorial arguing that the university should make this information more available to the student body. "The potential benefits of a comprehensive, campus-wide online facebook are plenty," the editors wrote. "Whether one is simply scoping an elusive classmate, or curious of a friend's first-year registration day photo—we all know the lure of that peculiar form of entertainment—a campus-wide facebook will facilitate the Harvard community with the names and basics of their peers, without worry of opening the site to unsolicited strangers." In a deposition years later, Zuckerberg cited the editorial as his real inspiration for Facebook. "I basically took that article that they wrote and made a site with those exact privacy controls, and that was Facebook," he said.[9]

But there was another, more insidious inspiration for Facebook. In November 2003, just three months before Facebook was launched, Zuckerberg met with two Harvard rowers to discuss a business proposition. The Winklevoss twins, Cameron and Tyler, held positions at the very top of Harvard's social pecking order, and not just because they stood an identical six feet, five inches tall. Both were members of the Porcellian Club, the secret society known to be the most elite of Harvard's already elite "final clubs." Both rowed in the varsity boat of Harvard's powerhouse heavyweight crew team, and, by all measures, they were the most talented of a talented team that went by the nickname "the God Squad" and swept all of collegiate rowing's most prized awards. They would later row for Oxford in the annual race against Cambridge on the Thames in London. In their junior year, they had begun working on a website that would serve as part social network, part dating site for the Harvard student body. But the Winklevoss twins did not have the coding knowledge necessary to make their site a reality, and so, in the fall of 2003, they turned to Zuckerberg. Just what was discussed during their November meeting is unclear, but email exchanges from the time suggest that they reached a handshake agreement for Zuckerberg to help revise the site's code. None of the parties thought to incorporate the arrangement into a formal written contract.

In the ensuing weeks, the Winklevoss twins grew increasingly frustrated with Zuckerberg's delay in finishing the Harvard Connection project. Zuckerberg gave various excuses for not doing the work, from catching up on homework to cramming for exams to losing his laptop charger. But the more important, and undisclosed, reason appears to have been that he had already started working on his Facebook site. In December 2003, just a week after meeting with the Winklevoss brothers, he texted friend and fellow Harvard student Eduardo Saverin about Harvard Connection. "Check this site out," he wrote, attaching the Harvard Connection address. "Someone is already trying to make a dating site. But they made a mistake haha. They asked me to make it for them. So I'm like delaying it so it won't be ready until after the facebook thing comes out." When Zuckerberg eventually launched Facebook, the Winklevoss brothers cried foul. At first, they reported him to Harvard's president, Larry Summers, alleging that he had violated the student honor code. Zuckerberg wrote a letter defending himself, saying, "Frankly, I'm kind of appalled that they're threatening me after the work I've done for them free of charge. I try to shrug it off as a minor annoyance that whenever I do something successful, every capitalist out there wants a piece of the action." Summers concluded that he would have nothing to do with the dispute. Next, the Winklevoss brothers sued Zuckerberg in a Massachusetts federal court for breach of contract, among other purported violations. Ultimately, the dispute was settled for $65 million—an amount that was paid partially in Facebook stock.[10]

The most convincing explanation of the origins of Facebook, though, is the simplest one: that lots of ideas and inspirations and ambitions had been percolating in Zuckerberg's mind, and they all played a role in forming his creation. Zuckerberg was a tinkerer at heart, and he thought that making the site would be fun. This is the image of Zuckerberg that comes out in a long interview he gave to the *Crimson* just a few months after launching Facebook. "I'm just like a little kid," he explained to the journalist. "I get bored easily and computers excite me. Those are the two driving factors here. . . . I just like making it and knowing that it works and having it be wildly successful is cool, I guess, but I mean, I dunno, that's not the goal." Uniquely, of all the factors driving his decision to create Facebook, money appears to have been near the bottom of the list, as he explained quite frankly to the interviewer. "[Selling Facebook] is just like not something we're really interested in. I mean, yeah, we can make a bunch of money—that's not the goal. . . . I mean, like, anyone from Harvard can get a job and make a bunch of money. Not everyone at Harvard can have a social network. I value that more as a resource more than like any money."[11]

Inspirations aside, what really mattered was implementation. Many people had imagined an online social network. Zuckerberg made one. And he made it remarkably quickly. On January 11, 2004, Zuckerberg registered the domain name "thefacebook.com." Later that month, he started coding. Within a week, it was done. The site went live on February 4, 2004, just as Harvard's spring semester was starting. The site was minimalist, lighthearted, techy, and fun. Visitors were met with a large blue ribbon on the top of the screen, showing a digitized face of an anonymous man fading into binary code and, on the right in large, lowercase letters, "[thefacebook]." Many people mistakenly took the image to be of a young Al Pacino, but internet sleuths eventually discovered it to be Peter Wolf of the J. Geils Band. Zuckerberg chose blue as the site's principal color because he was color-blind and couldn't distinguish between red and green. "Blue is the richest color for me—I can see all of blue," he told an interviewer. Beneath the ribbon, a welcome message appeared. "Welcome to Thefacebook. Thefacebook is an online directory that connects people through social networks at colleges. We have opened up Thefacebook for popular consumption at Harvard University." As the message indicated, Zuckerberg designed his site to be accessible only to Harvard students, which offered a sense of elitism to the site and reassured users that they could share more information about themselves. This was a closed ecosystem. Only people like them could see what they posted. At the bottom of the welcome page, a signature block appeared, identifying the site as "A Mark Zuckerberg production." On an "About" page, Zuckerberg claimed to be the "Founder, Master and Commander, Enemy of the State." His friend Eduardo Saverin was listed as the head of "business stuff, corporate stuff, Brazilian affairs." It all seemed very whimsical, in tune with Zuckerberg's general approach to programming. It was all fun and games.[12]

While its design may have been minimal, Facebook struck a chord with a Harvard student body that was eager to find more ways to interact with one another online. In four days, over 650 Harvard students had registered for the site. Within two weeks, four thousand had joined. Zuckerberg initially designed the site so that only students with a harvard.edu email address could register, but, recognizing that its success at Harvard could easily be replicated at other universities, he soon opened registration to new colleges. Facebook launched at

Columbia University in late February, then at Stanford, and then at Yale. By the end of March, Facebook had operations at eleven universities and claimed a total of thirty thousand users. Its reach was growing.

At around this time, Zuckerberg came to an important realization about the nature of his website. Facebook was a social network. And like all networks, it tended to become more valuable as more people joined. Consider, for example, telephones, the classic example of a network. If only one person in town has a telephone, he won't find it a particularly useful product. It may look pretty, and it may even be a technological marvel, but it doesn't serve much purpose. There is no one to call. But if other people in town start acquiring telephones, his phone suddenly becomes more valuable. Now he can call his friend down the street. He can reserve a table at his favorite restaurant. He can receive calls from neighbors or colleagues. What was once a curiosity has now become a necessity. The key question for every network is how to go from one person to many. In an interview with the *Crimson*, Zuckerberg explained why it was so important that Facebook had acquired so many users so quickly. "The nature of the site is that each user's experience improves if they can get their friends to join it," he said. Growth was good.

By the end of the spring semester, Facebook had become so successful that Zuckerberg decided to move out to Silicon Valley, the center of the technology world, to work full-time on the project. Along with two Harvard friends who had been helping him with the company and two freshman interns he had hired, Zuckerberg flew across the country to set up shop in a somewhat ramshackle five-bedroom house on a cul-de-sac named La Jennifer Way that he had found on Craigslist. That summer, the group worked relentless hours to keep the site functioning. On a typical day, they would program from noon until 5 a.m. It was hard work, but it still had the feeling of dorm life.

Zuckerberg would frequently stroll around the house in his pajamas, quoting from his favorite movie, *Wedding Crashers*. Later in the summer, Zuckerberg learned that Sean Parker, the infamous founder of the music-pirating site Napster, was living down the street. He invited him to join them in the house, and so Parker moved in as well.

But as Facebook grew—by June 2004, it had two hundred thousand users at thirty colleges throughout the country—the seriousness of the venture started to set in for Zuckerberg and the rest of his team. The company slowly became more formalized as a result. The first big decision point came when Zuckerberg opted not to return to Harvard for his junior year. Facebook's prospects were simply too great, its popularity too immense, for him to abandon it and return to school. This was his full-time job now.

Another important moment came when Zuckerberg decided to pursue venture capital funds. Ever since the 1970s, when the investment firms Kleiner Perkins and Sequoia Capital had started providing early-stage investments to technology companies, venture capital had become an essential part of most start-up tech companies' lives. Venture capitalists provided them with needed cash and, in return, received a big stake in the company. The start-up used the cash to fund its operations and get off the ground, without worrying about short-term profits and losses. The venture capitalists had a chance to make a big profit if the company was successful. It was a win-win. Venture capital firms dominated the Silicon Valley tech scene in the 1990s and early 2000s and controlled vast pools of capital. Receiving an investment from one of the more established venture capital firms, such as Sequoia or Kleiner Perkins, was a mark of honor in Silicon Valley, one that signaled to the world that you had a "big idea." By the summer of 2004, Zuckerberg realized that Facebook's growth was taxing the server space the company had been renting, and he needed cash to keep the site functioning smoothly. So in August he met with Peter Thiel, one of the most prominent venture capitalists in Silicon Valley. Thiel ended up investing $500,000 in the company for a 7 percent interest. Venture capital would play an important role in shaping the company's future.

That summer, Zuckerberg also decided to file papers in Delaware to incorporate TheFacebook, Inc. His website was now officially a corporation. This last development, turning Facebook into a corporation, proved more than a little contentious. Earlier that year, Zuckerberg had asked his friend and partner, Eduardo Saverin, to form a company, TheFacebook, LLC, in Florida. The Florida company was owned 65 percent by Zuckerberg, 30 percent by Saverin, and 5 percent by Dustin Moskovitz, Zuckerberg's roommate, who had been helping Zuckerberg code the site. But despite owning a significant portion of the company, Saverin did not come out to California with the rest of the crew. Over the summer, tensions mounted over the founders' differing expectations for the company and its needs. In the ensuing months, Zuckerberg became convinced that keeping Saverin as a major shareholder was no longer tenable. To that end, he had his lawyer prepare a set of documents that greatly diluted Saverin's stake in the newly formed Delaware corporation. In emails to his lawyer that were later leaked to the press, Zuckerberg made clear his deceptive intentions: "Is there a way to do this without making it painfully apparent to him that he's being diluted to 10%?" His lawyer warned him that there was a substantial risk that Saverin would sue him for breach of fiduciary duty if he proceeded, but, nonetheless, the transaction went forward. Sure enough, when Saverin figured out what had happened, a lawsuit quickly followed. After a long and acrimonious court battle, Saverin received a significant number of Facebook shares to settle his claims and, when the company went public, became an instant billionaire.[13]

Another early concern was privacy. As the FaceMash debacle showed, people cared deeply about who could see their personal information and how others were using it. Zuckerberg knew that reassuring users about the privacy of their posts was essential. As he explained to the *Crimson* in an interview, he had developed "intensive privacy options" for Facebook. "You can limit who can see your information, if you only want current students to see your information, or people in your year, in your house, in your classes. You can limit a search so that only a friend or a friend of a friend can look you up." As he concluded, "People have very good control over who can see their information."[14]

The reality, though, was less reassuring. The site controlled a growing mass of information about a large percentage of America's college students. And just what it was doing with all that information was obscure, at least to many users. An instant message from Zuckerberg soon after the site's launch showed the extent of the problem.

> **Zuck:** Yeah so if you ever need info about anyone at Harvard
> **Zuck:** Just ask.
> **Zuck:** I have over 4,000 emails, pictures, addresses, SNS
> [**Friend**]: What? How'd you manage that one?
> **Zuck:** People just submitted it.
> **Zuck:** I don't know why.
> **Zuck:** They "trust me"
> **Zuck:** Dumb f***s.[15]

And yet, despite the remarkable string of major controversies that dogged its first months in existence, Facebook kept expanding. By December 2004, it had a million users. In March 2005, it opened its first real office, on Emerson Street in Palo Alto. It raised more money—$12.9 million from the venture capital firm Accel Partners, which valued the company at $198 million. In 2005, it also changed its name. No longer would the company be known as "Thefacebook." It would now simply be Facebook.

A RELENTLESS DRIVE FOR EXPANSION MARKED FACEBOOK'S FIRST years. But it was a very peculiar kind of expansion, one that would have been inconceivable to corporations just a few decades before.

Facebook didn't sell spices, or cars, or train tickets, and so it was not looking to build bigger factories or rail networks or to speed up assembly times. Instead, it was simply trying to get more people to sign up for and use its free website. The aim was rapid growth in the number of daily active users, at any cost.

This focus on unbridled growth was a unique feature of the technology-driven capitalism of Silicon Valley in the 2000s. Two important factors drove it. The first was the concept of economies of scale. It had long been a foundational principle of economics that many goods are cheaper to make as you make more of them: once you build a factory and hire skilled workers, ramping up production from one car a day to two is easy. The cost of making additional cars decreases as you make more of them. Henry Ford had realized this a century before. But the invention of computers and the internet gave entirely new meaning to the idea. Once you made a website, allowing more people to access it was essentially free. Facebook could provide services to anyone in the world, at essentially zero additional cost. It simply needed to convince people to spend time on the site.

The venture capital firms that funded many of the most promising start-ups in San Francisco also drove the overriding focus on user growth. Over time, the venture capital playbook had zeroed in on a particular strategy that it believed led to outsized returns: rapid growth toward establishing a dominant, monopoly-type position in new markets. Of course, this strategy did not always work out so well. Extravagant spending with little revenue does not come without risks. As one venture capitalist would say, though, "Failures don't matter. You can only lose one times your capital." But every once in a while, these risky bets would pay out in giant windfalls. Even if most investments failed, the one or two every few years that succeeded tended to compensate for all the losses. Precisely this theory underlies venture capital's focus today on finding so-called unicorns, those rare start-up creatures that have such a magical business model that they are valued at $1 billion or more.[16]

It is no surprise, then, that Facebook, doubly steeped as it was in Silicon Valley culture and venture capital money, focused on growth above all else, including profits. Zuckerberg made clear to new employees that their priority was finding ways to attract new users. "He said that if any feature didn't do that, he was not interested," related one early employee of Zuckerberg's focus on growth. "That was the only priority that mattered." Zuckerberg later defended this decision as being in the best interest of users: "I think you can look at this from a cynical perspective that we were trying to grow because growth went in its own direction. But the reason people use social products is to interact with other people. The most valuable thing we could do for people was make sure that the people they cared about were on the service." Users wanted their friends on the site, and so Zuckerberg obliged. Networks only worked if other people were on them.[17]

One way of driving growth was simply letting new audiences onto the site. Initially, Facebook was only open to Harvard students. It later opened to Stanford and the Ivy League. Other colleges quickly followed. By November 2005, it had opened at over two thousand colleges and universities throughout the United States. Over 85 percent of all college students had an account. When Facebook ran out of colleges, it turned to high schools. And then, at the end of 2006, Facebook arrived at its inevitable conclusion: anyone could join. "It ended up going better than we thought," Zuckerberg told an interviewer about the shift to "open registration," or Open Reg. "Within a week of launching we'd gone from probably fewer than ten thousand people joining a day to sixty or eighty thousand people joining a day, and then it grew quickly from there."[18]

As part of the rollout, though, Facebook made an important change in the way that users interacted with one another. In the beginning, you couldn't browse profiles of people at other schools. Harvard students could connect with other Harvard students. Yale students could connect with Yale students. But Harvard students couldn't connect with Yale students, or vice versa. In 2005, when Facebook opened at high schools, this policy was changed. For the first time, people could start connecting with people outside their own schools. This raised new concerns about what private information might be shared with the public—a parent might snoop on a child's posts or an employer might discover embarrassing photos of an interviewee—but the company moved forward with it anyway. Zuckerberg seemed more preoccupied with ensuring that users kept migrating to the site. In scribbled notes in his notebook from the time, he considered how Open Reg might affect users' perceptions of the site. "What makes this seem secure," he asked himself, "whether or not it actually is?"[19]

Growth did not just require a more open ecosystem. It also required a better site. For the most part, this meant adding new and better features. The Accel investment from 2005 had allowed Facebook to ramp up its hiring of engineers and coders. Most new hires, at least at the beginning, were recent college graduates or people who had worked a year at a bigger company. They swiftly became initiated into the work culture at Facebook, which prioritized speed over precision. Most tech companies at the time would only "push out" new code after months of work and multiple layers of review. Facebook would do it several times a day. This was an unheard-of pace and often led to errors. Engineers broke the website so often that a tradition started of congratulating them when did they so. The company would send an email out to the entire engineering team: "Congratulations! You brought the site down—which means you're moving fast!" The focus on progress, at light speed, also birthed a slogan that has since become a Silicon Valley mantra. In an interview with *Business Insider* in October 2009, Zuckerberg said that his primary instruction to developers was to "move fast and break things." "Unless you are breaking stuff," Zuckerberg told the interviewer, "you are not moving fast enough." "Move fast and break things" was soon printed on posters pasted around the office as a daily reminder that velocity mattered.[20]

The emphasis on speed led to a dizzying array of changes to the site. Some were superficial: in 2005, the company replaced the Peter

Wolf image with a clean blue ribbon copied from the website of private equity firm the Carlyle Group. But others went to the heart of how users experienced the social network. In October 2005, for the first time, Facebook started to let users upload photos to the site, not just a single profile image. Users could add these photos and then "tag" other friends who appeared in them, thus turning the photos into a kind of communal memory on the site. In September 2006, Facebook launched News Feed—a long scroll of recent posts from friends, such as a new photo or a new comment. The News Feed was designed to increase user engagement. Before the News Feed, there was no way of knowing what other people were doing and saying without clicking on their profiles. "This felt very inefficient. Everyone is spending so much time clicking around on those profiles," said Adam D'Angelo, the company's chief technology officer. Of course, once the idea of the News Feed had been thought of, the big question was how to organize it. What should a user see at the top of the feed? Should it simply show the latest post, or should Facebook prioritize the latest photo uploaded? Or should it prioritize posts from people who hadn't posted lately? Or should it prioritize posts that tagged the user? All of these were plausible approaches to the problem and required active decisions by the Facebook team. Zuckerberg, in his notebook, wrote that the organizing principle behind it all should be "interesting-ness."[21]

But perhaps even more fateful for Facebook's future was a change internal to the corporation itself. Zuckerberg had long been preoccupied with growth, constantly fretting that user numbers were not increasing quickly enough or that activity levels were petering out. So in 2007 he created a group within the company whose sole purpose was to find ways to attract more users to the site. The Growth Circle, as it was called, quickly became the most powerful team within the company. Zuckerberg called it "the most important product feature" the company had ever invented. The group even created a metric to measure its success: the monthly active user. If someone visited the site at least once a month, the Growth Circle believed, that meant he or she was committed to the social network. The "monthly active user" became an obsessive focus for the company. "What you really need to think about," one member of the Growth Circle told an interviewer, "is what is the North Star of your company: what is that one metric, where everyone in your company is thinking about it and driving their product towards that metric and their actions towards moving that metric up? Monthly active people was the number Zuckerberg made the whole world hold Facebook to."[22]

Once the Growth Circle had identified a metric to measure success, it then went in search of ways to improve it. The team did studies on consumer psychology and internet usage and gathered huge datasets to analyze for patterns. An early discovery was that if new users who had just created accounts didn't quickly find their friends, they would often leave, never to return. To fix this problem, Facebook added a "Friends You May Know" feature in 2008 that notified you about new people to add to your network. It also allowed Facebook to download people's email address books and then send friend requests to people who did not already have a Facebook account. In another important change, a company-conducted study titled "Feed Me: Motivating Newcomer Contribution in Social Network Sites" concluded that privacy constraints tended to reduce engagement on the social network. So in 2009, the Growth Circle pushed for a new terms-of-service agreement that changed the default setting for users from sharing their activities with friends only to sharing them with everyone. Facebook's privacy chief argued against the change, believing that it violated privacy laws requiring user consent before changes in material terms, but Growth won, and the new terms of service went through.[23]

A rapidly expanding user base, combined with rapid-fire deployment of new features and structures, led to a constant stream of unintended consequences. The "Friends You May Know" feature led to some startling discoveries for users. One girl received a request to add her absent father's mistress. Sex workers were asked to friend their clients. People who visited the same psychiatrist were asked to friend

each other. The News Feed, on the other hand, unearthed some troubling quirks of being notified in real time about your friends and networks. Prior to the News Feed, when a user changed their relationship
status, people wouldn't know about it until they clicked on your page.
But now, it would be broadcast to all your friends: people could see on
their feed that so-and-so had just gone from being "in a relationship"
to being "single." This kind of public breakup could be humiliating
and emotionally fraught, particularly if one of the people in the relationship did not know that it had just been disclosed to the world. In a
backlash, a group of students started a Facebook group called Students
Against Facebook News Feed, asking for Facebook to shut the feed
down. Thousands of users complained. *TIME* wrote a story about it.
But despite all the complaints, Facebook saw that people started to
spend more time on the site. Zuckerberg wrote a dismissive blog post
titled "Calm Down. Breathe. We Hear You." "We agree: stalking isn't
cool; but being able to know what's going on in your friends' lives
is. . . . Use your privacy settings so you can feel most comfortable using
the site." In other words, if users had just taken the time to familiarize
themselves with the site's privacy features, they never would have been
so upset. Facebook later put together a new privacy tool letting users
control what would show up in feeds. It was not widely used, but the
uproar died down.[24]

But these stories were simply blips in the undeniable rise of the
all-conquering Facebook. By the beginning of 2008, it had one hundred million users. Seven months later, it had two hundred million.
By 2012, it surpassed the billion-user mark. Facebook had become the
greatest network the world had ever seen.

JUST ONE QUESTION REMAINED FOR FACEBOOK. HOW WOULD IT
ever make money? Facebook had become a phenomenally popular
website and even a dominant social force, but it was, at the end of the
day, a corporation. It had to make money. This might have seemed

like a simple proposition for a company with hundreds of millions of avid customers, but Facebook, unlike previous corporations, offered its services for free. Users could register, log on, play games, post updates, and look at their friends' pages for hours a day if they wanted and never pay Facebook a cent. Meanwhile, Facebook had to pay for its engineers and its servers, as well as satisfy its venture capital investors, who wanted to see a return. How could Facebook turn this into a sustainable business model?

The answer to the question lay in what Facebook called "monetization." Given Zuckerberg's insistence on keeping the site free for users, the one clear path to monetization was advertising. In the summer of 2006, Facebook hired Tim Kendall, an MBA from Stanford, as its head of monetization, and Kendall set to work developing the company's advertising strategy. One of Kendall's first achievements was to reach a deal with Microsoft, giving it the exclusive right to sell ads on Facebook to third parties. But in the summer of 2007, Kendall went further. He wanted to create an entirely new type of advertising, what he called "social advertising." "What worked on Facebook was learning about my friends," Kendall said. "And so learning about products and services through the lens of my friends seems like it should work, especially if the ads have pertinent, relevant information about my friends." The result of Kendall's efforts was Beacon, an initiative that heralded a new era of advertising.[25]

"Once every hundred years, media changes," Zuckerberg said in announcing the Beacon program. "The last hundred years have been defined by the mass media. In the next hundred years, information won't be just pushed out to people: it will be shared among the millions of connections people have." The idea behind Beacon was simple: people were more likely to buy things if their friends told them to buy them, or at least recommended them. "People influence people," Zuckerberg said. "Nothing influences people more than a recommendation from a trusted friend. A trusted referral influences people more than the best broadcast message. A trusted referral is the Holy Grail of advertising." In practice, though, the Holy Grail of advertising turned out to be significantly less saintly than it appeared on the surface. In connection with Beacon, Facebook entered into relationships with third-party web pages that would host monitors, or "beacons." When a Facebook user bought something on those pages, the beacon would send this information back to Facebook, and it would be shared on the News Feed of the user's friends. The idea was to replicate the kind of word of mouth that happens in the real world, like when you're at a party and you notice the host's new Instant Pot and decide to get one yourself. Hearing about your friends' purchases would hopefully make you more likely to buy something than just seeing a generic advertisement. But almost immediately, Beacon whipped up a storm of controversy. Stories emerged of people buying engagement rings online and, within minutes, receiving calls from their friends saying congratulations. Some users sued over the perceived violation of their privacy. Facebook disbanded the program, and Zuckerberg apologized.[26]

In response to these missteps, Zuckerberg decided to try something new. In the spring of 2008, he brought on a new chief operating officer, Sheryl Sandberg, and tasked her with building out Facebook's monetization strategy. Sandberg made a splash at Facebook almost immediately. On her first day, while attending a new-employee boot camp, she turned the tables on the trainers: instead of receiving the training, she gave it, delivering a speech on monetization to the attendees. Advertising, she explained, was an "inverted pyramid." At the bottom was demand fulfillment: someone wants to buy something and goes out looking for it, and advertising helps them fulfill the demand. This was the low-hanging fruit. It was easy to sell something when someone wanted to buy it. Google was good at monetizing demand fulfillment. But demand fulfillment required companies to wait until someone had developed an intention before targeting them. Facebook, Sandberg explained, was going for something much bigger, the large and untapped territory at the top, the much bigger part of the inverted pyramid: creating demand in the first place. As she would put it later, Facebook's "sweet spot" was "demand generation, before you know you want something, before you know you're interested in something."[27]

Sandberg turned Facebook into the perfect tool for generating demand. Most of the time, when people surfed the internet, they were looking for specific information. But when they were on Facebook, they were looking to learn, and this meant that they were particularly open to advertising messages. "You go to Facebook to share who you are and to hear about what other people are interested in," Sandberg told an interviewer. "So for the first time, these small businesses can get to you when you're in discovery mode in a way that they can afford." This wasn't just true for small businesses, though. Coke and Starbucks and other large retailers also advertised on Facebook. Sandberg told one interviewer, "Wendy Clark [the head of marketing at Coca-Cola] has this great quote, she says she's been able to go from the point of purchase to the point of thirst with her consumers. . . . Whenever they're thirsty, they'll think of Coke, because Coke's part of their life because it's in their Facebook feed. Think about how important that is for a marketer." Sandberg's strategy worked like a charm. Advertising revenue shot up from $764 million in 2009 to $1.9 billion in 2010, then to $3.1 billion in 2011. A decade later, when Zuckerberg appeared in congressional hearings before the Senate on April 10, 2018, Orrin Hatch asked him, "How do you sustain a business model in which users don't pay for your service?" Zuckerberg replied, "Senator, we run ads."[28]

In addition to developing Facebook's monetization strategy, Sandberg also introduced a subtle but fundamental change in the corporate culture at Facebook. Until Sandberg joined, the company still felt like a company run by kids. Zuckerberg had founded it at the age of nineteen, and most of his early hires were around his age (many of them, in fact, were his college classmates). When Sandberg joined, he was still just twenty-three. Sandberg, at thirty-eight, was the adult in the room. At times, this earned her grumbling from her subordinates. One employee called meetings with Sandberg "the Supreme Court of Sheryl." Once, when a problem emerged, she marched all the teams together and had them sit on the floor and talk it through. "A lot of us were kids and didn't know how to manage people and didn't have the skill sets to do nuanced communication. She put that stuff in place and brought a level of maturity," said another employee.[29]

With a sustainable business model, an enormous user base, and some of the tech world's brightest minds, Facebook seemed to have solved all of its problems. As the ultimate sign of its triumph, on May 17, 2012, Facebook went public in an initial public offering (IPO) that valued the company at $104 billion, the largest IPO ever. Speaking before ringing the bell at NASDAQ, Zuckerberg—who had just become a billionaire several times over—was breathless with excitement. "In the past eight years, all of you out there have built the largest community in the history of the world," Zuckerberg said. "You've done amazing things that we never would have dreamed of, and I can't wait to see what you're all going to do going forward."

Not everyone at the company, though, viewed the changes at Facebook so positively. Its focus on rapid growth and then rapid monetization seemed to many like a grand experiment on the human race. What would a social network that connected the entire world instantaneously do to its members? How would it work? What would happen when the corporation's priorities conflicted with those of its users? Some took a dim view of Facebook's new direction. One product manager on Facebook's ads team said, "Many people spent hours a day on Facebook . . . ignoring their surroundings, the imploring gaze of their wives, or their children's bid for attention. All those eyeballs, over hours, turned into cheap ads that gradually, as many raindrops make a river, amassed a torrent of revenue for Facebook." Another early employee complained, "The best minds of my generation are thinking about how to make people click ads. That sucks. . . . If instead of pointing their incredible infrastructure at making people click on ads, they pointed it at great unsolved problems in science, how would the world be different today?" Even Sean Parker, the Facebook evangelist who had moved into Zuckerberg's first house in Palo Alto, believed that the company had unleashed a dangerous product. In an interview in November 2017, he said,

> The thought process that went into building these applications, Facebook being the first of them . . . was all about: "How do we consume as much of your time and conscious attention as possible?" And that means that we need to sort of give you a little dopamine hit every once in a while, because someone liked or commented on a photo or a post or whatever. And that's going to get you to contribute more content, and that's going to get you more likes and comments. It's a social-validation feedback loop . . . exactly the kind of thing that a hacker like myself would come up with, because you're exploiting a vulnerability in human psychology. The inventors, creators—it's me, it's Mark [Zuckerberg], it's Kevin Systrom at Instagram, it's all of these people—understood this consciously. And we did it anyway.[30]

PRIVACY AND SOCIAL MEDIA WERE ALWAYS DESTINED TO BE STRANGE bedfellows. People used social media companies like Facebook in the first place because they wanted to give up their privacy for something else: the right to see and be seen. At the same time, they also wanted to believe that the information they shared was visible only to the people they chose to share it with—that their posts, photos, and activities were private to the world at large but public to their friends. This created a tension: in order to share things with your friends, you had to give those things to a company. Could people trust the company to do the right thing with their intimate information? And what precisely would the "right" thing be? The problem was devilishly difficult to solve.

To get a sense of the problem, one need only look at how Facebook handled "offensive" content posted to the site. Content moderation proved a constant thorn in the side at Facebook's headquarters. In its first years, Facebook had a small team of content moderators, and most of them received little more than a half hour of training. Rather than following a list of rules created at the outset about what constituted objectionable content, the team was forced to develop them as it muddled along from crisis to crisis. One of its rules of thumb was "three strikes and you're out," whereby users would be banned from the site if they posted objectionable content three times. Another was the "thong rule," meaning that if you could see a thong in a picture, it was too risqué and had to come down. But the way that content moderators handled complaints left much to be desired. Initially, when the team received a complaint about a photo, a moderator would log into the complainer's account using the complainer's own username and password to look at the photo and determine whether it was objectionable. If it was, the moderator would then turn to the poster's account, using the poster's username and password to log in and remove the photo. By the end of 2005, the support team still only numbered around twenty people implementing guidelines that were kept on a shared Word document. This was woefully inadequate for a website that now served millions and that anyone, from high schoolers to criminals and hackers, could join. In 2007, the New York attorney general launched a sting on Facebook in which investigators created fake profiles of underage girls. Within a matter of days, they were fielding suggestive messages from sexual predators.[31]

On the other side of the equation, some users complained that Facebook was *too* active in removing content. In 2008, a group of "lactivists," or mothers who celebrate breastfeeding, protested outside Facebook's headquarters to put a stop to the company's removal of breastfeeding photos. The company defended itself by citing its policy of prohibiting photos that contain a "visible nipple or areola." The lactivists were not satisfied with this answer, and protests continued in future years, leading Facebook to regularly clarify its breastfeeding photo policy. The difficulty of drawing ever more nuanced boundaries eventually led the company, in 2012, to set up a moderation center in the Philippines, where an army of content moderators screened the hundreds of millions of photos being uploaded to the site every day.[32]

But content moderation was just the tip of the iceberg. The more general issue the company faced was how to decide who had access to a user's information. An important turning point in this debate came in 2007, when Facebook began allowing developers to build services directly into the Facebook website. The project, called Platform, allowed outside companies and developers to create games, quizzes, polls, and other forms of content and then put them on Facebook. Since Facebook was a social media company, sharing became an integral part of these services. People could compete with each other, share their progress, and interact with their friends.

Initially, Zuckerberg had hoped that Platform might lead to more engaged citizens. His favorite app was Causes, an application that let people build communities devoted to solving issues of public importance, like climate change or world hunger. "Their vision was Causes," said Mark Pincus, founder of Zynga, a game developer on Platform. "They felt that the Platform was going to bring out our best selves." But while Causes attracted some attention, the killer apps, Facebook discovered, were mindless, time-consuming games. The biggest hit of all was a game called Farmville, where people tended a farm, planting seeds and raising livestock. The game was designed so that players had to wait increasing periods for crops and livestock to mature. They could pay for these things to move faster, though, and, it turned out, people were addicted to doing so. Zynga, the game's creator, turned enormous profits, so much so, in fact, that Pincus hid how much revenue Zynga had. "My customers were middle-aged women in Indiana who'd stopped watching soap operas to play Farmville," Pincus explained later. "Some of them were spending huge amounts, thousands of dollars a month with us. But I didn't want to get that story out." By the time Facebook went public, Pincus estimated that Zynga represented around 20 percent of Facebook's total revenue.[33]

Games and other applications, though, needed access to a certain amount of information about users from Facebook. And so a dilemma arose over exactly what information would be shared with them. A single user, after all, had access to lots of other people's information on the site—not just their own information but also any information their friends shared as well. So if a user chose to use an app, would the app get access to all that information? Even if the user's friends hadn't consented to it? Zuckerberg was inclined toward more sharing. "There was a lot of deliberation about which data to share," a Facebook executive said of the thought process. "There was a very strong thing coming from Mark that was: 'We need to be able to make it so that other developers can build things as good as what Facebook can build.' Facebook was a small company at the time, so they needed to give developers this data to just make the platform desirable."[34]

In the end, Facebook decided to put the onus on users to sort all these things out for themselves. Any time users accessed an app on Facebook, they would be shown an authorization dialog, stating that the app needed to access certain data: your name, your friend list, maybe your photos and your likes. The default information shared to the programs changed over time, but, initially, limiting access was largely left to the user, and app developers, as a result, tended to get lots of information. This included basic information like users' names, genders, friends, and profile pictures, but it also often went much further, to include locations, relationship statuses, likes, posts, and more. It even let users share information about their friends, such as status updates and interests, without the friends' consent.[35]

Facebook employees became concerned about the vast troves of data that companies were hoovering up about users. One former employee, who had led Facebook's efforts to resolve its privacy problems in its pre-IPO days, wrote an op-ed in the New York Times titled "We

Can't Trust Facebook to Regulate Itself." "What I saw from the inside was a company that prioritized data collection from its users over protecting them from abuse," she wrote. Facebook's developer platform had allowed third parties to access intimate information about users, and once they had the data, they could do nearly anything they wanted with it. The author recounted an instance when a developer had used Facebook data to generate profiles of children. When she called the company up, it claimed to have complied with Facebook's data policies. But there was no way to confirm that this was true. The developer had the data, and Facebook had no way of knowing what it did with it. When the op-ed author started pressing Facebook for more information about what companies were doing with user data, Facebook executives stonewalled her. After suggesting to one senior executive that Facebook needed to conduct a thorough audit of how developers were using consumer data, the executive replied, "Do you really want to see what you'll find?"[36]

Another problem was what Facebook itself was doing with all its data on users. In 2012, for example, Facebook researchers conducted a study examining whether the site could affect people's moods. The resulting article, titled "Experimental Evidence of Massive-Scale Emotional Contagion Through Social Networks," unsurprisingly found that it could. The article opened with a bang: "We show, via a massive ($N = 689,003$) experiment on Facebook, that emotional states can be transferred to others via emotional contagion, leading people to experience the same emotions without their awareness." The letter N here refers to the number of users that Facebook had conducted the experiment on: 689,003 of them. Perhaps even more surprising was how they conducted the experiment: without telling the users, the researchers intentionally tweaked their News Feeds to hide either positive or negative posts. As a result, the users tended to themselves become more positive or negative (as measured by what they shared on their own posts). But the idea that a large corporation was toying with hundreds of thousands of people's emotions just to see what would happen caused an immediate blowback. Sheryl Sandberg was forced to apologize for the furor, stating, "This was part of ongoing research companies do to test different products, and that was what it was; it was poorly communicated. And for that communication we apologize. We never meant to upset you."[37]

In the beginning, it wasn't entirely clear why all this data gathering mattered. After all, who cared if an outsider could see that you were friends with a college classmate or if you liked a picture of a cute cat? But by the 2010s, society began to understand that a paradigm shift had occurred. Facebook and other social networks had steadily eroded our realms of individual privacy. Companies now had access to enormous caches of information about more or less everyone, and they were using those caches for more and more purposes. In 2016, a news report came out that a group had gathered data on Facebook users expressing interest in Black Lives Matter and then sold it to police departments (the group was later banned). ProPublica found that Facebook's advertising options allowed property owners to discriminate based on race and gender in violation of the Fair Housing Act (the Department of Housing and Urban Development later sued Facebook over the practice).

Facebook approached privacy the same way it approached everything else on the site: move fast and break things. Facebook would launch something quickly, see how it worked, and resolve any problems later. Zuckerberg more or less admitted this in 2011, after mounting criticism of Facebook's privacy policies. "I think, related or unrelated to privacy, whenever we make a change of this magnitude, I think we should expect that some people will like it, some people won't, and then we'll have a rollout where we give people a chance to try it out if they want," Zuckerberg told an interviewer. "And then we'll take some period of time to adjust to all the feedback and we'll kind of go from there."[38]

But the move-fast-and-break-things approach, a reckless strategy even for a small start-up, became something entirely different in the hands of a $100 billion company controlling the user data of hundreds of millions of people.

But no one knew just how dangerous it could be until the election of 2016.

COULD FACEBOOK DECIDE AN ELECTION?

In 2010, a group of researchers at Facebook decided to find out. It might have seemed like an absurd proposition, when Zuckerberg first launched his website for finding friends, that it could potentially affect democracy itself. By 2010, not only was the idea not absurd; it seemed eminently plausible. Everyone at the company had long understood that Facebook now had the tools to directly influence how people communicated, how they acted, and even how they felt. As Facebook grew from a few thousand users to a few billion, the sheer scale of these effects became terrifying to conceive.

To answer the question, the Facebook researchers conducted an experiment on the 2010 midterm elections in the United States. The experiment came in the form of a randomized control trial, where the researchers randomly assigned sixty-one million (unknowing) users to different groups and subjected them to differing treatment. The first group, called the "social message" group, was shown a statement at the top of their News Feed encouraging them to vote and showing pictures of other friends who had voted. The second group, the "informational message" group, was shown the same message, but without any information about their friends' participation rates. A final "control" group received no messages at all. With their experiment in place, the researchers then sat back and waited to see what would happen. When the results started rolling in, the researchers were shocked at the extent of the effect. People who received the "social message" noting that their friends had voted were 0.4 percent more likely to have voted than people in the "informational message" group. Interestingly, turnout in the control group and the informational message group was around the same. In other words, what mattered was seeing that your friends had voted, not seeing generic pleas to "go vote." The authors estimated that their social messaging increased voter turnout by 340,000. In 2012, the researchers published their results in the journal *Nature* under the title "A 61 Million Person Experiment in Social Influence and Political Mobilization."[39]

It was a bombshell revelation. The researchers did not find out *how* these people voted—perhaps they skewed Republican, perhaps they skewed Democratic—but almost assuredly they had affected the ultimate vote totals in favor of one party or the other (it would have been even more improbable for the additional voters to have perfectly tracked voting proportions). Many observers cried foul. It was inappropriate for a technology company to be experimenting on American citizens to see how their algorithms affected people. Facebook had shown that it could not be trusted. Politicians, governments, hackers, even potentially enemy nations might seek to exploit Facebook's platform in the future for their own purposes. More importantly, now that the world had arrived at a place where billions of people were interacting and getting news from a single technology company, it seemed as if there was no way out of this conundrum.

All of these problems came to a head in the US elections of 2016. The 2016 presidential contest between the Republican candidate, Donald Trump, and the Democratic candidate, Hillary Clinton, was the most vitriolic and divisive campaign in recent memory (only outdone by the sequel between Trump and Joseph Biden in 2020). Both campaigns used social media in a major way, amplifying their messages through Facebook and Twitter. But it was hard to deny that Trump and his campaign were better at this game than Clinton. Rob Goldman, an advertising executive at Facebook at the time, described his interactions with the Trump campaign: "In every way, the way they used the product was different. The degree to which they measured their outcomes, the kinds of creative they used, the timing of their spend, the way they did their targeting. They took our best practices and operationalized them." Trump's campaign understood the digital consumer better than the Clinton campaign, and it used that knowledge to great effect, spending vastly larger sums on Facebook than Clinton's team did.[40]

Another troubling feature of the 2016 election was the marked rise in conspiracy theories and extremist rhetoric. Racism, sexism, and many other forms of hatred were everywhere, often promoted by Trump himself. Once again, Facebook played a role in creating the problem. In May 2016, a group of conservative commentators accused Facebook of political bias in how it crafted its "Trending Topics" feature, which showed a curated collection of news stories to users. At the time humans selected the articles, and many conservatives believed that the Facebook employees so tasked were, either intentionally or unintentionally, favoring "liberal" causes at the expense of conservative ones. In response to the criticism, Facebook replaced humans with algorithms, letting computer code make the decision of which topics to show. Soon far-right stories and disinformation were dominating the section. Later studies would help uncover why, as researchers found that false news spread much faster and farther on social media than true news. False news on Twitter, for example, was found to be 70 percent more likely to be retweeted than true news. Facebook researchers found that a sizeable majority of people joining extremist groups on the site were doing so because of Facebook's own recommendation tools.[41]

In the meantime, though, another hostile actor had its sights set on Facebook: Russian intelligence. Facebook was not entirely unaware of the possibility that foreign adversaries would seek to intervene in the election. Facebook's DC office even had a "Threat Intelligence" team aimed at tracking down espionage and malware during the campaign. In early 2016, the team had made a troubling discovery. Several accounts linked to the Russian military intelligence agency GRU had started searching on Facebook for people in government jobs, journalists, and Democrats in the Clinton campaign. Facebook informed the FBI about the activity. But the cyberespionage didn't stop. Later,

the accounts created a DCLeaks page on Facebook to spread embar-
rassing emails from the Democratic National Committee that had
been stolen by hackers. The page was nominally created by one "Alice
Donovan," but a subsequent investigation by special counsel Robert
Mueller uncovered that it had really been created by GRU officer
Aleksey Aleksandrovich Potemkin.

The primary thrust of these cyberattacks on the American election
by Russian military appears not to have been to get a particular candidate elected. Instead, the goal was to spread as much hate, anger, and,
ideally, violence among the American public as possible. For example,
in May 2016, the Russian hackers schemed to provoke a violent con-
frontation at an Islamic center in Houston, Texas. First, the Russians
created an account called "Heart of Texas," which catered to patriotic
Texans who believed in "guns, BBQ and secession," and announced
that the group would host a rally on May 21, 2016, at the Islamic center to "Stop Islamification of Texas." The group advised members to
bring their guns. At the same time, the Russians also created another
account, the "United Muslims of America," aimed at proud Muslim
Americans, and announced to this other group that it would be host-
ing a rally at the same Islamic center on the same day to "Save Islamic
Knowledge." So on May 21, both groups showed up, ready to stand
up for their side. Fortunately, there was no violence that day, but for
several hours, around a dozen Confederate-flag-bearing citizens and a
slightly larger group of Muslims and their supporters shouted at each
other from opposing sidewalks. Other Russian accounts targeted other
minority groups. One account, Blacktivist, shared content intended to
outrage its audience, posting videos of police violence against African
Americans. The page was more popular than the official Black Lives
Matter page. It also encouraged its followers to vote for the third-party
candidate: "Choose peace and vote for Jill Stein," one post read. "Trust
me, it's not a wasted vote."[42]

In the end, after a long and bruising campaign, Trump won a
shock victory over Clinton. All the polls had suggested that Clinton

had a strong lead, and, in fact, Clinton won more total votes than Trump. But due to the quirks of an Electoral College system in which presidents are elected by state-level votes rather than national-level ones, Trump eked out a win. Several swing states, like Pennsylvania and Michigan, were remarkably close, with Trump winning by less than a percentage point. Inevitably, in the aftermath, fingers started to point. Social media was squarely in the crosshairs.

Zuckerberg himself initially derided the claim that his company had played a role in undermining the election. "Personally, I think the idea that fake news on Facebook—of which it's a very small amount of the content—influenced the election in any way is a pretty crazy idea," Zuckerberg explained at a conference in Half Moon Bay, just south of San Francisco, two days after the election. "Voters make decisions based on their lived experience." Anyone who believed that Facebook had affected the election, Zuckerberg suggested, was simply out of touch with America. "I do think there is a certain profound lack of empathy in asserting that the only reason someone could have voted the way they did is they saw some fake news," Zuckerberg continued. "If you believe that, then I don't think you have internalized the message the Trump supporters are trying to send in this election." Of course, the accusation was not that Facebook was the sole reason why all voters voted the way they did. It was that the interventions on Facebook (ranging from the Trump campaign's sophisticated use of the platform, to the spread of false and divisive content on the site, to the active targeting of the site by the Russian military intelligence agencies) had affected voter preferences and turnout rates. And Facebook's own researchers had concluded that Facebook could in fact affect these things. It seemed not only plausible but even likely that Facebook had changed the path of the election.[43]

Eventually, the extent of the problem became clear to all observers, even within Facebook. Facebook launched an internal investigation of Russian interference in the election and turned up troubling information. Russian-affiliated actors had placed around

three thousand ads on the site and created almost five hundred accounts and groups, all for the price of just $100,000. The "vast ma-
jority" of the advertisements did not directly address the election but
rather "focused on amplifying divisive social and political messages
across the ideological spectrum—touching on topics from LGBT matters to race issues to immigration to gun rights." A few thousand ads
and a few hundred accounts may not sound like much. But on a social
network of Facebook's size, these small efforts reached a huge audience. A researcher at Harvard's Berkman Klein Center for Internet
& Society estimated that posts from just six of the accounts had been
shared 340 million times. Facebook would later disclose that 126 million users had been exposed to the Russian campaign, as had another
20 million on Facebook's subsidiary, Instagram. Facebook executives
who saw the Russian actions on the site came away disgusted. "We were
in a conference room looking through them and it was just revolting,"
Colin Stretch, Facebook's general counsel, told an interviewer. "It just
felt so exploitative and infuriating." One that stuck out to Stretch was
an image of someone shooting a flamethrower over an unidentified
mass labeled "Muslims," captioned "Let's burn them all!" "That sort
of violence and the idea it was being used to whip up people who may
carry certain prejudices was just awful," Stretch said.[44]

The departing president, Barack Obama, after the election, explained that the way people interacted with Facebook and other social media platforms presented deep challenges in a democracy. "An
explanation of climate change from a Nobel Prize–winning physicist
looks exactly the same on your Facebook page as the denial of climate
change by somebody on the Koch brothers' payroll," Obama explained.
"And the capacity to disseminate misinformation, wild conspiracy
theories, to paint the opposition in wildly negative light without any
rebuttal—that has accelerated in ways that much more sharply po-
larize the electorate and make it very difficult to have a common
conversation." In a democracy, citizens did not have to agree with one
another, but they did have to start from the same baseline of objective

information. Objective facts were supposed to be that: objective and indisputable. But because of the ways that lies and exaggerations spread on Facebook's platform, many citizens simply couldn't separate fact from fiction anymore.[45]

A year and a half after the election, Zuckerberg backtracked. In one of the more remarkable mea culpas ever pronounced by a corporate executive, Zuckerberg appeared before Congress in April 2018 and apologized for what his company had wrought.

> Facebook is an idealistic and optimistic company. For most of our existence, we focused on all the good that connecting people can bring. . . . But it's clear now that we didn't do enough to prevent these tools from being used for harm as well. That goes for fake news, foreign interference in elections, and hate speech, as well as developers and data privacy. We didn't take a broad enough view of our responsibility, and that was a big mistake. It was my mistake, and I'm sorry. I started Facebook, I run it, and I'm responsible for what happens here. . . . It's not enough to just connect people, we have to make sure those connections are positive. It's not enough to just give people a voice, we have to make sure people aren't using it to hurt people or spread misinformation. It's not enough to give people control of their information, we have to make sure developers they've given it to are protecting it too. Across the board, we have a responsibility to not just build tools, but to make sure those tools are used for good.

Zuckerberg's enlightenment came a little too late for the nation, but it marked an unusually candid acknowledgment of the role of the corporation in society, one that harkened back to earlier eras in corporate history. Facebook had created a corporation that, on most metrics, was undeniably successful. It had the world's most talented engineers and computer scientists, billions of customers, and a product that was as addictive as it was popular. And yet, as Zuckerberg acknowledged,

Facebook fell short when it mattered most. In its pursuit of growth and then profits, it had moved too fast and broken too many things. Much like the ancient Roman corporations had done during the first century BC, Facebook had ignored, dismissed, or simply not known how its behavior affected the common good. It had prioritized its own interests over those of society and, in the process, undermined democracy more broadly. Only time will tell whether our democratic institutions can recover.

※ ※ ※

THE AGE OF the Start-Up has barely begun. It has only been around for two decades. It took the Romans hundreds of years to resolve the problems of the *societates publicanorum*. It took Congress decades to respond to the perils of railroad monopolies. We should not expect at this point to fully understand the long-term effects of start-ups on the nature of capitalism, society, and democracy. We simply don't have enough experience with them.

And yet we are not entirely in the dark. We know some things, and we have inklings about others. We are likely to learn much more in coming years.

Any objective observer must be struck by the seemingly inexhaustible capacity that start-ups have for innovating and creating. They have shaken up tired and inefficient industries and invented entirely new ones. Today, we can call upon a global fleet of taxis at the tap of a finger. We can listen to any song ever recorded. We can buy toys and clothes and gadgets from the world's largest store and have them delivered to our doorsteps by the next day. Start-ups have transformed San Francisco into a hotbed of innovation and talent. The rise of the start-up company taught us that when we give small groups of intelligent, creative, and ambitious people the time and capital they need, they can tinker their way to brilliant, world-changing results.

But we have also begun to understand the pitfalls of this new era in corporate history. Start-ups can grow staggeringly quickly. Sometimes they achieve this growth by cutting corners, ignoring red tape, and not thinking through the consequences of their actions. Sometimes the consequences themselves may be hard to predict or simply unforeseeable. The move-fast-and-break-things culture of Silicon Valley tends to exaggerate tendencies already present in corporations, from excessive risk-taking, to consumer manipulation, to short-termism. Start-ups have often ignored, tolerated, or even encouraged problematic behavior on their platforms.

Society, long aslumber, has begun to awaken to these problems. It is starting to fashion responses. Governments are asking hard questions about data and privacy and cybersecurity, about Big Tech and artificial intelligence and social media. Consumers, shareholders, employees, and even some CEOs are pressing for change. Facebook itself has decided to stop breaking things—although it still wants to move fast.

If history is any guide, this is not the end of the story. The corporation will survive—perhaps in a different form, but still, in its spirit, the same thing. It will continue to take the world in hand and shape it in its image. It is up to us to decide whether the world it creates is to our liking.

CONCLUSION

IT IS TRENDY TO WRITE AGAINST CONVENTIONAL WISDOM. To show that everyone else is wrong. To offer some insight never before conceived. To remind us that the world is complex. But sometimes, the conventional wisdom is precisely that: wisdom. This does not mean that it is always true or does not come with exceptions or caveats. It is simply, as Aristotle said of political philosophy, "for the most part true, roughly and in outline." Sometimes the best thing we can do is not to destroy old truths but rather to recover them.

This book has sought to unearth what we have learned about corporations over their two thousand years of history. It has aimed to recover and, in some ways, rehabilitate our conventional wisdom about what corporations are and why they exist. It has focused in particular on one simple foundational principle: the purpose of corporations is, and has always been, to promote the common good. Corporations have existed for thousands of years and have sprung up in radically different social contexts and milieus, but they have always been closely connected to the state and its interests. In ancient Rome, they were viewed as the "sinews of the state," tasked with upholding the public obligations of a republic that had grown too large, too fast. In Renaissance Florence, they were seen as a tool for financing the ambitions of nobles, churchmen, and a burgeoning class of merchants across the European continent. In Elizabethan England, they were created to expand the borders of the kingdom and open up new markets for trade and navigation. During the American Civil War, they were viewed as the saviors of the Union, capable of laying a transcontinental railroad that would knit the country back together again. Simply put, corporations exist to promote society, not to oppose it.

But just because corporations were created to protect the interests of society does not mean that they will, in fact, end up doing so. History is littered with examples of them failing spectacularly in this respect. The corporations that were supposed to be collecting taxes for the Roman Republic ended up enslaving subject populations and corrupting the Senate. The Medici Bank usurped political power from the guilds and used the bank's assets to fund the personal ambitions of Medici family members. The East India Company entangled the English Crown in disputes across the globe, from India to Boston. And after the Civil War, the Union Pacific defrauded the American government and raised railroad rates on poor farmers.

Is it inevitable that corporations will always fall into vice and greed? Is the history of corporations simply a story of great expectations and disappointing results? Are societies simply naive about the role that corporations play on the world stage? I would argue that the answer to these questions is no. Throughout history, corporations have demonstrated a remarkable ability to channel human effort into productive enterprise. There is something magnificent in the tale of Henry Ford figuring out how to make a car and, within the span of just two decades, assembling a team capable of making ten thousand of them in a day. There is something awe-inspiring about Exxon's engineers hunting the world for hidden caches of oil and then inventing ways to extract them from the bottom of the ocean and the frost-ridden lands of the Arctic. There is something grand about Mark Zuckerberg's team of coders building Facebook into a website that reached billions of people around the globe. There is roguery, here, to be sure, but there is also something mystical. The corporation is, at its heart, a testament to the power of cooperation, of people working together toward a common goal. Corporations work economic miracles because people can accomplish more together than they can apart. This is a cause for celebration and optimism, both about human nature and about our capitalist system.

If we created corporations to serve the interests of society, how do we know if they are doing their job? This is where things get tricky. People disagree vehemently about what society's interests are. Some believe that we should restrict immigration; others that we should increase it. Some believe that we should increase wealth redistribution; others that we should decrease it. Some believe that we should have free education; others that we should privatize it. If we as a society can't agree on what the common good is, how can corporations be expected to guide their actions by it? Should corporations wade into these debates at all, or should they simply pursue profits in the blind belief that doing so is the best thing they can do for society?

The history of corporations provides some insight on these questions. When corporations wade into politics, they tend to bear an outsized role in shaping it. The East India Company created an army that conquered Bengal and ruled the subcontinent for over a century in order to protect its interests in the Indian textile trade. Exxon shaped American foreign policy and environmental regulation for decades. Today, Facebook's algorithms determine what we see and know, shaping the very discourse that citizens engage in. This suggests that, at the very least, businesses should be cautious before seeking to craft society's values—their actions are magnified beyond what any individual could ever hope to achieve. I would go further. Businesses should stay out of the politics game entirely. They do not have access to some essential wisdom about what the common good is. They should instead respond to and comply with the norms and expectations set by democratic governments. This isn't to say that individual employees of firms shouldn't participate in politics in their capacity as citizens. They should. And it is good, even essential, for governments to consider the interests of workers and investors and the economy. Founders, capitalists, and executives are people too. But when they use the corporation as a means of shaping public opinion and setting goals, they fundamentally distort its nature, turning it from an instrument to promote the common good into one that defines the common good in the first place. This is not the spirit of capitalism. It is a rigged game, and one that we should refuse to play.

While it will always be hard to define precisely what policies best promote the common good, the very act of asking the question is a step in the right direction. Henry Ford asked himself how he could use his company to serve both the public and his employees, and it led to cheap cars and high wages. Grenville Dodge believed that America needed a transcontinental railroad, and so he constantly fought against any measures by other executives at the Union Pacific to skimp on costs and pay excess dividends to shareholders that would detract from the railroad itself. Just as importantly, while there are certainly hard questions about the common good, there are also easy ones. A corporation that profits by exploiting unsophisticated investors acts wrongly. A corporation that pays its managers millions while sending the company into bankruptcy acts wrongly. A corporation that hides information about its harmful effects on the environment acts wrongly. A corporation that looks the other way when its customers' data is stolen acts wrongly. Encouraging executives to reflect on how their actions and the actions of their businesses affect others is fully consistent with the founding purpose of the corporation. Keeping that value in mind wouldn't solve every ethical question a corporation faces, but it would solve many of them.

On the other hand, the blind belief that the pursuit of profit will always redound to the benefit of society as a whole is both flawed and dangerous. It is flawed because, in any number of arenas, there are profitable strategies that may prove harmful. Facebook crafted its website to be as addictive as possible in order to lure in advertisers, but society has suffered as false and divisive posts have proliferated. Exxon lobbied against climate change regulation in order to improve its profits, but society has paid the price in the form of long-term environmental damage. Kohlberg Kravis Roberts & Co. (KKR) unleashed a wave of leveraged buyouts to enormous success, but much of it came from financial engineering aimed at lowering taxes paid to the government and cost-cutting aimed at reducing worker counts. The glorification of profit seeking is not just flawed; it is also dangerous. It is dangerous because it leads executives and managers into a particular kind of thinking that valorizes numbers over ideas. Focusing on profits to the exclusion of all else can blind us to the harm that we are doing. It can crowd out mental space that we might otherwise devote to broader questions about the role our corporations should play in improving our societies. And it also leads to a certain type of smugness. It is one thing to be happy that your company earned a profit last year. It is another to think that the best thing you can do for the world is to make your company earn as much profit as humanly possible. Pursuing profit as an end in itself, and not as a means to something greater, is simply greed. Yet the caricatured view of capitalism so common today makes it into a virtue. This kind of thinking does real harm to the fabric of society, as well as to the project of capitalism. Employees who see their managers making ten, twenty, one hundred times their salaries are naturally suspicious about how much the corporation truly values them. Dispirited workers hurt businesses. And even when they don't, alienation and division are evils worth combatting.

Despite the endless argument today over what the purpose of a corporation is, whether social goals can be considered, and whether directors must focus entirely on maximizing profit, when we examine the corporation as a historical phenomenon, a clear picture emerges of their true raison d'être, their true founding purpose, and that is to promote the common good of the nation. Corporations were created to pursue national goals, which, to be sure, included expanding commerce, but also included exploration, colonization, and religious aims. If you told a member of Parliament in seventeenth-century England that, as Milton Friedman said in 1970, the purpose of a corporation was to "make as much money as possible," he would have been shocked. Everyone knew that joint stock companies were intimately connected with the national interest—the monarch granted them charters for a reason, and it wasn't simply to enrich the few dozen merchants on Philpot Lane.

But somewhere along the line, between Adam Smith and today, this connection between the corporation and the public good became obscured. Today, not only it is *not* obvious that corporations should consider the common good, but it is even considered quite controversial. This book has traced the shift from the corporation as public entity with a public purpose to the corporation as mindless engine of profit.

There are also more specific lessons from the world's experience with corporations. Each corporation we've encountered in this book—from the Roman *societas publicanorum* to the East India Company to the Ford Motor Company—created some new way of organizing human industry. They pioneered limited liability or stocks or mass production. But once these innovations had gained sway, corruptions and abuses inevitably arose. When society eventually learned the full extent of these abuses, law and policy evolved to correct them. In ancient Rome, the emperor Augustus replaced the flawed tax-farming system that relied on the *societates* with new, centrally administered taxation. In the Gilded Age, Congress passed the Sherman Antitrust Act to rein in the abuses of monopolistic railroad companies. With the New Deal, Franklin Delano Roosevelt enacted labor laws protecting workers from the dehumanizing consequences of mass production and the assembly line. This dynamic—innovation, exploitation, reformation—has played out over and over again in the history of corporations. When one looks at its evolution over hundreds of years of history, we get a remarkable picture of how the corporate infrastructure of today is laid on the bones of these historical moments of insight and catastrophe.

Today, corporations are immensely powerful. Their decisions shape our lives in innumerable ways, from how we spend our days to what we care about and value. But, unleashed from their guiding purpose, corporations have the capacity to do great harm. Law takes time to develop, and in the meantime society can pay a steep price. I, for one, hope that we will rediscover the vision of the corporation as an engine for the common good.

ADAM SMITH, THE FOUNDING PHILOSOPHER OF CAPITALISM, BElieved that an invisible hand guides our markets. It nudges, pulls, and sometimes shoves profit seekers toward the greater good. It leads corporations to invent, innovate, and grow. It makes them sensitive to scarcity, consumer demand, and the welfare of workers. These incentives are often good. They align the interests of corporations and society.

But Adam Smith was no Pangloss. He understood that the invisible hand falters. It grows weary. It sometimes drops the ball. For the good of everyone, we need to learn when the invisible hand is most likely to fail us and when it will lead us down dangerous or harmful paths. We also need to learn what we can do about it when it does.

In this final section of the book, I would like to offer a few guiding principles for fixing corporations. These lessons are not foolproof (nothing ever is). But they provide a useful road map, based on real-world examples. If corporate executives, government policymakers, and citizens keep these rules in mind, they will have a handy tool kit for making wise decisions in the years to come.

I. DON'T OVERTHROW THE REPUBLIC

Regardless of the potential for profit, corporations should avoid taking actions that undermine the foundations of democracy itself. The first corporation was founded in a democracy. The corporation has always been the product of society, receiving privileges and rights not bestowed on anyone else. In return, it owes obligations to society. It is expected to serve the greater good. At the very least, this means not destroying the pillars of democracy.

The fate of the original corporations, the *societates publicanorum* of ancient Rome, provides a lesson. In the Roman Republic, these special companies collected taxes, constructed roads, and built aqueducts. They were so important that Cicero called them the "ornament of the state." But over time, as the *societates* grew more powerful, cracks emerged. They were accused of oppressing the provinces, enslaving foreign citizens, and bribing the Senate. As Harvard classicist Ernst Badian put it, the companies "were the curse and the scourge of the conquered nations, largely responsible for the detestation of the Roman name among the subjects of Rome, and perhaps even for the downfall of the Roman Republic." The companies encouraged Rome to launch aggressive wars to conquer new territory (which they could then exploit for profit). They made speculative bets on future prospects that threatened to draw in the fortunes of the republic itself. They grew "too big to fail" and demanded bailouts from the government. They favored the rise of the Triumvirate of Caesar, Pompey, and Crassus that would soon spell the end of the republic and the transition of Rome to an empire.

The ancient Roman corporation represented the world's first attempt to craft a vessel purpose-built for business and commerce, and it worked quite well. Its basic structure, while crude, has endured in one form or another to this day. But it was also a dangerous vessel. Its interests often diverged from those of the state that created it. Its capacity to magnify the fortunes and wealth of its owners meant that the interests of the corporations often trumped those of other interests within the country. In the end, it deformed government policy and hastened the decline of democracy.

The failures of the Roman corporation hint at two ways that business can undermine good government. The first is that it can throw a wrench in the gears of democratic process. Corporations should be careful to ensure that their actions do not hinder democratic decision-making—by limiting or distorting the information available to voters, say, or by lobbying for government policies they know to be harmful for citizens as a whole (it goes without saying that bribing legislators is also off the table). We have seen this happen again and again throughout history. The Union Pacific regularly interfered in the doings of state legislatures, striking down unfavorable bills and defeating candidates who might champion them. Exxon backed industry groups that undermined the growing scientific consensus about climate change. Facebook failed to police how its platform could be used to interfere in elections. These actions strike at the very heart of our democracy. They also represent a betrayal of the spirit of capitalism.

The second way that business can undermine good government is by taking on excessive risk. Businesses take risks all the time—about whether consumers will buy their products, their research will lead to innovations, or employees will live up to expectations. Risk is unavoidable in an unpredictable world. Ordinarily, though, companies bear these risks themselves. If the product fails to catch on, if the research fails, or if employees underperform, the company might lose money or even close, but these losses fall on its shareholders, executives, and employees. Sometimes, though, businesses create risks not just for themselves but for others. When risks are so great that the company cannot bear them alone, they sometimes fall on the government and society more generally. The Roman corporations bet that they could reap great rewards from new Roman provinces, but when those re-wards didn't surface, the resulting losses threatened not just individual corporations but the Roman economy as a whole. These kinds of systemic risks place a great burden on society. Sometimes, like in ancient Rome, they require society to come in and bail the corporations out because the consequences of failure are simply too dire. The East India Company ushered in an entirely new kind of systemic risk when it introduced the English public to stock exchanges, leading to the South Sea Bubble and other economic crises. More recently, KKR and other private equity firms have greatly increased the debt loads of corporations, generating new risks that bankruptcies among utility companies, hospitals, and other industries might destroy services that are necessary to the public. Corporations must avoid taking these kinds of risky bets when they threaten systemic risk, even if profit can be made from them.

The first rule provides a principle of action for corporate executives and government regulators alike. Will their new social media app debase public discourse? Will their lobbying campaign distort democratic decision-making? Will their financial innovation create excessive risk for the economy? If the answer is yes, then executives should say no. Even if it feels like the invisible hand is guiding them toward it, executives must understand that profit is not always synonymous with virtue. And if executives fail to police themselves, governments are justified in stepping in. History has shown that markets have a disturbing tendency to encourage excessive risk-taking, precisely because risk-taking is sometimes profitable. But the invisible hand is not infallible, and where it mistakenly guides corporations in antidemocratic directions, governments must slap it down.

II. THINK LONG TERM

Corporations focus overwhelmingly on the here and now. They fail to plan for the soon to come, let alone the far-off. But to prosper as institutions, corporations must consider the consequences of their actions, not just for this month's revenue or this year's profit but for the overall long-term prosperity of the company. Not all profits are created equal. Sometimes, higher profits today mean lower profits tomorrow. Markets may well reward companies for making shortsighted decisions, but where they do, corporations should be prepared to push back.

The Medici Bank serves as a reminder of what can happen when corporations fail to think for the long term. The Medici Bank was the most powerful financial institution of the Renaissance, acting as banker to the pope and financing the artistic genius of such figures as Michelangelo, Leonardo da Vinci, and Donatello. When Giovanni di Bicci de' Medici founded the Medici Bank in 1397, Florence was still recovering from the ravages of the Black Death. It was dominated by the intrigues of competing guilds and the warfare of rival kingdoms. But the chaotic political situation also presented an opportunity. Wealthy nobles, rulers, and priests needed a safe place to store their wealth, and less fortunate nobles, rulers, and priests needed money to stay in power. The Medici Bank stepped in to fill these needs. Through a complex system of accounting, bills of credit, and currency exchanges, it helped forge an international banking system that transcended the petty squabbles and conflicts of local lords and, importantly, avoided the draconian usury laws of the Catholic Church. Over the next several decades, the Medici family would navigate the complex political situation to perfection, taking control of the bankers' guild, winning over the Vatican, and turning Florence into the financial center of all of Europe. The Medici then lavished their great riches on arts and learning, and their largesse in a very real sense ushered in the Renaissance.

But by the end of the century, the Medici Bank was gone, the Medici family had been exiled, and the friar Savonarola was conducting bonfires of the vanities in Florence's piazzas. The causes of this dramatic decline were many and complicated—resentment, negligence, malfeasance, and wider economic conditions all played a role—but at the heart of the matter was a failure to think for the long term. This might strike a casual observer as surprising: the Medici, after all, spent lavishly on the art and architecture of Florence, the results of which still redound to the glory of the city and the genius of its artists today—and didn't they make these donations for the sake of eternity and their everlasting souls? But the business of the Medici Bank, particularly in the second half of the fifteenth century, was marked by a lack of care for the future. A bungled succession plan led the Medici Bank to fall into the hands of a string of uninterested, arrogant, or simply incompetent elder sons: Piero the Gouty, Lorenzo the Magnificent, and Piero the Unfortunate. These sons then made a string of decisions that hastened the collapse of the bank. Piero the Gouty forced the bank's creditors to repay their loans immediately, temporarily strengthening the bank's balance sheet but devastating its reputation as a reliable lender. Lorenzo forced the bank into speculative ventures, like alum mining, that had nothing to do with the bank's expertise and ended up distracting him and the rest of the bank's managers from more pressing concerns. And more generally, the Medici failed to consider that their dizzying wealth, combined with the Machiavellian political scheming that underlay it, would inspire the resentment of powerful players in Italy, especially the pope, on whom they depended for profits. In the end, all of these short-term decisions played a part in destroying the bank.

The history of the Medici Bank provides a cautionary tale about why corporations are drawn into the losing game of preferring short-term returns over long-term ones. Sometimes it is perfectly rational to do so. The future is uncertain. We don't know what tomorrow's demand will look like or where the economy will go or whether a depression lies ahead. In the face of this uncertainty, it often makes sense to chase profit today rather than wait and play the long game. Sometimes a dollar today is preferable to two dollars a year from now. But there are also more pernicious reasons for preferring the short term. CEOs and other executives often don't expect to stay at their companies for an indefinite period and so might prefer to juice up short-term returns to boost their bonuses and stock options. They may no longer be at the company when the long-term consequences of those actions are eventually felt, and so they disregard them. They might skimp on investments in research and technology in order to cut short-term costs. They might let worker pay stagnate, hoping that morale won't fall enough to hurt this year's revenues. The always-on feature of today's stock markets, in which managers can see how every small piece of news contributes to their stock rising or falling, only exacerbates this problem. It attunes managers even more to short-term fluctuations over long-term patterns.

In order to counteract these short-term biases, corporate executives should ask themselves, whenever they make a significant decision, how it will affect the long-term prospects of the company. Is it inconsistent with the company's core mission? Does it endanger the company's future revenue streams? Does its success undermine other, more important values? If the answer is yes, executives should tread carefully. The invisible hand often encourages short-term thinking at the expense of long-term planning. If companies ask these questions, they may avoid repeating the worst failures of the past.

The second rule also suggests an important role for law. Not every corporation will be able to resist the pull of short-term thinking. Not every executive will be able to say no to a business decision that will result in a lavish year-end bonus. Law can step in to help resolve these problems. Strong fiduciary duty rules can ensure that executives have obligations to protect the long-term interests of the company. Public-disclosure rules can force companies to explain why they are making decisions and how they will affect the company's future performance. Liability rules can protect constituencies from long-term harms. There is nothing interventionist or anti-market about these rules. They are necessary to make the invisible hand work.

III. SHARE WITH SHAREHOLDERS

Corporations must render unto shareholders what is rightfully theirs. When companies sell their stock to the public, they commit to sharing ownership of the business with them. Shareholders should be treated fairly and forthrightly. This means providing them with meaningful information about the company and its prospects, as well as distributing the fruits of the company's labors with them. Too often, executives view shareholders as burdens, as landed gentry eager to get rich off the work of others. But shareholders are a fundamental feature of the corporation itself. Without shareholders, the corporation does not exist. Their capital is the foundation of capitalism. Corporations must be run with the interest of shareholders in mind, and a healthy relationship between the corporation and its shareholders is essential to the capitalist system.

The British East India Company brought to light many of the stress points of the joint stock system. The East India Company began as an enterprise of London spice merchants with a charter from Queen Elizabeth I to trade with Asia. The company's joint stock structure gave it an advantage, allowing it to raise large amounts of money from the public to equip merchant fleets to sail the seas. The company's stock formed the basis of a new stock exchange set up in London's Exchange Alley. Soon the joint stock corporation and its shareholder-oriented model came to dominate all competitors.

But the rise of the almighty stock led to new schemes and scams, from insider trading conspiracies to stock bubbles. It also created new pressures for companies to generate greater profit to feed shareholders clamoring for dividends. When the new ruler of Bengal threatened to shut down the company's access to India's textile market, the East India Company outfitted an army and conquered the nation. When unscrupulous managers learned of good news from abroad, they hid it and instead spread rumors of war and pestilence among stock traders, then quickly bought up stock on the cheap, reselling it at huge profits when the good news finally leaked. The London Stock Exchange gave way to wild fluctuations and frauds, ruining many and forcing Parliament to pass new laws governing the sale of stock to the public (and even, for a period, banning new corporations from coming into existence). The "pernicious art of stock-jobbing"—that is, the sale of shares in corporations to the public—was widely denounced throughout England.

The history of corporations suggests that the relationship between a corporation and its shareholders is a tricky one in which the market often fails. East India Company directors regularly duped their shareholders into buying shares at inflated prices. Henry Ford constantly fought with his shareholders about profits and policy. KKR charged public-minded investors (like teachers' pension funds and college endowments) enormous fees for the privilege of participating in its buyout funds. There are simply too many opportunities for shortsighted managers to take advantage of unsophisticated investors. The invisible hand needs a corrective here.

This is not to say that there aren't hard issues involving shareholders. Shareholders are entitled to a share of the profits that corporations make, but how much? If raising the wages of employees will reduce dividends, who should win? How should corporations deal with activist shareholders who seek to make a quick profit by flipping the corporation's shares? There are no easy answers here, and reasonable minds can disagree about the best solutions.

A wise executive understands the role of shareholders in making the corporation thrive. He does not have to cave in to their every demand. There is a time and a place for resisting shareholders—particularly when meeting their demands would come at the expense of society. But thoughtful leadership means listening and responding to shareholders about their interests. It means not frustrating their right to vote. It means not hiding relevant information from them. It means not exploiting information advantages to extract as much as possible from them—even if the executive can make a windfall by doing so.

But because we cannot expect every corporate executive to be so virtuous, and we cannot expect the market to constrain them, society is justified in imposing rules governing the relationship between corporations and their shareholders. We need rules preventing insider trading. We need rules prohibiting pump-and-dump schemes. We need securities laws forcing companies to share information with shareholders. We need stock exchanges monitoring the markets for telltale signs of bubbles and irrational exuberance. We cannot expect shareholders to be able to protect themselves, and so society must sometimes step in to do it for them.

IV. COMPETE, BUT FAIRLY

The fourth rule of the invisible hand is for corporations to compete, but fairly. Corporations should seek to provide better products than their competitors and offer them at lower prices. It is good for the world when they do. But they must do so fairly. It is one thing to sell a product for lower prices in order to attract more customers; it is another to sell it for less than its cost in order to bankrupt a rival. It is one thing to buy a technology company because you think its technology could improve your own business; it is another to do so in order to prevent it from emerging as your competitor. Too often corporations are driven by a desire to eliminate competition in any way possible. And the invisible hand has shown a disturbing tendency to push corporations toward these kinds of anticompetitive strategies.

No corporation better embodied this dangerous predilection than the Union Pacific. The story of the railroad empire that the Union Pacific built during the Gilded Age was uniquely American. It began with Abraham Lincoln, a railroad lawyer in Illinois who believed in the potential of railways to transform the United States and spearheaded the Pacific Railroad Act. Over the next decade, the nation would witness the power of pure competition as the Union Pacific and the Central Pacific raced to complete a transcontinental railroad. The two corporations would overcome almost unimaginable difficulties in surveying, grading, and laying tracks across the deserts, mountains, and plains of the continent, much of this terrain entirely unexplored. When the road was finally completed, the Civil War was over, and the railroad helped rejuvenate the devastated American economy, opening up commerce, communication, and travel throughout the country.

At the same time, the network of railroads that the Union Pacific owned provided an opportunity for a new breed of unscrupulous capitalists, the so-called robber barons, to create monopolies and exploit vulnerable farmers and ranchers. Jay Gould, the most notorious of the robber barons, acquired control of the Union Pacific and then used every means at his disposal to eliminate its competitors and establish a monopoly. He spread malicious rumors about competitors to get them investigated by federal authorities. He secretly acquired competitors' stock and then took control of their boards. Once he had consolidated control and eliminated options, he raised rates. The rising tension between the giant railroad corporations and regular citizens would eventually lead to calls for antitrust regulation to rein in the abuses of the Gilded Age.

Government has an important role in enforcing the obligation to compete fairly. Antitrust rules created in the 1890s have only grown more important in recent years as large corporations like Facebook, Amazon, and Google have taken over vast swathes of our lives, leaving us with few meaningful alternatives. Government must police corporations to ensure that competition occurs for the right motives and in the right ways. Again, this raises difficult questions. How do we know whether someone is lowering prices to eliminate a competitor or simply to win more business? Should we break up large corporations simply because they have a monopoly or only if they raise prices on consumers? What types of mergers and acquisitions should be scrutinized? There are no easy answers. But the invisible hand often fails to direct corporations toward fair and open competition, and where it does, governments must step in to ensure that corporations promote the greater good rather than simply lining the pockets of their executives.

V. TREAT YOUR WORKERS RIGHT

Corporations must compensate employees fairly, offer safe workplaces, and establish boundaries between work and home. For increasingly large portions of our waking lives, we devote ourselves to serving the interests of corporations. Society has a legitimate reason for ensuring that this relationship is a positive one. To be sure, work can provide a path to prosperity and growth. But it can also demoralize and debase. The free market is not always capable of correcting abuses when they occur, and so we must be mindful of how corporations treat their workers.

Ford Motor Company provides both a point and a counterpoint here. It is no exaggeration to say that America's obsession with the automobile—and with it, roads, highways, motels, suburbs, and oil—began with Henry Ford and his Model T. But what made the Model T such a revolutionary invention was not the car itself; other companies were making automobiles too, and many of these other cars were superior in performance, comfort, speed, or some combination thereof. The Model T's advantage was the corporate structure behind it. Henry Ford was deeply devoted to efficiency, and the Ford Motor Company incorporated his ideas in everything from the design of its factory in Highland Park, to its system of assembly lines, to its standardization of components. Ford's ideas about mass production led to more cars being made for less, and soon cars were flying off the assembly line in record numbers—at one point, half of all cars on the road in America were Model Ts. Recognizing that mass production of cars required consumers with money and leisure, Ford pioneered the five-day, forty-hour workweek and increased the wages of his workers. The rise of mass production and cheap consumer goods wrought great changes in the daily lives of Americans, who could suddenly afford a level of prosperity unimaginable to previous generations. The success of Ford Motor Company's strategy was undeniable, and its innovations in production, labor, and advertising marked the start of a new era in consumer capitalism.

But there was a dark side to Fordism as well. Mass production could be dehumanizing for workers, who were reduced to mindless cogs in an endless assembly line. Ford's paternalistic approach to employment introduced a new and intrusive aspect to capitalism, as his Sociological Department visited homes and demanded strict compliance with Ford's standards of good moral character. And Ford's deep commitment to the uplifting elements of work ("Work is our sanity, our self-respect, our salvation," he was fond of saying) led him to turn a blind eye to the worsening working conditions of his employees and to violently resist efforts to unionize at his factories. The rise of Ford made it crystal clear to society that a vast disparity in power between the individual and the corporation now existed. By the 1930s, growing awareness of the labor problem led to the passage of a raft of new laws seeking to protect workers from exploitation and establish a right to collective bargaining.

Corporate leaders have a role to play in enforcing the fifth rule. Too often, firms exalt profits over workers. They handsomely reward CEOs who increase share prices, regardless of the cost to employees. In 1965, the average CEO was paid twenty times more than the average worker; today, they are paid almost three hundred times as much as their workers. KKR executives reaped salaries of hundreds of millions of dollars a year, even while their companies were laying off thousands of employees. This is not creative destruction; it is simply destruction. Directors and officers must recognize that they have a social duty to protect workers and promote their interests, even when doing so may dent corporate profits. Again, there is room for disagreement about what precisely fairness requires. Treating workers fairly does not mean paying them all the same. Talent, industry, and skill should be rewarded. And the proper balance between shareholder returns and employee pay is a tricky one that necessarily involves conflict. But too often the invisible hand simply sweeps workers aside. CEOs would do better to embrace them.[1]

VI. DON'T DESTROY THE PLANET

Not destroying the planet sounds like a low bar. But the invisible hand has displayed a disturbing tendency to miss the forest for the trees. Corporations are often so focused on their own internal measures of success that they fail to see how those measures affect the world around them. The problem is well known among economists, who term the effects *externalities*. Our actions often create harms that are borne, not by ourselves, but by others. Without some mechanism to force corporations to shoulder responsibility for these harms, they will tend to create too many of them. And while any single decision of a corporation likely will not destroy the planet on its own, collectively, the decisions of thousands of corporations around the world acting without regard for the well-being of outsiders may well lead to catastrophe. Climate change is one of the most pressing of these problems. Others exist as well. Chemical plants can leach dangerous toxins into water supplies. Airports can cause noise pollution that degrades the quality of life for thousands living under flight paths. Technology companies create a slew of externalities when they unleash new programs that threaten free speech, civic discourse, or even simply our ability to relate to the world. Many of these costs are not borne by the companies that incur them, and society suffers as a result.

Exxon provides a case in point. Exxon's origins lay in Standard Oil, the giant conglomerate that John D. Rockefeller constructed in the late 1800s and that was eventually broken up in the trust-busting days of the early twentieth century. But by the 1970s, Exxon had started putting the broken pieces back together and emerged as one of the few companies in the world with the expertise and the international reach to find and extract oil from wherever it might be. As countries became increasingly dependent on oil to keep their citizens fed and warm and mobile, Exxon took the lead in the furious global hunt for petroleum. In the process, Exxon created a new breed of multinational corporation, with borderless operations around the globe aimed at finding cheap resources wherever they might be. But the multinational corporation created new risks. In some of its international deals, Exxon had to negotiate with corrupt or antidemocratic governments, and its ventures forced it to defend uncomfortable alliances back at home. Questions arose about where global corporations' allegiances might lie, whether they were less-than-ideal corporate citizens, and whether they might exploit dependent nations. Most worryingly of all, Exxon's interest in spurring ever greater oil consumption led it to hide growing evidence that greenhouse gases were contributing to global climate change. In many minds, Exxon became synonymous with planetary destruction.

Corporate leaders can help ensure their companies are good planetary citizens. They can take pledges to promote sustainable development and follow industry-leading safety precautions. They can commit funds to research green innovation. They can foster a culture of good corporate citizenship that devotes time and energy to thinking about how corporate policy contributes to the greater good. Sometimes, perhaps often, these decisions can reduce profits. But they are fully consistent with a thriving capitalist system—and indeed, necessary for its survival.

Government also has a role. Not every corporation will have the kind of farsighted leadership that takes into account the welfare of the planet. In some cases, corporations gain a competitive advantage by *refusing* to act as good corporate citizens. They can cut corners in complying with environmental, waste-disposal, or cybersecurity regulations and protections. Where this occurs, governments must step in to level the playing field. They can draft, enact, and enforce rules to reward good behavior. They can fine polluters. They can tax carbon emissions. They can set consumer-protection rules governing Big Tech. Much of the past century has been spent trying to craft these rules. But more work must be done to ensure that the invisible hand cultivates the garden of Earth.

VII. DON'T TAKE ALL THE PIE FOR YOURSELF

Corporations exist to promote the common good. They do so by channeling our work into productive avenues, from growing crops to building houses to inventing new technologies. Their goal is to create value and increase the size of the economic pie. When the pie gets bigger, everyone can have more of it. It is not a zero-sum game. But there is nothing inevitable about just how much of that extra pie goes to one group versus another. One piece might go to the corporation's executives, another might go to the workers, another might go to the corporation's customers, and perhaps another piece might go to society. But all too often, corporate executives take the lion's share of the pie and leave only crumbs for others. When this happens, it is both unfair and inconsistent with the spirit of capitalism. The fruits of capitalism must be divvied up fairly and reasonably, with some attention both to merit and to need.

Consider, for example, the case of KKR. By the 1970s, it appeared that corporations had reached their final form: massive multinational companies with shares listed on national stock exchanges, a class of professional managers to run them, and mass-produced goods and services. The corporation had manufactured the American dream. But then, seemingly out of nowhere, a new type of corporation emerged and suddenly threatened the old-line corporation. Going by various names, from leveraged buyout shops to private equity firms to corporate raiders, these new firms were the antithesis of the corporate giants of the day. They were small, nimble, and leanly staffed, operating out of single offices. But they were all united in a belief that, somewhere along the line, the corporation had lost a step. Management had gotten fat and lazy. Directors had grown cocky. Executives lacked discipline. And so, slowly at first, then faster and faster, corporate raiders took aim at these corporations and took them over. They all followed a similar playbook first developed by the undisputed champion of them all, Kohlberg Kravis Roberts & Co. KKR's fix was the hostile takeover: money could be made by acquiring poorly run companies, whether they liked it or not, fixing them up, and then reselling them a few years later. KKR's sharp-elbowed tactics made them the scourge of Wall Street, but they also forced big companies to adapt to a new world of shareholder empowerment—particularly after KKR successfully took over RJR Nabisco, a mainstay of corporate America. Soon, even the country's largest corporations trembled in fear that the barbarians would arrive at their gates next. The leveraged buyout proved an almost unimaginably profitable tactic, and an entire industry of private equity firms sprang up to copy KKR's methods. This new era of hypercapitalism, fueled by ever more sophisticated financial engineering, transformed the very nature of stock markets and spawned the modern mergers and acquisitions industry.

At the same time, the private equity revolution generated new risks. Companies, weighed down by the copious debt that private equity firms layered on them, went bankrupt. The ruthless focus on efficiency fueled layoffs. The slash-and-burn strategies of private equity managers favored short-term profits at the cost of long-term destruction. But nothing got in the way of the vast paydays earned by private equity managers. Observers across the political spectrum wondered whether financial engineering was siphoning value out of the American economy. As Robert Reich put it, "Never have so few exercised such power over how the slices of the American pie are rearranged." Today, top private equity managers routinely take home tens of millions of dollars a year; in 2020, Blackstone's top two executives earned a combined $827 million.

The question of fairness and desert is, of course, complicated. If a private equity firm buys a company for $100 and sells it for $200, how much is it entitled to? Its managers might argue that it should receive all $100, since, without them, the extra $100 would not have existed in the first place. But what about the pension funds that gave them the capital to buy the company at the outset? Or the workers who actually performed the company's daily work? Should it matter if some of the profit came from reducing taxes paid to the government? Or from laying off workers? One might conclude that the fair result is simply the one that the market reaches. If the private equity firm negotiates for 20 percent of the profits, then that is the fair result. But this requires an awfully rosy view of the way that deals get done. We know that the world is filled with inefficiencies and biases and coercion. We know that sometimes negotiations are tainted by favoritism or pride or self-interest or simply ignorance, and sometimes these flaws are borne not by the negotiator but by wider society. The fact that something has been negotiated is not enough for it to be fair. Or, as Paul Newman said in *Cool Hand Luke*, "Calling it your job don't make it right." We have broader ethical obligations to consider what is conducive to the common good, what is just, and what is proportionate. Corporations cannot turn a blind eye to generosity.

There is plenty of room here for creative and thoughtful business leaders to share the pie more equitably. They can arrange compensation structures to shift as profits rise and fall. They can give shares to workers. They can disclose compensation practices more clearly and let more parties have a say in them. They can place caps on maximum and minimum compensation. Governments can help as well by implementing systems of progressive taxation, closing tax loopholes, and regulating executive pay. Some argue that these schemes are inconsistent with free markets and disincentivize hard work and ingenuity. But the invisible hand's grasp is porous and imperfect. For the greater good of all, society must ensure that corporations share the pie with everyone at the table.

VIII. DON'T MOVE TOO FAST OR
BREAK TOO MANY THINGS

The corporation was designed as an institution to let people take risks and shoot for ambitious targets. Its limited liability granted owners protection from the worst outcomes of these blunders. Many companies fail. Not all products catch on. Sometimes the market turns against you. In these instances, the corporation provides a fail-safe. Even if your company fails, you will not be ruined. Shareholders have limited liability, and they don't put their personal assets at risk when they invest in a company.

But the corporation was not intended to promote *reckless* risk-taking. It was not supposed to provide a blank check for entrepreneurs to play fast and loose with the rules of society, with no respect for the potential harms. And yet, sometimes, it has been used precisely for these things, as a veneer to protect consciously irresponsible behavior. Joint stock companies in seventeenth-century England raised money from the unsuspecting public for palpably infeasible projects, knowing that the promoters would get rich before anyone got wise. Railroad companies in the nineteenth century took out massive amounts of debt that they knew would likely never be repaid. And today, technology companies launch products that create big risks without thinking through the consequences. No place better embodies this than the Silicon Valley start-up culture, which views failure as having no consequences (and indeed, often thinks of it as a badge of honor).

Few arenas demonstrate the tremendous power of corporations to shape our lives more clearly than the internet. We search on Google, shop on Amazon, connect on Facebook, and do all of these things on our iPhones. The decisions of a few large technology companies determine the daily lived experience of billions of people around the globe. Perhaps even more remarkably, with the exception of Apple, none of these companies existed thirty years ago. The era of the start-up began with the invention of the internet. Facebook was founded by a nineteen-year-old college sophomore out of his Harvard dorm room and, within a year, had a million users. Today, it has 3.3 billion users, who spend, on average, fifty minutes a day on the site—its reach is vast and deep. Facebook's success was founded on the innately human desire to connect with each other but also on the extraordinary ambition of its founder, Mark Zuckerberg, who assembled a crack team of computer scientists to help implement his dream of a global social network within a shockingly short time.

In order to reach this kind of scale, though, Facebook often acted recklessly. "Move fast and break things" became the company mantra. The strategy worked but came at a cost to its users and society. Facebook used endless feeds, notifications, and other tactics to engage users and entice them to spend more time on the site, driving social media addiction. Facebook tracked users across the web and gathered troves of data about them, then turned around and used this data to sell advertising aimed at them. And in 2016, the platform became a target for election interference, as Russian military intelligence agencies and extremist groups spread false, hateful, and polarizing information to voters. The move-fast-and-break-things culture of the start-up corporation may have made sense when Facebook was operating off a laptop in a college dorm room, but it had dangerous ramifications when Facebook matured into a global network serving billions of people.

Unlike with the previous ages of the corporation, we still live in this one. We have yet to sort out its repercussions. Society is still grappling with how to respond. This brings us to the eighth rule of the invisible hand: don't move too fast or break too many things. Corporations must not use the shield of limited liability as an excuse for reckless behavior. Corporations may gain a competitive advantage from launching a product as soon as possible and growing their user base as exponentially as they can. But before they do so, they have an obligation to think through the risks and rewards, not just for themselves but for their users and society more broadly. If the risks are too great, they should refrain from moving forward, even if there is an opportunity for substantial profit. Governments can help provide cover for responsible corporate decision makers by, again, leveling the playing field to ensure that reckless behavior is not rewarded. They can impose broad product-liability rules on companies and their executives. They can actively investigate bad behavior and protect whistle-blowers who come forward to report abuses. They can develop regulatory sandboxes where companies considering a new technology can interact closely with regulators to understand the relevant rules and policies. Democracy and capitalism must be allies, not antagonists. They should work hand in hand to ensure that corporations are institutions for the common good, as has always been the intention behind them.

※ ※ ※

AFTER READING THIS laundry list of problems, one might be tempted to conclude that the invisible hand is a myth. That the corporation, the building block of modern capitalism, is hopelessly corrupt. That it is simply a tool for the rich and the powerful to impose their will on society. That we are all helplessly dependent on a destructive institution bent on exploiting us. And that the dream of a corporation that serves the public is just that, a dream.

But it is important to remember that the corporation has been behind humankind's greatest creations. It helped build ancient Rome and Renaissance Florence. It opened the world to trade and exploration in the Age of Discovery. It tied America together through a network of railroads and automobiles. It provided the energy that powered the twentieth century's path to unparalleled prosperity and the finance that helped pay for it. Today, it has spearheaded an explosion of new technology that has opened the world's knowledge to us all. These great works are nothing less than marvelous.

What is more, corporations are not just soulless, faceless entities. They are institutions for bringing people together to work toward common ends. The achievements of the corporation are, at heart, a testament to the human capacity for cooperation. Countless men and women worked together to create the breakthroughs that today inspire us with awe. It is their stories—of ambition, of bravery, of hope, and of trust in their companions—that we should celebrate as the true legacy of capitalism. And while corporations have often failed in their obligations to society, society has, time and again, risen to the challenge, correcting, disciplining, and putting these powerful vessels of commerce on a better path. The history of the corporation reminds us of a simple truth. Humanity works best when it works together.

Acknowledgments

Many people have contributed to the ideas in this book. While I cannot thank them all, I can at least thank some. For wisdom and style, I would like to thank Michael Coenen. For essential comments and encouragement, I would like to thank Jacob Eisler, James Coleman, Mark Ramseyer, Reinier Kraakman, Seth Davis, Harold Koh, Katharina Pistor, Randy Gordon, Adam Winkler, Tim Mulvaney, Bobby Ahdieh, Vanessa Casado-Perez, Orly Lobel, Elisabeth de Fontenay, BJ Ard, Heinz Klug, Yaron Nili, John Ohnesorge, Nina Varsava, Jason Yackee, Greg Shill, Chris McKenna, Andrew Tuch, John Fleming, Jack Goldsmith, Ann Lipton, Matt Perault, Elizabeth Pollman, Felix Mormann, Steve Harrigan, Martha Levin, John Micklethwait, Adrian Wooldridge, and Douglas Brinkley. For improving the book in innumerable ways, I would like to thank my brilliant editor at Basic Books, Emma Berry. For believing in this project and shaping it into a coherent whole, I would like to thank Howard Yoon. For sparks of imagination, I would like to thank my father. For moments of peace and love, I would like to thank my mother. For blazing the way, I would like to thank my sister. For inspiration, I would like to thank Jane, Catherine, and Emma.

Notes

INTRODUCTION

1. William Blackstone, *Commentaries on the Laws of England*, Vol. 1 186 (1876); *The Case of Sutton's Hospital*, 5 Co. Rep. 23, 32b (1526–1616).

2. Milton Friedman, *Capitalism and Freedom* 133 (2d ed., 1982).

3. Letter from Thomas Jefferson to Tom Logan (Nov. 12, 1816); Karl Marx, *Das Kapital: A Critique of Political Economy*, Vol. 3, part 5, ch. 27 (1867); Matt Taibbi, "The Great American Bubble Machine," *Rolling Stone*, Apr. 5, 2010.

CHAPTER 1. CORPUS ECONOMICUS

1 Livy, *History of Rome*, bk. 23, ch. 49 (Frank Gardener Moore, trans., 1940).

2. Livy, *History of Rome*, bk. 23, ch. 49.

3. Dante Alighieri, *De monarchia* 39 (Donald Nicholl and Colin Hardie, trans., 1954); *Plutarch's Lives and Writings* (A. H. Clough, ed., 1909), 2:351.

4. For a sample of these debates, compare Ulrike Malmendier, "Roman Shares," in *The Origins of Value: The Financial Innovations That Created Modern Capital Markets* (William Goetzmann and K. Geert Rouwenhorst, eds., 2005), with Andreas Martin Fleckner, "Roman Business Associations," in

Roman Law and Economics: Institutions and Organizations, Vol. 1 (Giuseppe Dari-Mattiacci and Dennis P. Kehoe, eds., 2020).

5. Luke 5:27–30.

6. William Blackstone, *Commentaries on the Laws of England*, Vol. 1 187 (1876); Dionysius of Halicarnassus, *Roman Antiquities*, bk. 6, ch. 17; Pliny, *Natural History*, bk. 10, ch. 26; Livy, *History of Rome*, bk. 5, ch. 47.

7. Livy, *History of Rome*, bk. 24, ch. 18; Malmendier, "Roman Shares" 32–33.

8. Cassius Dio, *Roman History*, Vol. 4193 (Earnest Cary, trans., 1954); Michael Lovano, *All Things Julius Caesar: An Encyclopedia of Caesar's World and Legacy*, Vol. 1 805 (2015).

9. Livy, *History of Rome*, bk. 24, ch. 18.

10. *The Orations of Marcus Tullius Cicero*, Vol. 3 112 (C. D. Yonge, trans., 1852).

11. *Digest* 46.1.22; Ulrike Malmendier, "Law and Finance at the Origin," 47 *J. Econ. Lit.* 1076, 1090 (2009); Cicero, *In Vatinium* 29. Pomponius wrote, "Upon the death of a partner, the *societas* is dissolved, so that we cannot state without reservation that the heir of a partner inherits membership in a partnership. This is indeed the case with regard to private partnerships, but in the case of the society of tax collectors, the partnership remains in existence even after the death of one of the partners, as long as the deceased partner's share was bequeathed to his heir, so that it must be conferred upon him." See Malmendier, "Roman Shares" 36.

12. Ernst Badian, *Publicans and Sinners: Private Enterprise in the Service of the Roman Republic* 72 (1983).

13. Badian, *Publicans and Sinners* 29, 67; Lovano, *All Things Julius Caesar* 807.

14. Georg Brandes, "High Finance in the Time of Caesar," in *The Living Age* 156 (Jan. 1923); Badian, *Publicans and Sinners* 58.

15. Keith Hopkins, "The Political Economy of the Roman Empire," in *The Dynamics of Ancient Empires* 178, 183 (Ian Morris and Walter Scheidel, eds., 2009); Polybius, *Histories*, bk. 6, ch. 17; Michail Rostovtzeff, *The Social and Economic History of the Roman Empire* 31 (1957); William Cunningham, *An Essay on Western Civilization in Its Economic Aspects* 164 (1898).

16. Livy, *History of Rome*, bk. 24, ch. 3–5.

17. Diodorus Siculus, *Library of History* 5.38, in Matthew Dillon and Lynda Garland, *Ancient Rome: A Sourcebook* 311 (2013); Badian, *Publicans and Sinners* 69.

18. Livy, *History of Rome*, bk. 45, ch. 18; Badian, *Publicans and Sinners* 11.

19. Commentators generally agree that Roman senators were prohibited from participating in the *societates publicanorum*, but some have cast doubt on whether the prohibition came from the lex Claudia rather than some other

law. See William V. Harris, *War and Imperialism in Republican Rome*, 327–70 B.C. 80 (1979).

20. *Select Orations of M. T. Cicero* 153–54 (C. D. Yonge, trans., 1877).

21. Cicero, *Letters to Quintus and Brutus* 33 (D. R. Shackleton Bailey, trans., 2002); *Cicero's Letters to Atticus*, Vol. 3 115 (D. R. Shackleton Bailey, trans., 1968).

22. Charles Oman, *Seven Roman Statesmen of the Later Republic* 170 (1903).

23. *Cicero's Letters to Atticus*, Vol. 1 99–100 (D. R. Shackleton Bailey, trans., 1999).

24. Lovato, *All Things Julius Caesar* 808; Cicero, *Vatinius* 29.

25. Max Weber, *The Agrarian Sociology of Ancient Civilizations* 315–25 (R. I. Frank, trans., 1976).

26. Adrian Goldsworthy, *Caesar: The Life of a Colossus* 70–74 (2006).

27. Peter A. Brunt, "Publicans in the Principate," in *Roman Imperial Themes* (Peter A. Brunt, ed., 1990).

CHAPTER 2. THE BANK

1. Richard Stapleford, *Lorenzo de' Medici at Home* 18 (2013).

2. John Kenneth Galbraith, *Money: Whence It Came, Where It Went* 23 (2017).

3. *The Works of Walter Bagehot*, Vol. 5 365 (1891).

4. Raymond de Roover, *The Rise and Decline of the Medici Bank, 1397–1494* 2 (1999).

5. Giovanni Boccaccio, *The Decameron* 11 (Wayne A. Rebhorn, trans., 2014); de Roover, *Rise and Decline* 35.

6. John V. Fleming, *An Introduction to the Franciscan Literature of the Middle Ages* 258 (1977).

7. de Roover, *Rise and Decline* 11–12.

8. Richard Goldthwaite, *The Economy of Renaissance Florence* 221 (2009).

9. de Roover, *Rise and Decline* 132–34.

10. de Roover, *Rise and Decline* 103.

11. Mandell Creighton, *A History of the Papacy During the Period of the Reformation* 202–4 (1882); Goldthwaite, *The Economy of Renaissance Florence* 612; Mary Hollingsworth, *The Family Medici: The Hidden History of the Medici Dynasty* 66 (2018).

12. de Roover, *Rise and Decline* 194.

13. de Roover, *Rise and Decline* 293, 309. Some commentators conclude that the Medici giraffe died while in Florence. See Marina Belozerskaya, *The Medici Giraffe and Other Tales of Exotic Animals and Power* 127–28 (2006).

14. Goldthwaite, *The Economy of Renaissance Florence* 231–32.

15. de Roover, *Rise and Decline* 77–81. In some places, such as Naples and Geneva, the Medici Bank registered as a *societa' in accommandita,* or "limited partnership," which provided formal rights of limited liability.

16. de Roover, *Rise and Decline* 75–88.

17. de Roover, *Rise and Decline* 47–48; Stapleford, *Lorenzo de' Medici at Home* 14.

18. de Roover, *Rise and Decline* 143; Harold Acton, *The Pazzi Conspiracy: The Plot Against the Medici* 11 (1979).

19. de Roover, *Rise and Decline* 51; Alfred von Reumont, *Lorenzo de' Medici: The Magnificent,* Vol. 1 36 (Robert Harrison, trans., 1876).

20. de Roover, *Rise and Decline* 47–70; Niccolò Machiavelli, *History of Florence and of the Affairs of Italy* 190 (Hugo Albert Rennert, ed., 1901); Francesco Guicciardini, *Florentine History,* ch. 9; Jean Lucas-Dubreton, *Daily Life in Florence in the Time of the Medici* 58 (A. Litton Sells, trans., 1961).

21. Christopher Hibbert, *The House of Medici* 19, 49 (1975).

22. de Roover, *Rise and Decline* 361–63.

23. Guicciardini, *Florentine History,* ch. 9.

24. Guicciardini, *Florentine History,* ch. 9.

25. Marcello Simonetta, *The Montefeltro Conspiracy: A Renaissance Mystery Decoded* 69 (2008).

26. Simonetta, *The Montefeltro Conspiracy* 1.

27. Lauro Martines, *April Blood: Florence and the Plot Against the Medici* 179 (2003); de Roover, *Rise and Decline* 160–61; Hibbert, *The House of Medici* 157.

CHAPTER 3. THE STOCK

1. *The Journal of John Jourdain, 1608–1618* 47 (William Foster, ed., 1905).

2. *Journal of John Jourdain* 303–4.

3. *Journal of John Jourdain* 304.

4. *Journal of John Jourdain* 304–6.

5. E. A. Bond, *Speeches of the Managers and Counsel in the Trial of Warren Hastings,* Vol. 1 15 (1859).

6. Glenn J. Ames, *Vasco da Gama: Renaissance Crusader* 50 (2005).

7. Robert Leng, *Sir Francis Drake's Memorable Service Done Against the Spaniards in 1587* 51 (1863).

8. Richard Hakluyt, *Voyages and Discoveries* 312 (Jack Beeching, ed., 2006).

9. John Shaw, *Charters Relating to the East India Company from 1600 to 1761* 1 (1887); William Blackstone, *Commentaries on the Laws of England,* Vol. 1 185 (1876). For an enlightening discussion of Blackstone's theory of the

corporation, I highly recommend Adam Winkler's *We the Corporations: How American Businesses Won Their Civil Rights* (2018). For a history of corporate purpose clauses, see Elizabeth Pollman, "The History and Revival of the Corporate Purpose Clause," 99 *Tex. L. Rev.* 1423 (2021).

10. Alexander Brown, *The Genesis of the United States*, Vol. 1 99 (1890); John Davis, *The Voyages and Works of John Davis the Navigator* 71 (Albert Hastings Markham, ed., 1880).

11. James Lancaster, *The Voyages of Sir James Lancaster to the East Indies* 63–64 (Clements R. Markham, ed., 1877).

12. John Keay, *The Honourable Company: A History of the English East India Company* 15–17 (1994); Lancaster, *The Voyages of Sir James Lancaster* 94; William Dalrymple, *The Anarchy: The East India Company, Corporate Violence, and the Pillage of an Empire* 20 (2019).

13. Gary Taylor, "*Hamlet* in Africa 1607," in *Travel Knowledge: European "Discoveries" in the Early Modern Period* (Ivo Kanps and Jyotsa G. Singh, eds., 2001); Keay, *The Honourable Company* 113–14.

14. Stephen R. Bown, *Merchant Kings: When Companies Ruled the World, 1600–1900* 38 (2010).

15. Nick Robins, *The Corporation That Changed the World: How the East India Company Shaped the Modern Multinational* 46 (2006).

16. John Blanch, *An Abstract of the Grievances of Trade Which Oppress Our Poor* 10–13 (1694).

17. *Historical Manuscripts Commission, Calendar of the Manuscripts of the Marquis of Salisbury* 445 (1904). Scholars have vigorously debated whether East India Company shareholders truly benefited from limited liability. For a sampling of some of the divergent opinions, see Edward H. Warren, "Safeguarding the Creditors of Corporations," 36 *Harv. L. Rev.* 509 (1923) (arguing that, with respect to English trading corporations from the sixteenth century on, "an opinion that the members of a chartered corporation were liable for the debts of the corporation, simply because they were its members, is not well founded"); Ron Harris, "A New Understanding of the History of Limited Liability: An Invitation for Theoretical Reframing," 16 *J. Inst. Econ.* 643 (2020) (arguing that limited liability only became a "corporate attribute" around 1800); John Armour et al., "What Is Corporate Law?," in *The Anatomy of Corporate Law: A Comparative and Functional Approach* (2017) (arguing that "limited liability was not a standard feature of the English law of joint stock companies until the mid-nineteenth century").

18. Keay, *The Honourable Company* 242; *Records of Fort St. George, Despatches from England, 1717–1721* 15–16 (1928); James Long, *Selections from Unpublished Records of Government*, Vol. 1 127–28 (1869).

19. James Talboys Wheeler, *Early Records of British India* 68–69 (1878).

20. Robins, *The Corporation That Changed the World* 47.

21. Dalrymple, *The Anarchy* 109; Richard B. Allen, *European Slave Trading in the Indian Ocean, 1500–1850* 38 (2015).

22. P. G. M. Dickson, *The Financial Revolution in England: A Study in the Development of Public Credit, 1688–1756* 490 (1967).

23. Kirti N. Chaudhuri, *The Trading World of Asia and the East India Company, 1660–1760* 77 (1978); Daniel Defoe, *The Anatomy of Exchange-Alley* 14–15 (1719).

24. *Journals of the House of Commons*, Vol. 11 595.

25. John Francis, *Chronicles and Characters of the Stock Exchange* 37 (1850); *The Manuscripts of the House of Lords, 1695–1697*, Vol. 2 11 (1903); Captain Cope, *A New History of the East Indies* 285 (1754).

26. James Mill, *The History of British India*, Vol. 1 24 (1858); George Herbert Perris, *A Short History of War and Peace* 141 (1911); Philip Anderson, *The English in Western India* 82 (1854).

27. Stephen Pincus, "Whigs, Political Economy and the Revolution of 1688–89," in *Cultures of Whiggism: New Essays on English Literature and Culture in the Long Eighteenth Century* (David Womersley, Paddy Bullard, and Abigail Williams, eds., 2005); Romesh Chunder Dutt, *History of India*, Vol. 6 57 (1907).

28. Dalrymple, *The Anarchy* 15; William Hunter, *A History of British India* 248 (1900).

29. Keay, *The Honourable Company* 247.

30. Robins, *The Corporation That Changed the World* 11; Dalrymple, *The Anarchy* 69–70; Keay, *The Honourable Company* 323.

31. *A Vindication of Mr. Holwell's Character* 93 (1764); Dalrymple, *The Anarchy* 62; Robins, *The Corporation That Changed the World* 72. Historians disagree about the precise number that died after the capture of Calcutta—some say that only sixty-four people were imprisoned and forty-three died. See Stanley Wolpert, *A New History of India* 185 (2009).

32. See P. J. Marshall, *Problems of Empire: Britain and India, 1757–1813* 17 (1968).

33. Samuel Charles Hill, *Bengal in 1756–1757: A Selection of Public and Private Papers*, Vol. 1 240 (1905); John Malcolm, *The Life of Robert, Lord Clive*, Vol. 3 133 (1836).

34. Robins, *The Corporation That Changed the World* 79; George Forrest, *The Life of Lord Clive*, Vol. 2 258 (1918).

35. W. W. Hunter, *The Annals of Rural Bengal* 26–27 (1868).

36. *Life and Writings of John Dickinson*, Vol. 2 460 (Paul Leicester Ford, ed., 1895).

37. Adam Smith, *An Inquiry into the Nature and Causes of the Wealth of Nations*, Vol. 2 225 (1869).

38. Karl Marx, "The Government of India," *New York Daily Tribune*, July 20, 1853.

CHAPTER 4. THE MONOPOLY

1. *The Complete Works of Abraham Lincoln*, Vol. 7 253 (John G. Nicolay and John Hay, eds., 1894).

2. Grenville M. Dodge, *How We Built the Union Pacific Railway* 10 (1910); *Report of the Select Committee of the House of Representatives on Credit Mobilier and Union Pacific Railroad* 551 (1873).

3. Edwin Legrand Sabin, *Building the Pacific Railway* 130 (1919).

4. See, generally, Alfred B. Chandler, *The Visible Hand: The Managerial Revolution in American Business* (1977).

5. Stephen Ambrose, *Nothing Like It in the World: The Men Who Built the Transcontinental Railroad, 1863–1869* 28 (2000); John H. White, *A History of the American Locomotive: Its Development, 1830–1880* 211–12 (1979).

6. Horace Greeley, *An Overland Journey from New York to San Francisco in the Summer of 1859* 272 (1860).

7. John P. Davis, *The Union Pacific Railway* 89–90 (1894).

8. Horace Greeley, "The Pacific Railroad," 19 *Am. R.R. J.* 592 (1863).

9. *Railroad Record*, Sept. 11, 1862, 339.

10. George Francis Train, *My Life in Many States and in Foreign Lands* 285 (1902).

11. Maury Klein, *Union Pacific: The Birth of a Railroad* 24–25 (1987); Dodge, *How We Built the Union Pacific Railway* 12.

12. Ambrose, *Nothing Like It in the World* 125–26.

13. J. R. Perkins, *Trails, Rails and War: The Life of General G. M. Dodge* 35 (1929); Dodge, *How We Built the Union Pacific Railway* 11.

14. Ulysses S. Grant, *Personal Memoirs*, Vol. 2 47, 352 (1886).

15. Union Pacific, *Progress of the Union Pacific Railroad* 9 (1868).

16. Klein, *Union Pacific* 76.

17. George Bird Grinnell, *The Fighting Cheyennes* 256–58 (1915).

18. Henry Morton Stanley, *My Early Travels and Adventures in America and Asia*, Vol. 1 156–57 (1895).

19. *Report of Major General John Pope to the War Committee* 204–5 (1866).

20. Klein, *Union Pacific* 70.

21. Klein, *Union Pacific* 165; Perkins, *Trails, Rails and War* 222.

22. Dodge, *How We Built the Union Pacific Railway* 29. David Haward Bain has called the veracity of the story into question, noting, "There is, however, no evidence in all the telegrams, letters, reports, journals, and contemporary newspapers to support this myth of corporate race warfare." David Haward Bain, *Empire Express: Building the First Transcontinental Railroad* 658 (1999).

23. Robert Glass Cleland, *A History of California* 395 (1922). There is some debate about whether Stanford and Durant really swung and missed.

Some conclude that this was a legend made up by later commentators wishing to disparage them. Bain, *Empire Express* 666.

24. Klein, *Union Pacific* 269.

25. Stanley, *My Early Travels and Adventures in America and Asia* 165–66.

26. *Federal Coordinator of Transportation, Public Aids to Transportation,* Vol. 1 110 (1940); Josiah Bushnell Grinnell, *Men and Events of Forty Years* 86 (1891).

27. *The Congressional Globe,* Vol. 41 536 (1869).

28. *The Works of Ralph Waldo Emerson,* Vol. 2 293 (1901); Martin W. Sandler, *Iron Rails, Iron Men, and the Race to Link the Nation* 176 (2015); *Annual Report of the Auditor of Railway Accounts for the Year Ending June 30, 1889* 322 (1880).

29. *North American Review,* Vol. 108 145 (1869).

30. Robert T. Swaine, *The Cravath Firm and Its Predecessors* 158 (2007).

31. *North American Review,* Vol. 108 145–48 (1869).

32. Harold Crimmins, *A History of the Kansas Central Railway* 24 (1954).

33. Klein, *Union Pacific* 307.

34. Maury Klein, *The Life and Legend of Jay Gould* 457 (1986); Klein, *Union Pacific* 308–10, 482.

35. Klein, *Union Pacific* 308–16.

36. Klein, *Union Pacific* 402–13; Henry Villard, *Memoirs* 283 (1904).

37. Klein, *Union Pacific* 360.

38. Henry George, *Progress and Poverty* 173 (1996).

39. Charles Postel, *Equality: An American Dilemma, 1866–1896* 43 (2019); Solon Justus Buck, *The Granger Movement* 58 (1913); Jonathan Periam, *The Groundswell* 286 (1874).

40. Charles Francis Adams, "Railway Problems in 1869," 110 N. Am. Rev. 123 (1870).

41. 21 Cong. Rec. 2,457 (1890).

42. Crimmins, *A History of the Kansas Central Railway* 24.

43. *Scribner's Magazine,* Vol. 5 429 (1889); Klein, *Union Pacific* 495.

44. Edward Chase Kirkland, *Charles Francis Adams, Jr, 1835–1915: The Patrician at Bay* 126 (1965); Thomas Warner Mitchell, *The Collateral Trust Mortgage in Railway Finance,* 20 Qu. J. Econ. 443 (1906); Klein, *Union Pacific* 655–57.

CHAPTER 5. THE ASSEMBLY LINE

1. "New Industrial Era Is Marked by Ford's Shares to Laborers," *Detroit Free Press,* Jan. 6, 1914.

2. Garet Garrett, "Henry Ford's Experiment in Good-Will," *Everybody's Magazine,* Apr. 1914.

3. "An Industrial Utopia," *New York Times,* Jan. 7, 1914.

4. *The American Flint*, Vol. 5 No. 4 25 (Feb. 1914); Daniel M. G. Raff and Lawrence H. Summers, "Did Henry Ford Pay Efficiency Wages?," 5 *J. Lab. Econ.* S57, S57 (1987).

5. Henry Ford, "How I Made a Success of My Business," *System: The Magazine of Business* 448–49 (Nov. 1916).

6. Enzo Angelucci and Alberto Bellucci, *The Automobile: From Steam to Gasoline* 115 (1976).

7. *The American Flint*, Vol. 5 No. 4 25 (Feb. 1914).

8. James Truslow Adams, *The Epic of America* 404 (1931).

9. John Cote Dahlinger, *The Secret Life of Henry Ford* 118 (1978).

10. Henry Ford, *My Life and Work* 200 (1922).

11. Henry Ford and Samuel Crowther, "The Greatest American," *Cosmopolitan*, July 1930, 191.

12. Ford, *My Life and Work* 33.

13. Dixon Wecter, *The Hero in America* 418 (1941); Allan Nevins and Frank Ernest Hill, *Ford: The Times, the Man, the Company* 167 (1954); Ford and Crowther, "The Greatest American" 36–38.

14. Douglas Brinkley, *Wheels for the World: Henry Ford, His Company, and a Century of Progress* 28–30 (2003).

15. J. Bell Moran, *The Moran Family: 200 Years in Detroit* 126 (1949).

16. Brinkley, *Wheels for the World* 35.

17. Steven Watts, *The People's Tycoon: Henry Ford and the American Century* 60 (2006); Ford, *My Life and Work* 86.

18. Bruce W. McCalley, *Model T Ford: The Car That Changed the World* 8 (1994); Ford, *My Life and Work* 56.

19. Richard Crabb, *Birth of a Giant: The Men and Incidents That Gave America the Motorcar* 202 (1969).

20. Ford, *My Life and Work* 18. Some commentators have cast doubt on Ford's version of how vanadium steel was discovered and instead ascribe it to metallurgist Wills's learning about it from another metallurgist. See Brinkley, *Wheels for the World* 102.

21. Ford, *My Life and Work* 73.

22. Ford, *My Life and Work* 80; Nevins and Hill, *Ford: The Times* 471–72 (1954); David Hounshell, *From the American System to Mass Production, 1800–1932: The Development of Manufacturing Technology in the United States* 255 (1985).

23. Watts, *The People's Tycoon* 139.

24. Julian Street, *Abroad at Home* 93–94 (1914).

25. Stephen Meyer, *The Five Dollar Day: Labor Management and Social Control in the Ford Motor Company, 1908–1921* 72–80 (1981).

26. Nevins and Hill, *Ford: The Times* 533. In other renditions of the story, it was James Couzens who first had the idea for a five-dollar day and proposed

it to Ford. Brinkley, *Wheels for the World* 167–68; Harry Barnard, *Independent Man: The Life of Senator James Couzens* 85–90 (1958).

27. Allan Nevins and Frank Ernest Hill, *Ford: Expansion and Challenge, 1915–1933* 91 (1957); Robert Lacey, *Ford: The Men and the Machine* 168 (1986).

28. Ford, *My Life and Work* 162; cross-examination of Henry Ford, *Dodge v. Ford Motor Co.*, 170 N.W. 668 (Mich. 1918) in Linda Kawaguchi, "Introduction to *Dodge v. Ford Motor Co.*: Primary Source and Commentary Material," 17 *Chap. L. Rev.* 493 (2014).

29. *Dodge v. Ford Motor Co.*, 204 Mich. 459, 507 (1919).

30. Charles Madison, "My Seven Years of Automotive Servitude," in *The Automobile and American Culture* (David L. Lewis and Laurence Goldstein, eds., 1983).

31. Anthony Harff, *Reminiscences* 18–19 (Benson Ford Research Center, 1953).

32. John A. Fitch, "Ford of Detroit and His Ten Million Dollar Profit Sharing Plan," *The Survey*, Feb. 7, 1914, 547–48.

33. James O'Connor, *Reminiscences* 31 (Benson Ford Research Center, 1955); Ida Tarbell, *New Ideals in Business: An Account of Their Practice and Their Effect upon Men and Profits* 129 (1917).

34. Ford, *My Life and Work* 120; "'Shun Unions,' Ford Advises Workers," *New York Times*, Feb. 20, 1937; F. Raymond Daniell, "Ford Confidently Faces a Labor Duel," *New York Times*, Oct. 17, 1937; Frank Cormier and William J. Eaton, *Reuther* 98 (1970).

35. "Final Report and Testimony Submitted to Congress by the Commission on Industrial Relations," Senate Documents, Vol. 26, 64th Cong., 1st Sess., 7627–28; W. J. Cunningham, *"J8": A Chronicle of the Neglected Truth About Henry Ford and the Ford Motor Company* 38–40 (1931).

36. "Ford Men Beat and Rout Lewis Union Organizers," *New York Times*, May 27, 1937.

37. Henry Ford, "Why I Favor Five Days' Work with Six Days' Pay," *World's Work*, Oct. 1926, 613–16; Ford, *My Life and Work* 154.

38. Henry Ford, "When Is a Business Worthwhile?," *Magazine of Business*, Aug. 1928.

39. Bruce Barton, "'It Would Be Fun to Start Over Again,' Said Henry Ford," *American Magazine*, Apr. 1921, 7; Norval A. Hawkins, *The Selling Process: A Handbook of Salesmanship Principles* 216–18 (1920).

40. John Maynard Keynes, *The General Theory of Employment, Interest and Money* 92 (2018).

41. Alfred D. Chandler Jr., *Giant Enterprise: Ford, General Motors, and the Automobile Industry* 3–7 (1964).

42. Brinkley, *Wheels for the World* 526.

43. Allan Louis Benson, *The New Henry Ford* 99 (1923).

CHAPTER 6. THE MULTINATIONAL

1. Bernard Weinraub, "Oil Price Doubled by Big Producers on Persian Gulf," *New York Times*, Dec. 24, 1973.

2. Richard Eder, "U.S. Chief Target," *New York Times*, Oct. 18, 1973; "Saudis Cut Oil Output 10% to Put Pressure on U.S.," *New York Times*, Oct. 19, 1973.

3. Robert B. Stobaugh, "The Oil Companies in the Crisis," *Daedalus*, Vol. 104 179, 184 (1975); US Congress, Senate, Foreign Relations Committee, Subcommittee on Multinational Corporations, Multinational Corporations and United States Foreign Policy, part 7 546–47 (1975).

4. Richard Nixon, "Radio Address About the National Energy Crisis," Jan. 19, 1974.

5. US Congress, Senate, Foreign Relations Committee, Subcommittee on Multinational Corporations, Multinational Corporations and United States Foreign Policy, part 7 515–17 (1975).

6. Daniel Yergin, *The Prize: The Epic Quest for Oil, Money, and Power* 613 (2008).

7. Joseph A. Pratt and William E. Hale, *Exxon: Transforming Energy, 1973–2005* 15 (2013); Exxon, 1972 Annual Report 18.

8. Federal Energy Administration and Senate Multinational Subcommittee, *U.S. Oil Companies and the Arab Oil Embargo: The International Allocation of Constricted Supply* 8–10 (1975).

9. Raymond Vernon, *The Oil Crisis in Perspective* 179–88 (1976); "We Were Robbed," *The Economist*, Dec. 1, 1973; Anthony Sampson, *The Seven Sisters: The Great Oil Companies and the World They Shaped* 313 (1975).

10. Thomas L. Friedman, "The First Law of Petropolitics," *Foreign Policy* 28, 36 (May/June 2006).

11. Harold F. Williamson and Arnold R. Daum, *The American Petroleum Industry: The Age of Illumination, 1859–1899* 320 (1959).

12. Ron Chernow, *Titan: The Life of John D. Rockefeller* 132 (2004); Yergin, *The Prize* 43–53; Allan Nevins, *Study in Power: John D. Rockefeller, Industrialist and Philanthropist* 402 (1953).

13. Ralph W. Hidy and Muriel E. Hidy, *Standard Oil*, Vol. 1 213–14 (1955); Yergin, *The Prize* 104; Ida M. Tarbell, *The History of the Standard Oil Company*, Vol. 2 288 (1963).

14. Theodore Roosevelt, Message to Congress on Worker's Compensation, Jan. 31, 1908.

15. Harold F. Williamson et al., *The American Petroleum Industry*, Vol. 2, *The Age of Energy, 1899–1959* 443–46 (1963).

16. Winston S. Churchill, *The World Crisis*, Vol. 1 130–36 (1928).

17. H. A. Garfield, *Final Report of the U.S. Fuel Administration* 261 (1921); Yergin, *The Prize* 176; Burton J. Hendrick, *The Life and Letters of Walter H. Page*, Vol. 2 288 (1930); R. W. Ferrier, *The History of the British Petroleum Company*, Vol. 1, *The Developing Years, 1901–1932* 248–49 (1982).

18. Yergin, *The Prize* 178, 194; US Energy Information Administration, US Field Production of Crude Oil.

19. Bennett H. Wall and George S. Gibb, *Teagle of Jersey Standard* 48–49 (1974).

20. Wall and Gibb, *Teagle of Jersey Standard* 71–72.

21. George Otis Smith, "Where the World Gets Oil and Where Will Our Children Get It When American Wells Cease to Flow?," *National Geographic* 292 (Feb. 1929); Secretary of State Memo to Diplomatic and Consular Officers, Aug. 16, 1919.

22. George Gibb and Evelyn H. Knowlton, *History of Standard Oil Company (New Jersey)*, Vol. 2, *The Resurgent Years, 1911–1927* 384–90 (1956).

23. Yergin, *The Prize* 233–35.

24. Yergin, *The Prize* 176.

25. E. H. Carr, *The Bolshevik Revolution, 1917–1923*, Vol. 3 352 (1985); Wall and Gibb, *Teagle of Jersey Standard* 222–25.

26. Yergin, *The Prize* 330.

27. Harold L. Ickes, "After the Oil Deluge, What Price Gasoline?," *Saturday Evening Post*, Feb. 16, 1935.

28. Arthur J. Marder, *Old Friends, New Enemies: The Royal Navy and the Imperial Japanese Navy* 166–67 (1981); US Strategic Bombing Survey, *Oil Division Final Report* 36–39 (1947); B. H. Liddell Hart, *The Rommel Papers* 328 (Paul Findlay, trans., 1953).

29. Yergin, *The Prize* 373; John G. Clark, *Energy and the Federal Government: Fossil Fuel Policies, 1900–1946* 337–44 (1987).

30. Erna Risch, *Fuels for Global Conflict* ix (1945); Everette Lee De-Golyer, "Petroleum Exploration and Development in Wartime," *Mining and Metallurgy* 188–90 (Apr. 1943); Yergin, *The Prize* 384; Harold Ickes, *Fightin' Oil* 6 (1943).

31. Yergin, *The Prize* 410; "Jersey Standard Lists Dip in Profit," *New York Times*, Jan. 27, 1959.

32. Douglas Martin, "The Singular Power of a Giant Called Exxon," *New York Times*, May 9, 1982.

33. Exxon, 1975 Annual Report 4; Pratt and Hale, *Exxon* 112.

34. Daniel Yergin, "Britain Drills—and Prays," *New York Times*, Nov. 2, 1975; Pratt and Hale, *Exxon* 151.

35. Pratt and Hale, *Exxon*, 159.

36. Bennett H. Wall, *Growth in a Changing Environment: A History of Standard Oil Company (New Jersey), 1960–1972, and Exxon Corporation, 1972–1975* xxxviii–xxxvix (1988).

37. US Congress, Senate, Foreign Relations Committee, Subcommittee on Multinational Corporations, The International Petroleum Cartel, the Iranian Consortium, and US National Security 57–58 (1974).

38. "A Conversation with Lee Raymond," *Charlie Rose* (PBS), May 6, 2004; Steve Coll, *Private Empire: ExxonMobil and American Power* 71 (2012).

39. Detlev F. Vagts, "The Multinational Enterprise: A New Challenge for Transnational Law," 83 *Harv. L. Rev.* 739, 745 (1970).

40. "Incident Archive—Taylor Energy Oil Discharge at MC-20 Site and Ongoing Response Efforts," Bureau of Safety and Environmental Enforcement, www.bsee.gov/newsroom/library/incident-archive/taylor-energy-mississippi-canyon/ongoing-response-efforts.

41. Ad Hoc Study Group on Carbon Dioxide and Climate, *Carbon Dioxide and Climate: A Scientific Assessment* vii (1979); James Hansen et al., "Climate Impact of Increasing Atmospheric Carbon Dioxide," 213 *Science* 957 (1981).

42. Brian Flannery, "Global Climate Change: Speech to Esso Italiana," Sept. 14, 1996.

43. Lee Raymond, "Energy—Key to Growth and a Better Environment for Asia-Pacific Nations," Address to the World Petroleum Congress, Oct. 13, 1997.

44. Draft Global Climate Science Communications Action Plan, American Petroleum Institute (1998).

CHAPTER 7. THE RAIDER

1. Smith, *Wealth of Nations* 326.

2. Michael C. Jensen and William H. Meckling, "Theory of the Firm: Managerial Behavior, Agency Costs, and Ownership Structure," 3 *J. Fin. Econ.* 305, 312 (1976).

3. George Anders, *Merchants of Debt: KKR and the Mortgaging of American Business* 6, 29 (1992).

4. Anders, *Merchants of Debt* 5.

5. Anders, *Merchants of Debt* 7; George P. Baker and George David Smith, *The New Financial Capitalists: Kohlberg Kravis Roberts and the Creation of Corporate Value* 53–54 (1998).

6. Bryan Burrough and John Helyar, *Barbarians at the Gate: The Fall of RJR Nabisco* 136 (2009); Anders, *Merchants of Debt* xix.

7. Burrough and Helyar, *Barbarians at the Gate* 138.

8. Anders, *Merchants of Debt* 14.

9. Baker and Smith, *The New Financial Capitalists*; Anders, *Merchants of Debt* 45.

10. Robert Metz, "Takeover Hope and Houdaille," *New York Times*, July 7, 1978.

11. Anders, *Merchants of Debt* 26.

12. Anders, *Merchants of Debt* 33–34.

13. Anders, *Merchants of Debt* 34–36.

14. David Carey and John E. Morris, *King of Capital: The Remarkable Rise, Fall, and Rise Again of Steve Schwarzman and Blackstone* 13–14 (2012).

15. Carey and Morris, *King of Capital* 13.

16. Burrough and Helyar, *Barbarians at the Gate* 140.

17. Sarah Bartlett, "Gambling with the Big Boys," *New York Times*, May 5, 1991.

18. Anders, *Merchants of Debt* 44; Sarah Bartlett, *The Money Machine: How KKR Manufactured Power and Profits* 118 (1992); Baker and Smith, *The New Financial Capitalists* 79–80; Anders, *Merchants of Debt* 54.

19. Allen Kaufman and Ernest J. Englander, "Kohlberg Kravis Roberts & Co. and the Restructuring of American Capitalism," 67 *Bus. Hist. Rev.* 52, 71 (1993); Anders, *Merchants of Debt* 54.

20. Anders, *Merchants of Debt* 23.

21. Carey and Morris, *King of Capital* 38; Anders, *Merchants of Debt* 83.

22. Anders, *Merchants of Debt* 160.

23. Lawrence M. Fisher, "Safeway Buyout: A Success Story," *New York Times*, Oct. 21, 1988; Anders, *Merchants of Debt* 158–61.

24. Anders, *Merchants of Debt* 158; "N.Y. Fed President Takes Swipe at Junk Bond King," Associated Press, May 1, 1989; Carey and Morris, *King of Capital* 43.

25. Susan C. Faludi, "The Reckoning: Safeway LBO Yields Vast Profits but Exacts a Heavy Human Toll," *Wall Street Journal*, May 16, 1990; Anders, *Merchants of Debt* 180; Fisher, "Safeway Buyout."

26. Baker and Smith, *The New Financial Capitalists* 207; Anders, *Merchants of Debt* 36.

27. Burrough and Helyar, *Barbarians at the Gate* 144; Anne de Ravel, "The New Formalities: The Menus," *New York Times*, Oct. 26, 1986; "Those Gilded Moments," *Esquire*, June 1990.

28. Anders, *Merchants of Debt* 179; *Toledo Blade*, March 21, 1987.

29. Laura Saunders, "How the Government Subsidizes Leveraged Takeovers," *Forbes*, Nov. 28, 1988; Anders, *Merchants of Debt* 158. Alvin Warren, a tax-law scholar at Harvard, summarized the state of opinion: "Originally conceived as a temporary concession to the World War I excess profits tax,

full deductibility for corporate interest payments, coupled with the non-deductibility of dividends, has since been a persistent problem of the federal tax on corporate income." Alvin C. Warren Jr., "The Corporate Interest Deduction: A Policy Evaluation," 83 *Yale L. J.* 1585, 1618–19 (1974).

30. Anders, *Merchants of Debt* 243.

31. Theodore Forstmann, "Corporate Finance, Leveraged to the Hilt," *Wall Street Journal*, Oct. 25 1988; Colin Leinster, "Greed Really Turns Me Off," Fortune, Jan. 2, 1989.

32. Burrough and Helyar, *Barbarians at the Gate* 142.

33. Burrough and Helyar, *Barbarians at the Gate* 144–45; Anders, *Merchants of Debt* 149.

34. Burrough and Helyar, *Barbarians at the Gate* 71–72, 93.

35. Alison Leigh Cowan, "Investment Bankers' Lofty Fees," *New York Times*, Dec. 26, 1988; Smith, "KKR to Receive $75 Million Fee in RJR Buy-Out," *Wall Street Journal*, Feb. 1, 1989; Burrough and Helyar, *Barbarians at the Gate* 508.

36. Frederick Ungeheuer, "If I Fail, I'm on the Hook," *Time Magazine*, Dec. 5, 1988.

37. Jim Hightower, "Where Greed, Unofficially Blessed by Reagan, Has Led," *New York Times*, June 21, 1987.

38. Baker and Smith, *The New Financial Capitalists* 26–27; Robert B. Reich, "Leveraged Buyouts: America Pays the Price," *New York Times*, Jan. 29, 1989.

39. See Peter Lattman, "KKR Duo: $1.65 Billion Stock Stake," *Wall Street Journal*, July 7, 2010.

40. Bartlett, *The Money Machine* 214.

41. Anders, *Merchants of Debt* 152.

CHAPTER 8. THE START-UP

1. US Bureau of Labor Statistics, American Time Use Survey 2019.

2. Meerkats are not quite as gentle as they appear. One study found that, of all mammals, meerkats are the most likely to be murdered by their own species. Jose Maria Gomez, "The Phylogenetic Roots of Human Lethal Violence," 538 *Nature* 233 (2016).

3. John Cassidy, "Me Media," *New Yorker*, May 14, 2006; Michael M. Grynbaum, "Mark E. Zuckerberg '06: The Whiz Behind thefacebook.com," *Harvard Crimson*, June 10, 2004.

4. Claire Hoffman, "The Battle for Facebook," *Rolling Stone*, Sept. 15, 2010; S. F. Brickman, "Not-So-Artificial Intelligence," *Harvard Crimson*, Oct. 23, 2003.

5. Steven Levy, *Facebook: The Inside Story* 13 (2020).

6. Interview with Mark Zuckerberg, "How to Build the Future," Y Combinator, Aug. 16, 2016.

7. Katharine A. Kaplan, "Facemash Creator Survives Ad Board," *Harvard Crimson*, Nov. 19, 2003.

8. Kaplan, "Facemash Creator Survives Ad Board"; Hoffman, "The Battle for Facebook."

9. "Put Online a Happy Face," *Harvard Crimson*, Dec. 11, 2003.

10. Nicholas Carlson, "At Last—the Full Story of How Facebook Was Founded," *Business Insider*, Mar. 5, 2010.

11. Grynbaum, "Mark E. Zuckerberg '06."

12. Jose Antonio Vargas, "The Face of Facebook," *New Yorker*, Sept. 13, 2010; Hoffman, "The Battle for Facebook."

13. Nicholas Carlson, "Here's the Email Zuckerberg Sent to Cut His Cofounder Out of Facebook," *Business Insider*, May 15, 2012.

14. Alan J. Tabak, "Hundreds Register for New Facebook Website," *Harvard Crimson*, Feb. 9, 2004.

15. Nicholas Carlson, "Well, These New Zuckerberg IMs Won't Help Facebook's Privacy Problems," *Business Insider*, May 13, 2010.

16. Sebastian Mallaby, *The Power Law: Venture Capital and the Making of the New Future* (2022).

17. Levy, *Facebook* 214, 525.

18. Levy, *Facebook* 144.

19. Levy, *Facebook* 110.

20. Levy, *Facebook* 108; Henry Blodget, "Mark Zuckerberg on Innovation," *Business Insider*, Oct. 1, 2009.

21. Levy, *Facebook* 123–27.

22. Hannah Kuchler, "How Facebook Grew Too Big to Handle," *Financial Times*, Mar. 28, 2019.

23. Levy, *Facebook* 267.

24. Levy, *Facebook* 141.

25. Levy, *Facebook* 180.

26. Dan Farber, "Facebook Beacon Update: No Activities Published Without Users Proactively Consenting," *ZDNet*, Nov. 29, 2007.

27. Levy, *Facebook* 195–96.

28. Robert Hof, "Facebook's Sheryl Sandberg: 'Now Is When We're Going Big' in Ads," *Robert Hof*, Apr. 20, 2011; Emily Stewart, "Lawmakers Seem Confused About What Facebook Does—and How to Fix It," *Vox*, Apr. 10, 2018.

29. Antonio Garcia Martinez, *Chaos Monkeys: Obscene Fortune and Random Failure in Silicon Valley* 5 (2018); Levy, *Facebook* 197.

30. Martinez, *Chaos Monkeys* 275; Ashlee Vance, "This Tech Bubble Is Different," *Bloomberg*, Apr 14, 2011; Mike Allen, "Sean Parker Unloads on

Facebook: 'God Only Knows What It's Doing to Our Children's Brains,'" *Axios*, Nov. 9, 2017.

31. Levy, *Facebook* 247–48.

32. "Facebook Nudity Policy Angers Nursing Moms," Associated Press, Jan. 1, 2009.

33. Levy, *Facebook* 166.

34. Levy, *Facebook* 153.

35. Josh Constine, "Facebook Is Shutting Down Its API for Giving Your Friends' Data to Apps," *TechCrunch*, Apr. 28, 2015.

36. Sandy Parakilas, "We Can't Trust Facebook to Regulate Itself," *New York Times*, Nov. 19, 2017.

37. R. Jai Krishna, "Sandberg: Facebook Study Was 'Poorly Communicated,'" *Wall Street Journal*, July 2, 2014.

38. Levy, *Facebook* 272–73.

39. Robert M. Bond, "A 61-Million-Person Experiment in Social Influence and Political Mobilization," *Nature*, Sept. 2012.

40. Levy, *Facebook* 354.

41. Soroush Vosoughi, Deb Roy, and Sinan Aral, "The Spread of True and False News Online," 359 *Science* 1146 (2018).

42. Donie O'Sullivan and Dylan Byers, "Fake Black Activist Accounts Linked to Russian Government," *CNN*, Sept. 28, 2017; Indictment, *US v. Internet Research Agency*, Feb. 16, 2018, 1:18-cr-00032-DLF.

43. Casey Newton, "Zuckerberg: The Idea that Fake News on Facebook Influenced the Election Is 'Crazy,'" *The Verge*, Nov. 10, 2016.

44. Alex Stamos, "An Update on Information Operations on Facebook," *Facebook Newsroom*, Sept. 6, 2017; Craig Timberg, "Russian Propaganda May Have Been Shared Hundreds of Millions of Times, New Research Says," *Washington Post*, Oct. 5, 2017; Levy, *Facebook* 373–74.

45. David Remnick, "Obama Reckons with a Trump Presidency," *New Yorker*, Nov. 28, 2016.

CONCLUSION

1. Lawrence Mishel and Julia Wolfe, "CEO Compensation Has Grown 940% Since 1978," Economic Policy Institute, Aug. 14, 2019.

Index